The Arabic Print Revolution

In a brief historic moment, printing presses, publishing ventures, a periodical press, circulation networks, and a mass readership came into being all at once in the Middle East, where none had previously existed, with ramifications in every sphere of people's lives. Among other outcomes, this significant change facilitated the cultural and literary movement known as the Arab *nahḍa* ("awakening").

Ayalon's book offers both students and scholars a critical inquiry into the formative phase of that shift in Arab societies. This comprehensive analysis explores the advent of printing and publishing; the formation of mass readership; and the creation of distribution channels, the vital and often overlooked nexus linking the former two processes. It considers questions of cultural and religious tradition, social norms and relations, and concepts of education, offering a unique presentation of the emerging print culture in the Middle East.

Ami Ayalon is Professor Emeritus in the Department of Middle Eastern and African History at Tel Aviv University. His scholarly interest focuses on the cultural and political history of Arabic-speaking societies in modern times, with a recent accent on the entry of printing into the Middle East and its wide implications. Ayalon has published numerous studies on these subjects, including *Language and Change in the Arab Middle East* (1987); *The Press in the Arab Middle East: A History* (1995), and *Reading Palestine: Printing and Literacy, 1900–1948* (2004).

The Arabic Print Revolution

Cultural Production and Mass Readership

Ami Ayalon

Tel Aviv University

Windsor, 8 December 2022

Dear Ahmed (if I may),

Merry Christmas!!!

I saw this book and immediately thought of you.

Hope you find it of interest.

Sincerely,

Esther Mª Villegas de la Torre

(your very happy new employee)

CAMBRIDGE
UNIVERSITY PRESS

CAMBRIDGE
UNIVERSITY PRESS

University Printing House, Cambridge CB2 8BS, United Kingdom

One Liberty Plaza, 20th Floor, New York, NY 10006, USA

477 Williamstown Road, Port Melbourne, VIC 3207, Australia

314-321, 3rd Floor, Plot 3, Splendor Forum, Jasola District Centre, New Delhi - 110025, India

79 Anson Road, #06-04/06, Singapore 079906

Cambridge University Press is part of the University of Cambridge.

It furthers the University's mission by disseminating knowledge in the pursuit of education, learning and research at the highest international levels of excellence.

www.cambridge.org
Information on this title: www.cambridge.org/9781316606025

First published 2016
First paperback edition 2018

A catalogue record for this publication is available from the British Library

Library of Congress Cataloging in Publication data
Ayalon, Ami, author.
The Arabic print revolution : cultural production and mass readership /
Ami Ayalon, Tel Aviv University.
New York : Cambridge University Press, 2016.
LCCN 2016028985 | ISBN 9781107149441
LCSH: Printing, Arabic – History – 19th century. | Books and reading – Middle East – History – 19th century. | Book industries and trade – Middle East – History – 19th century. | Middle East – Intellectual life – 19th century.
LCC Z186.M628 .A93 2016 | DDC 686.2/192709034–dc23
LC record available at https://lccn.loc.gov/2016028985

ISBN 978-1-107-14944-1 Hardback
ISBN 978-1-316-60602-5 Paperback

For Keren and Sophie

Who bring so much light to the “tribe”

Contents

Preface and Acknowledgments

> As you know, I have received no money from the *jabal* [Mount Lebanon] nor have I received the [newspaper's] dues from Tunis. As for the other agents, some of them delay payment, while still others send in only a quarter or half of what they owe me. I have lost 700 francs to my agents in Algiers ... He who gives, gives. I am not going to sue those who don't.[1]

Thus wrote Aḥmad Fāris al-Shidyāq, owner of the weekly *al-Jawā'ib*, to a member of his family in 1866. Shidyāq, a celebrity of the Arab *nahḍa*, is remembered for his pioneering literary, scholarly, and journalistic work and his major contribution to his society's awakening. Seldom do we associate his role in Arab cultural history with financial hitches and agent malperformance. Even more rarely do we care to consider the debtors and agents themselves. Yet, hitches, malperformance, and other material and organizational factors were integral features of Shidyāq's literary routine, at once facilitating and encumbering it. They affected the work of all makers of the cultural change, eminent and lesser ones alike. Such constraints had a substantial impact on the scope and pace of producing written works, their dissemination in the region, and their availability to the emerging reading publics. Writers and thinkers who are known to us as trailblazers of modern Arabic thought and literary production were all subject to these checks. They also played an important role in advancing the necessary technical and logistic underpinnings, along with a body of auxiliary personnel of all stripes. Yet, in the rich and expanding literature on Arab cultural development of the time, these banal facets are seldom noticed and the many men involved in them remain largely unknown. Historians have usually focused on ideas, contents, and genres of the writings and on their broader historic implications. This book sets the spotlight on the other, less-known aspects of the story, without which there would have been no literary awakening.

[1] Letter to Ẓāhir al-Shidyāq, 14 October 1866, quoted in ʿImād al-Ṣulḥ, 99.

Save for some modest precursors, it was only in the nineteenth century that Arabic texts began to be printed in the Middle East on a big scale, and only in its last third that printing became a considerable industry. Until then, the region's rulers and societies had shown little interest in Gutenberg's invention: The existing political order, sociocultural norms, and time-honored writing practices seemed to render printing redundant. The grand historic changes of the nineteenth century altered this aloof attitude and led potentates and some creative local entrepreneurs to open the gates for printing and its products. They set up presses and publishing projects, drawing on the local literary heritage and encouraging new creation, different in substance and format from the old. Concomitantly, a set of circulation channels and functions – from postal services to bookshops, from subscription arrangements to public libraries – emerged to sustain the flow of printed works and make them accessible to potential consumers. The growing public thirst for news and orientation and the advent of schooling systems gave birth to an inquisitive reading public. Overall it was a dramatic shift. In a brief historic moment, a publishing industry, diffusion networks, and a mass readership came into being all at once. Books and other writings, hitherto of limited use, became central to public and interpersonal communication and other vital everyday practices. Developments that had taken place in Europe over several centuries were telescoped here into a condensed process, with visible repercussions in every sphere of the society's life. Together they amounted to a far-reaching cultural transformation. By the eve of World War I, printing had become a prime device of spreading news and ideas and enabling a lively public discourse across the region. The emergence of printing and publishing, and the shift from illiteracy to reading, formed a crucial platform on which more extensive and profound cultural changes rested. This book examines this platform as such.

The history of the book, printing, and reading is by now a well-established subfield of cultural history, with a focus on the European and North American experience. In the Middle East and the Islamic world, however, research on this subject is still in its infancy. We already have a substantial corpus of excellent research on many other aspects of the cultural changes, but little on publishing and reading. Serious interest in this has begun some fifteen years ago and it is rising, as reflected in a series of international symposia (notably Mainz, 2002; Paris, 2005; Leipzig 2008; Berlin 2015); in published works (contributions by Geoffrey Roper, Orlin Sabev, Nelly Hanna, Konrad Hirschler, Ian Proudfoot, Dana Sajdi, Beth Baron, and Marilyn Booth have been especially significant); and recently also in several doctoral dissertations (notably by Kathryn Schwartz, Hala Auji, and Hoda Yousef). Such an output is impressive and exciting, but on the whole the efforts made so far are rather modest in relation to the questions that beg exploration, especially with regard to the period of mass printing. A volume recently published by Ashgate and entitled *The History of the Book in the Middle East* – an ambitious, 570-page tome with 27 essays (only a handful of them dealing with the post-1800 period) – mirrored the rudimentary state of the field: Containing important and even groundbreaking studies by leading scholars, it still resembles a net full of holes. Clearly much remains to be explored in the Middle Eastern context.

This book seeks to contribute to that endeavor by studying developments in the Arabic-speaking provinces of the Ottoman Empire during the formative phase of the cultural change, from 1800 to 1914. I became aware of the substantial lacuna in the field some twenty-five years ago while working on the history of the Arabic press, an undertaking that was seriously hampered by the want of a systematic map of Arab printing, publishing, and reading. Reckoning that an exploration of these matters across the entire region was too ambitious a task for a single project, I chose instead to conduct a narrower study by way of a pilot, dealing with a limited case that would serve as a lab for testing key questions in a single community. Published as *Reading Palestine* (University of Texas Press, 2004), the study looked into central cultural issues related to publishing and reading in Palestine's Arab society from 1900 to 1948. After another decade of research, reflection, and reconsideration of previous concepts, I am feeling more comfortable to take a broader look.

This book focuses on the Arab region's "eastern" parts, the *mashriq*, with which I am better familiar: Egypt, the countries of the Fertile Crescent, and to some extent the Arabian Peninsula. It should be borne in mind, however, that this was just one of several arenas in the Islamic lands where such developments took place at about the same time, triggered everywhere by the entry of printing. In countries of North Africa, Iran, India, and farther in Southeast Asia, such changes unfolded concurrently and often in close association with those examined here – in technology, diffusion mechanisms, and above all consumption. This book, then, is essentially about a link in a chain, but one that bears many of the genetic attributes of the other links as well.

The inquiry revolves around three axes: production, that is, printing and publishing; consumption, namely the emergence of mass readership; and the creation of diffusion channels, the indispensable nexus linking the previous two. Each of these comprises a varied set of functions and mechanisms. It goes without saying that in casting such a wide net the book can offer no more than an introductory statement on the workings of the cultural-literary activities. Each component of the scene by itself may be a subject of a book-size inquiry. For example, Arab printing, narrowly speaking, could be a topic for a colorful study that should address technological and mechanical matters, issues of typography and lithography, book formats and graphic images, social aspects of the printer's trade, the routine of printers' working with authors, publishers and sellers, and so on. My purpose here is different, and broader: To trace and explore the constituent processes of the entry of printing into the region, delineate their historic phases, and examine the ways by which the new medium affected the cultural transformation. This includes looking at practical sides of publishing, considering the emergence of diffusion conduits, and scrutinizing readers' accommodation to the practice in its early stage. To shed light on these, I shall follow the personal stories of several typical representatives of the process: Khalīl Sarkīs, the semi-aristocratic Lebanese publisher; his humbler Palestinian peer, Jurjī Ḥabīb Ḥanāniyā; the Tripoli resourceful bookseller ʿAbdāllāh al-Rifāʿī; the book-diffusion entrepreneur, Yūsuf al-Shalfūn; and individual book readers such as the Cairo youth Hudā Shʿrāwī and her rural compatriot, Sayyid Quṭb, a teenager who was exposed to the world of reading in an Egyptian village on the eve of World War I. Certain sides of the story had to be left out: aspects of printing technology; the contents and themes of the published products (save for a limited categorization of them, in Chapter 3); and the wider political, economic, social, and cultural ramifications of the entry of printing, along the lines pursued by Elizabeth Eisenstein and her many followers (and critics) in the wide subdiscipline of book history. These are subjects for further inquiry, which is indeed highly needed. I do, however, consider questions of cultural tradition, social norms and relations, concepts of education, and religious faith that are pertinent to publishing and reading. One can tell a multifaceted story of a society's development by examining the emergence and role of printing in it. This book illuminates certain central chapters of that story.

I now come to the pleasant duty of thanking the many who helped me in various ways as this study was taking shape. I am indebted to my students in the Department of Middle Eastern and African History at Tel Aviv University, especially those who participated in my graduate seminars on modern Arab cultural history during the last decade. Each of these seminars served as a workshop for testing new ideas and examining new studies in the company of bright students, ever an enlightening and enjoyable experience. I remain forever obliged to all of them. I learned so much from my colleagues and friends Miri Eliav-Feldon and Elchanan Reiner of Tel Aviv University, with whom for several years I taught joint courses on printing and reading in Christian, Jewish, and Muslim societies. I owe them more than they would admit, for exposing me not only to the rich saga of the book and publishing in Christian and Jewish Europe but also to some of the central dilemmas involved in studying them, and the field in general. Numerous other friends and colleagues helped me with advice, insights, and references, of whom I wish to single out for special thanks: Beth Baron, Guy Burak, Dagmar Glass, Uri Kupferschmidt, Amalia Levanoni, Kathryn Schwartz, Sasson Somekh, Alon Tam, Mira Tzoreff, and Fruma Zachs. Yaron Ayalon, Miri Elieav-Feldon, Jacob M. Landau, and David J. Wasserstein read parts of the manuscript, offered invaluable comments, and saved me from some shameful slips, as did the three anonymous readers of my MS for Cambridge University Press. I am beholden to all of them. They all share whatever merits this book might have but none of its faults or errors it must still contain, for which I alone am responsible.

Most of the research for this study was conducted when I was a visiting fellow at the Department of Near Eastern Studies in Princeton, in 2007. The department people and the marvelous university surroundings proved as inspiring as ever and made my work there a sheer delight. I was immensely fortunate to have been invited to attend Robert Darnton's PhD seminar on book history at Princeton's History Department, which proved a highly instructive experience for me in more ways than one. And Firestone Library did not cease to amaze me with its treasures of even the most obscure items. My heavy debt to its phenomenal collection and to the librarians who put it together over the years should be clearly evident in the pages below.

At Cambridge University Press, Maria Marsh, Cassi Roberts, Amanda George, and James Gregory executed the task of turning my manuscript into a book with remarkable efficacy and much grace, as did the project manager Aishwariya Ravi and my superb copyeditor Jothilakshmi Ganesh at Integra-PDY. I am grateful to them all. I also thank Salim Tamari and *The Jerusalem Quarterly* for their kind permission to reproduce the Ḥanāniyā family image, first published in issue 32 (2007) of the journal. Finally, I wish to record my incalculable debt and intense gratitude to members of my dear family, who accompanied me in this long journey with admirable tolerance: my wife Yael, who knows best how vital her role in this was; our sons Yaron and Gil; our grandchildren Yuval and Omri; and our daughters-in-law Keren and Sophie, who have brought so much joy to our circle and to whom this book is dedicated.

The research for this book was supported by the Israel Science Foundation (grant no. 732/09), which I gratefully acknowledge.

A Note on Transliteration

The frequent mention of Arabic names – people, books, journals – has led me after much hesitation to apply a full system of transliterating Arabic into English. Students of Arab societies should need no guidance for this self-explanatory system, which may help them identify Arabic names and terms with precision. The non-specialist should simply ignore the screen of dots, macrons, and inverted apostrophes and easily proceed without them.

Introduction

The Question of Genesis

The first book in Arabic script to be printed with movable type in any Arabic-speaking country appeared in Aleppo, in 1706.[1] The psalter *Kitāb al-zabūr al-sharīf* was printed by the Christian deacon ᶜAbdāllāh Zākhir under the guidance of Athanasius Dabbās, the Melkite Patriarch of Antioch. This casual venture in an Ottoman province, though duly recorded in historical annals,[2] has been given less scholarly attention than the printing project launched two decades later in the Ottoman capital by the enterprising Ibrahim Müteferrika, a Christian convert to Islam. In 1727, in the wake of a *firman* by Sultan Ahmet III, which permitted printing in Arabic script in the empire, Müteferrika was given an imperial clearance to launch his own press. It took him two years to publish the first work, a Turkish rendition of an eleventh-century Arabic lexicon in two volumes, and more printed books followed. Müteferrika's enterprise has been the focus of extensive historical discussion, in which he has often been hailed as "the first Ottoman printer."[3]

Zākhir and Müteferrika were pioneers, but neither of them could claim the honor of being the world's first-ever printer in Arabic letters. Their initiatives were preceded by printing schemes in Europe, begun in the early sixteenth century. Presses in Italy, France, the Netherlands, Germany, and England produced printed works in several Islamic languages, including printings of the Qur'ān, for religious-missionary, scholarly, and sometimes commercial purposes, copies of which reached Ottoman collections.[4] Zākhir and Müteferrika were also preceded by

[1] As distinct from Arabic bloc printing and amulets, known at least from the tenth century CE; Schaefer, 1–39.

[2] E.g., Kaḥḥāla; Dabbās-Rashshū, 37–81; Feodorov (I owe this reference to Jacob M. Landau).

[3] Müteferrika's enterprise is mentioned in almost every work on Muslim printing history. For some recent critical studies, see: Sabev, "First Ottoman"; Sabev, "Virgin"; Kunt; and van den Boogert.

[4] Roper, *Arabic Printing in Malta*, 9–104; Roper, "Early Arabic"; Balagna; al-Sāmarā'ī; Wilson, 32–36.

printers in the empire itself, non-Muslim subjects of the sultan who produced books in their own languages and scripts. Jewish exiles from Spain opened Hebrew printing shops in Istanbul as early as the mid-1490s, and Jews later set up presses in Salonika, Edirne, Izmir, and Safad. A press in Armenian opened in Istanbul in 1567 and one in Greek in 1627. We also know of printing in a Mount Lebanon monastery which produced at least one item, a prayer book in Arabic (in the Syriac/*karshūnī* script), in 1610, and of several other small plants owned by Jews or Christians elsewhere in the empire.[5] Such sporadic endeavors by non-Muslim minorities aside, it was only in the early eighteenth century that books began to be printed in the languages of Islam under an Islamic-Ottoman rule; to wit, two centuries and a half after Gutenberg.

Mass Arabic printing in the Ottoman Empire was also slower to evolve than its European antecedent, gaining real momentum only in the nineteenth century. Zākhir's 1706 printing initiative yielded a total of eight religious tracts in a modest edition before closing forever five years later. Müteferrika produced sixteen books in some 10,000 copies altogether in his more famous print shop, until his death in 1746 and the folding of his press. Another eight titles with a similar print-run appeared in the Ottoman capital between that last point and the end of the century.[6] On the whole, then, twenty-four books in a total of ca. 13,000 copies were produced in Istanbul from 1727 to 1800, a period stretching over more than seven decades and marked by long intervals of inactivity. Another twenty-nine titles with a comparable number of copies were produced during that time in Syria and Lebanon, according to one count.[7] It was a humble yield. If Zākhir and Müteferrika blazed a trail for Ottoman and Arab printing, that trail remained largely deserted for many more years thereafter. The expectation implied in the 1727 *firman* licensing printing – that a whole new era in text production would soon follow[8] – turned out to be premature; the venture that ensued marked no historic turning point. The appearance of the "first Ottoman printer" in the eighteenth century has recently been described as a kind of historic

[5] Schwartz, 30–32 (with a detailed list of such ventures). See also the studies by Tamari, Pehlivanian, and Glass/Roper in Hanebutt-Benz and others; and Roberts.

[6] The date of Müteferrika's death is in some doubt; see Sabev, "First Ottoman," 64–65. A list of his printed titles appears on p. 83. The last of his sixteen books (one of them comprising two volumes) was published in 1742. For works published in Istanbul from Müteferrika's death to the end of the century, see Kut and Türe; Oman et al.

[7] Gdoura, 249–64.

[8] An English translation of Sultan Ahmet's *firman* of 1727 appears in Atiyeh, *Book*, 284–92. The *firman* goes to great length in explaining the benefits of printing, laying out as many as ten of them, and anticipates that henceforth books "shall become numerous" through the printing process.

accident, "a pure chance" in an environment that was not ready for him.[9] The history of printing in the Turkish- and Arabic-speaking parts of the Ottoman Empire would begin in earnest only in the subsequent century.

The scope of book production once the machines started rolling under Ottoman sway – thousands of copies within a few years – was impressive for the region. But it looks strikingly modest when contrasted with the pace of European printing in the decades after Gutenberg. There, almost overnight a network of print shops spread all over western and central Europe, from Lisbon to Krakow and from Naples to Stockholm. During the five decades up to 1500 CE (the "*incunabula*" phase), some 30,000 titles in an estimated fifteen to twenty million copies were printed in Europe[10] – conceivably more than all the books produced by man in six millennia of writing. Thereafter, the numbers continued to increase exponentially. Printing came to play a vital role in Europe's grand historic developments, including the late Renaissance, the Protestant Reformation, and the scientific revolution, the expansion of literacy, and the emergence of reading publics. While its actual role in these changes is a matter of controversy among scholars,[11] even those who tend to play it down acknowledge its major contribution to mankind.

The considerable gap in timing and pace between the two scenes seems to beg some "why" questions: Why did the Ottoman Empire refrain from adopting printing in its own languages before the eighteenth century, despite being amply aware of its existence? Why did the advent of printing, once it had begun under Ottoman rule, generate no excited momentum similar to that of fifteenth-century Europe? Why did it take another century for the endeavor initiated by Zākhir and Müteferrika – its benefits now explicitly acknowledged – to become a mass enterprise? And, we may also ask, what caused the heirs of these two pioneers to be so much more successful in the following century?

Before embarking on exploring these questions, let us briefly consider the methodological validity of such an exploration. Would studying Ottoman printing by contrasting it with the European antecedent help

[9] Sabev, *In Search*, 6–7: "Because the Ottomans themselves were not in a dramatic wait for printing, the time of Müteferrika's appearance seems to be really senseless." In a revised published version of his paper, Sabev modified this statement somewhat: "In my opinion, Ibrahim Müteferrika was 'an agent of change,' though not an 'agent of immediate change'"; Sabev, "Waiting," 105.

[10] Dondi. The British Library's online Incunabula Short Title Catalogue contains 30,375 extant editions printed before 1501; www.bl.uk/catalogues/istc (last consulted 16 September 2015).

[11] See e.g., the exchange between Elizabeth Eisenstein and Adrian Johns in the *American Historical Review*, 107, 1 (February 2002), 87–128; Grafton; and Eisenstein, *Printing Revolution*, "Afterword."

us in comprehending the Ottoman case? Wouldn't our habitual, almost axiomatic, association of printing with progress perforce impose on us a prejudiced outlook that would preclude a fair-minded appraisal of the Ottoman scene? It has recently been suggested that studying Ottoman printing by asking the above "why" questions would be "ahistorical," in that it would "predicate Ottoman printing on the European experience of print": Applying criteria molded by one historic case to another historic case, such an approach would inevitably produce a distorted understanding of the latter.[12] Would it not be more useful, then, to probe the emergence of Ottoman printing as a facet of Ottoman history, studied from within, with no relation to the European model?

It seems to me that examining Ottoman printing history against the backdrop of the European experience might become ahistorical only if one is oblivious to the methodological pitfalls on the way, which are, admittedly, more real than visible. The risk of such unawareness is ever there when studying a society other than one's own, even when no comparison between cultures is openly attempted, let alone when a comparison is at the heart of the probe. The biased attitude typical of the study of another society through one's own sociocultural prism had, until recently, marred much of the European scholarship on the Muslim world. Among other things, it had been reflected in European views on the "late entry" of printing into the region: Deeming printing as a clear mark of progress and its absence as regression, scholars have tended to interpret the Ottoman shunning of printing as opting for backwardness and to regard their subsequent adoption of printing as a "belated" embracing of modernity. As historian Orlin Sabev has observed, educated Westerners – who "cannot imagine a society without printing" – had been exploring a quandary of their own making when erroneously assuming that the Ottomans were preoccupied with a "dilemma, to print or not to print."[13]

Perpetual awareness of our cultural filters should help us in skirting such dangers. We ought to check and recheck our alertness at every turn – a demanding but attainable requirement. If keen and alert, there would be nothing ahistorical in our comparative inquiry. Grand comparisons between civilizations are too exciting and gratifying to avoid and should not be given up because of avertible methodological hazards. They have much to offer to the inquisitive researcher and often yield insights unobtainable otherwise. Historian David Landes, who chose to investigate the

[12] Schwartz, 18, and extensive discussion in chapter 2 of her thesis. Schwartz argues that much of the existing scholarship on Ottoman printing, including some recent works, is thus tainted.

[13] Sabev, *In Search*, 3–5.

enigmatic absence of scientific and industrial revolutions in China's history, ascribed his choice of topic to a simple, healthy historical curiosity: "Why should one not expect China to be interested in economic growth and development? . . . to want to do more work with less labor?" Why, we may likewise ask, would the Ottoman state and its subjects in the Middle East turn their backs for such a long time on a device which had proven to hold so many benefits in neighboring Europe? The questions about the long absence of mass printing in the Ottoman Empire are among the historic dilemmas related to the major disparities between European and Middle Eastern civilizations, like those that concern feudalism, nationalism, or democracy. They invite judicious comparisons between their divergent historic courses and choices. These are ever-elusive questions and their probing is intricate. But, as Landes has noted, "that is what history is all about."[14]

Asking why a certain development, known in one society, did not occur in another entails more methodological difficulties. The sources of a studied society do not usually discuss phenomena or ideas that were not a part of its own experience, and rarely explicate their absence. Such is the case with printing in the pre-eighteenth-century Middle East. The local sources, so rich on so many other matters, say little about the foreign technology and do not care to expound the choice not to adopt it for several centuries. The historian is thus left to rely on indirect evidence and on inferences as much as, or more than, on explicit testimonies and come up with explanations that are inevitably tentative. This will be all too obvious in the discussion below.

The "Late Début": Opting for the Sidelines?

Until recently, historians did not examine the reasons for the Ottoman disinterest in printing very closely. Scholars who discussed that historic fact usually did so hastily and were content with certain simplistic explanations. Grounded in some crude assumptions regarding Muslim culture and the Ottoman Empire, their superficial treatment of the issue was uncritically recycled in the literature. It reflected the long-familiar problematic tendency to ascribe one's own concepts and priorities to another society under scrutiny.

The standard account attributed the Muslim-Ottoman choice to avoid printing to three main causes: government objection, *ᶜulamāʾ* disapproval, and opposition by the many book copyists in the capital. Ottoman sultans were said to have been wary lest printing introduce alien concepts and

[14] Landes, 16.

habits that would weaken the Islamic order on which their power and the imperial order rested. Two sultans, Bāyezid II and Selim I, were reported to have issued *firmans* (edicts), in 1485 and 1515, respectively, which explicitly prohibited the use of printing in the languages of Islam under penalty of death, and these presumably remained in force in subsequent centuries. The *ʿulamāʾ*, for their part, were believed to have been opposed to the foreign technology mostly on conservative religious grounds. To them, printing represented a *bidʿa*, objectionable innovation of the worst kind, the kind borrowed from infidels. For these guardians of the faith, it was "veneration of the Arabic language as the medium for revealing the word of God" that made them "oppose the use of a metal object, coming from Christendom, to reproduce the honored language of revelation," one scholar has suggested.[15] Like the sultans, they must also have been concerned about the threat the imported medium held to their standing as the overseers of all written guidance to the community. Müteferrika's words about the *ʿulamāʾ* fearing that printing would place "more than the necessary amount of books" into circulation were taken as an accurate expression of their stance.[16] In the centralized empire, such a shared opposition by sultans and *ʿulamāʾ* should have sufficed to prevent the entry of printing by an order from above. But there was also opposition from below, by the Istanbul scribes and book copyists. They made up a sizeable group – 80,000 strong in the late seventeenth century, according to one testimony[17] – and hence influential enough to pressure the government to ban the tool that would undercut their livelihood. Both the government and the *ʿulamāʾ* had high esteem for the scribes and copyists as a vital brick in the edifice of the existing order, and both were keen to protect them. Other possible reasons for the "belated" genesis of Ottoman printing were also mentioned, as subsidiary complements to those noted above: economic factors – the high cost of establishing a press and the dearth of public demand, given the society's widespread illiteracy and poverty; and, somewhat more hazily, cultural factors – a time-honored preference for oral expression, coupled with a reverence for the written word and for the craft of calligraphy. Both would impede the adoption of printing.[18]

On the whole, this multilayered explanation seemed to make sense, and for a long time scholars accepted it as adequate. It was comfortably consonant with modernization theories, which regarded printing as

[15] Atiyeh, "Book," 235.
[16] Quoted in Göçek, 113.
[17] The figure is taken from a report by the Bolognese scholar and soldier Luigi Ferdinando Marsigli, who visited Istanbul in 1682 as a young man; quoted in Oman et al. See also the sources cited in Sabev, "Formation," 313.
[18] Oman et al.; Robinson, 234.

a key to progress and its absence as a mark of underdevelopment. By depriving itself from its benefits, it was assumed, the Muslim Ottoman state opted to remain on the sidelines of human progress, way behind Europe, which was racing ahead. To some observers, this was yet another proof of Muslim societies being intellectually and scientifically "inert" in recent centuries.[19] Only rarely did scholars question the soundness of the explanation or the credibility of its underlying historic evidence.[20] It was thus presented in the article on printing ("Maṭbaᶜa") in the authoritative *Encyclopaedia of Islam*, second edition, and was perpetuated as a matter of course in the historical literature, including works as recent as the present decade.[21] "One can avoid the need to explain a great deal by relying on this conviction," historian Ian Proudfoot has observed.[22]

A closer look at this reading of the issue brings up questions which the above explanation leaves unresolved. One may wonder, how come government disapproval and *ᶜulamā'* resentment sufficed to prevent printing by Muslims throughout that vast empire for centuries, while in Europe printing thrived despite similar obstacles. One may also wonder, with regard to the scribes and copiers – who would naturally strive to avert the danger posed by printing – what made those in the Ottoman Empire more effective than the corresponding class in Europe, who had also tried to check the danger to their livelihood and soon lost the battle. In the same vein, illiteracy and poverty, two obstacles to mass production and consumption of written texts, were not unique to the Middle East. They also prevailed in Europe, which was overwhelmingly illiterate when printing appeared and for a long time thereafter and in large part also indigent, but these did not prevent the remarkable success of the printing press. Finally, perhaps most puzzling about the standard interpretation is the historic fact that the Zākhir and Müteferrika initiatives of the early eighteenth century had no follow-up for many decades. State approval and *ᶜulamā'* consent were already there, as were the eager entrepreneur and the machinery; but the enterprise failed to take off. Why? This last puzzle is

[19] E.g., Huff, 153–59, 307.

[20] Notably André Demeerseman, who, in a seventy-six-page-long study published in 1954, cast doubt on some of the accepted assumptions and proposed a more nuanced analysis. His essay passed largely unheeded, as can be seen from the many works referred to in the next note below, most of which appeared much later.

[21] Oman et al. (article published in 1989). For studies that endorsed this explanation in whole or in part, see, e.g., Pedersen, 133–34; Nasrallah, 17–25; Ṣābāt, 17, 21–22; Dabbās-Rashshū, 14; Szyliowicz, 251; Atiyeh, "Book," 234–35; Bagdadi, 85–86; Lewis, *Middle East*, 268; Bloom, 217–24; Finkel, 366–68; Harding, 432; Huff, 307; Wilson, 36–37, and (admittedly) Ayalon, *The Press*, 166.

[22] Proudfoot, "Mass Producing," 184.

not accounted for by the regular explanations. Perhaps other, more subtle, factors were at play here, beyond the calculated interests of the usual actors.

In recent years, especially in the last decade, scholars have begun to look into these questions more critically. Doubts have been raised concerning the alleged imperial ban on printing, casting it as, apparently, a myth. It has been noted that no copies of the presumed decrees by Bāyezid II and Selim I have been found in the archives so far, and that the assumption that these two sultans – who were generally known for their favorable view of learning – should issue such a command was unlikely. To be sure, the notion that Ottoman rulers would be distrustful of printing has not in itself been disputed. What has been is the use of this notion as a blanket explanation for the absence of Muslim printing, without trying to probe the roots of that possible distrust. Doubts have also been raised about the likelihood that fifteenth- and sixteenth-century decrees should effectively retain their prohibitive force until the eighteenth century all over the vast and diverse empire.[23] Similar skepticism has been voiced about the notion of *ʿulamāʾ* opposition to printing. It has been argued that the sources studied so far contain no unequivocal evidence of their hostility to printing and that, moreover, when the practice was seriously considered in the eighteenth century, the stance of many *ʿulamāʾ* was rather supportive. It could also be shown that, historically, they tended to approve of novel technologies more often than not.[24] "Instead of stating that the *ʿulamāʾ* were against printing, we may note that printing was opposed by some *ʿulamāʾ*," one scholar has suggested.[25] The assumption that printing was rejected from above, through dictates by the community's rulers and spiritual guides, has thus been rendered questionable.

[23] Ghobrial, 1–4; Sabev, "Formation," 311–14; Schwartz, 54–55, 62–68. Doubts concerning the authenticity of the sultan's decrees were voiced already in 1928 by Gerçek, 9, but have passed largely unnoticed. The Tunisian historian Wahid Gdoura (Waḥīd Qaddūra) has traced the roots of the account on the decrees to a report by André Thevet, a sixteenth-century French traveler to the East, which was apparently based on unsubstantiated rumors (Thevet, 515) and which later historians accepted as a fact; Gdoura, 86–89, and see also Sabev, "Virgin," 392–97.

[24] Gdoura, 81–83; Kunt, 96; Proudfoot, "Mass Producing,"167; Sajdi, "Print," 117ff; Skovgaard-Petersen, 77ff. As against this, a forthcoming study by Guy Burak argues that *ʿulamāʾ* of the established hierarchy did object to Müteferrika's scheme and to the adoption of printing. They adhered to the traditional "manuscript culture," with the practice of canonizing texts and their copies as its cornerstone principle; See Burak. I am grateful to the author for allowing me to consult and refer to a draft of this article. Burak is reminding us here that some (or perhaps many) *ʿulamāʾ* did retain an unfavorable view of printing, an assessment compatible with that of Skovgaard-Petersen's, quoted immediately below.

[25] Skovgaard-Petersen, 78.

Likewise, the common wisdom on the copyists as a major obstacle to Ottoman printing has been cast in doubt.[26] That this sector had a genuine interest in blocking the entry of printing is obvious, but historians are required to prove, not just conjecture, that these practitioners had sufficient influence, as an organized guild or otherwise, to attain such a goal. Recent studies have reminded us that we still do not know enough about the role of Ottoman guilds to reach such conclusions, and that the little we do know seems to indicate that copyists might not have been thus organized.[27] Similarly, the idea that Muslim reverence for the scriptures and the sacred language led them to object to printing has come under attack. Historians have criticized the notion of "a purported timeless Muslim suspicion of the written word"; there was "no general 'sacred refusal to print'," Dana Sajdi has argued, presenting examples of Islamic block-printing of various texts, including the Qur'ān itself from the tenth century onward.[28]

An explanation that once seemed satisfactory has thus been rendered shaky. But if it was not sultanic reluctance, *ᶜulamā'* dogmatism, pressures by copyists, or the overriding sacredness of writing, what explains the long abstention of the Ottomans from printing? The difficulty in devising an answer is exacerbated by the silence of local sources on the matter. "We have never set much store on strange and ingenious objects, nor do we need any more of your country's manufactures," the emperor of China told King George III of England in 1793, stating his mind explicitly.[29] We know of no like remark by an Ottoman ruler. The recent search by scholars has revealed no more than a handful of references to printing by Muslims before the eighteenth century. We know of two Ottoman authors who addressed the matter sketchily, both in the seventeenth century: Ibrahim Peçevi (1574–1649), who in his history of the empire briefly mentioned the European practice of printing, noting its technical benefits; and Katip Çelebi (1609–1657), who in his universal history (*Cihannüma*) referred to printing in ancient China. Both of them dealt with printing in foreign contexts; neither considered its relevance to Ottoman needs, nor did they openly recommend its adoption.[30] At about the same time, in another corner of the region, Muḥammad bin ᶜAbd al-Wahhāb al-Wazīr al-Ghasānī wrote an account

[26] Marsigli's oft-quoted fantastic figure of 80,000 book copyists in seventeenth-century Istanbul is patently implausible: In a city of some 800,000 souls at the time – namely, ca. 200,000–250,000 adult males – this would make one out of every three breadwinners a scribe or a bookmaker.

[27] Sabev, *In Search*, 3–4; Ghobrial, 2, quoting Eujeong Yi, *Guild Dynamics in Seventeenth-Century Istanbul: Fluidity and Leverage* (Leiden: Brill, 2004). See also Berger, 15–16.

[28] Sajdi, "Print," 118–20. See also Cole, 348.

[29] Quoted by Landes, 18.

[30] Sabev, "Formation," 314; Sabev, "Virgin," 396; Kunt, 91.

of his 1690 trip to Spain as an official Moroccan emissary, in which he noted the existence of print shops and newspapers there, presenting them as odd curiosities of the infidels.[31] Such fleeting references – there might have been a few more here and there – tell us little about Muslim views on printing as a practical option, beyond reflecting indifference to it. This resonant silence leaves the striking gap between the Muslim world and Europe with regard to printing an open question for anyone to speculate on, cursorily or systematically.

Another Explanation: Printing Redundant

A sound analysis of the absence of mass printing in the Middle East should take into account cultural, religious, social, and political factors. All of these should be considered, even though their respective weight might be hard to assess. Let us first look at the essence of these different ingredients and then try to understand how they worked to delay the entry of mass printing.

A good place to begin is the cultural sphere. It is a commonplace that Muslim societies accorded a limited role to writing and written texts in the community's routine functioning. To examine this view more closely, we must go beyond simplistic notions such as the Arab "superior oral tradition" and the invariable sacredness of anything inscribed in Arabic. Speech and writing were two modes of retaining and transmitting knowledge which complemented, not negated, each other. There was a role division between them, one that changed according to function. Vocal utterance of written texts was essential in religious contexts: God was believed to have delivered His message to His community in speech, and sacred and doctrinal writings were deemed most valid when cited out loud. This preference for oral usage was extended to other kinds of texts, sometimes only partly sacred and at other times not at all. Such was the case with legal testimonies, which were considered weightier than written ones. Likewise, in Muslim learning and the imparting of traditional knowledge, special value was placed on audible recitation, usually regarded as superior to silent reading, even when written copies were at hand.[32] Poetry and literary prose, too, were considered to be at their

[31] Ghasānī, 67. Wahid Gdoura has suggested that, rather than being silent on the issue, Muslims had engaged in a "*long débat*" on the pros and cons of printing between the sixteenth and eighteenth centuries. As evidence for this extended "debate" he cited a set of episodic and laconic Ottoman references to the importation of European books into the Empire; Gdoura, 83–86. It seems that Gdoura has taken intermittent and unrelated points for a line.

[32] Berkey, *Transmission*, 26–30.

fullest expression when read out loud. Legal court testimonies, *madrasa* teaching, and poetry recitation, all had their respective rationales for preferring speech over writing, and in all of them orality was of the essence.

As already noted, the special value placed on the spoken word led some observers to assume that, in Muslim tradition, the penchant for the oral was so overriding as to treat writing as a lesser medium. Muslims, it has been suggested, "were always fundamentally skeptical of the written word."[33] This is surely a rash generalization, for had this been the case, their written legacy in every field of knowledge would not have been as rich as it is. While venerating vocal articulation for specific purposes, these societies had equally high esteem for books and writing, as indispensable devices for retaining knowledge, teaching, and disseminating ideas of every kind. The old tradition of book copying and collecting hardly needs to be elaborated here. The status of books underwent changes in different historic periods,[34] hence there is no simple way of characterizing their overall role in Muslim cultural life. But it is certainly true that reverence for the oral and high esteem for the written had existed side by side, at least from the tenth century onward, without one of them obviating the other. If so, we may also assume that it was not veneration for the spoken word as such which barred a technology designed for mass production of books.

It could have contributed a good deal to our inquiry if we could somehow measure the proportion of written to oral modes in society's practices during the era before printing. Available evidence, however – or rather, that which has so far come to light – allows for no more than a very general and loose impression of that relationship. The problem of evidence is especially acute with regard to praxes that leave no recorded traces, such as reading (as we shall see later on) or interpersonal oral communication. From this restricted vantage point, it seems that the number of people who read and wrote prior to the entry of printing was rather small. Those who did engage in these activities often did so while fulfilling specific public roles: primarily the *ʿulamāʾ*, including those in the various legal and educational institutions, who were entrusted with retaining the community's legal and spiritual heritage; and state officials and scribes, who performed administrative and clerical tasks. There were also book

33 Robinson, 236–37. See the criticism of Robinson's approach by Proudfoot, "Mass Producing," 167–68; Messick, 158–59; and Sajdi, "Print," 117–18, and passim. Sajdi is far pricklier in her censure of Dan Diner's *Versiegelte Zeit: über den Stillstand in der islamischen Welt* (Berlin: Propyläen, 2005), in which Diner is said to have argued that Muslim preference for the oral bred aversion to books; Sajdi, "Print."

34 Hirschler, 12–25, showing that these changes were not necessarily a linear development.

copyists, who made their living from rendering services to the public; individual scholars, who wrote chronicles, theological tracts, poetry, and more; and sometimes common people such as farmers, soldiers, merchants, and even a barber – the "nouveau literates" in Dana Sajdi's study[35] – who had acquired reading skills and sometimes had enough curiosity in them to read and even write.

All of these together must have made up a minority section of the community, apparently no more than a thin social layer. The rest were essentially illiterate and remained beyond the circle of such activities. It was not a rigid division but rather a porous line: Entering the circle was open to anyone with sufficient motivation to do so; few actually did. The society did not regard reading and writing as useful skills for everyone to acquire and offered training in them to its members rather unsystematically, or sporadically. This was taken to be the right order of things.

For the most part, then, written knowledge was the designated territory of specified groups, not quite exclusive yet distinct. Those outside their ranks had little use for it or for the skills to access it. "In the Ottoman intellectual world," historian Metin Kunt has observed, "learning was by nature elitist both by the limited number of people with real understanding and penetrating minds, and by the limited number [*sic*] of worthy and useful reading matter."[36] How big, or small, was the "limited number" of enlightened people and of worthy texts it is impossible to quantify, but as an intuitive consideration that underscores their fewness, the observation seems sensible. Most daily functions throughout the community were performed by oral/aural channels, from transmitting state messages to the subjects and circulating news across society to leisure-time activities, based as they were on listening, not reading. These channels served the community well, and the modest quantities of written texts it needed to various ends could be adequately produced by handwriting. It was, in Kunt's words, "a classic case of old technology too efficient to be easily displaced by a new technology too cumbersome and too expensive to become an immediate alternative."[37]

The above explanation concerns practical considerations as much as cultural ones. Another possible cause was more strictly cultural, and

[35] See the story of the barber, and other commoners, who ventured to write history books and chronicles in eighteenth-century Damascus, in Sajdi, *The Barber*. Recent scholarship has suggested that this last group was slowly expanding already before the entry of printing. This point will be discussed in Chapter 2.

[36] Kunt, 98. An Egyptian physician in the mid-seventeenth century who discussed Ottoman aversion to printing with a French traveler remarked that a profound reading of a few texts was superior to a superficial reading of many; quoted in Demeerseman, 56–57. Also Berger, 18, 22–23.

[37] Kunt, 97.

a rather nebulous one at that: dislike for printing on esthetic grounds. That users of Arabic had special esteem for the written letters of their language and for the practice of inscribing them is a worn-out notion, whose sense has often been extended beyond its reasonable bounds. It is valid when related to sacred texts: These were to be produced conscientiously, not light-heartedly, and to be marked by grace and elegance. This, however, is merely one facet of the matter. Only a small part of all written Arabic texts, a tiny fraction, were thus revered; the rest were texts of lesser stature, whose production or copying did not require such careful attention. Works of scholarship and wisdom, e.g., in philosophy or medicine, if neatly executed would be treasured both for their contents and as precious objects. Otherwise, they, like countless other items of nonsacred nature – e.g., state documents or commercial paperwork – would be deemed only as valuable as is the information they carry, with no regard for their decorative quality. The esthetic norms of Arabic writing, then, featured a gamut rather than one rigid standard. European-printed Arabic books which entered the region usually failed to meet the upper level of this gamut of norms and did not represent an especially attractive option of text reproduction. Their printing was less pretty than manuscript writing, "a travesty of scribal form" as one scholar put it.[38] Evidence from different times and places in the Muslim world indicated a preference for manuscript over printed versions of the same books: from Antoine Galland's famous seventeenth-century report out of Istanbul,[39] through eighteenth-century accounts from that same city and from the Yemeni highlands, to an early nineteenth-century testimony from Muslim eastern Asia.[40]

Like some of the other factors examined here, the esthetic factor is easier to point out than to appraise; in a way, it is more elusive than the other social and cultural causes. Still, it does seem to have played a role in delaying the entry of printing into the region and slowing down its

[38] Proudfoot, "Mass Producing," 171–74. Typographic print, Proudfoot noted, "was less densely clustered than readers [of Arabic] were accustomed to, comprising lines of dark, stilled and uniform units, not the subtly varied strokes and styles of the manuscript." Proudfoot, "Lithography," 121. See also Sabev, "Formation," 315.

[39] "The Arabs, Persians and Turks ... like reading handwritten books in their languages much better than printed ones ... I saw in an Istanbul bookshop a copy of Ibn Sina (Avicenna) printed in Rome, which surpasses in beauty all other printed editions and which was produced in the finest Arabic script most closely resembling handwriting. This copy has been left [unsold] in the shop for a long time, even though its price was cheap ... while that bookshop and other ones are selling the same book in manuscript for a much higher price"; Galland, xix.

[40] Proudfoot, "Mass Producing," 172; Proudfoot, "Lithography," 121 (quoting a testimony from Batavia); Messick, 159–60 (quoting Carsten Niebuhr's remarks on Yemen). See also Berger, 16–17; Demeerseman, 36–45; Sabev, "Waiting," 112–13 (quoting testimonies to that effect from the late-nineteenth century).

assimilation, as the testimonies quoted above seem to suggest. This problem would be alleviated in part with the invention of lithography in Europe at the close of the eighteenth century, based as it was on hand-produced texts. Allowing adherence to the Arabic standards of calligraphic beauty through the use of skilled scribes, lithography was adopted in some Muslim countries in the nineteenth century – mostly India, East Asia, Iran, certain parts of North Africa, and to some extent Egypt. In other Ottoman Arab provinces, however, typographical print remained predominant.[41] The dislike for the visual quality of its products would persist for some time, and we may guess, if not yet prove, that it encumbered the acclimatization of printing in these parts.

An order in which all writing needs were effectively served by existing methods, along with dislike for the imported printed exemplars, together placed a barrier between Middle Eastern society and printing. The public acceptance of this basic order rendered unlikely a popular demand for written texts beyond the modest quantities that could be adequately produced by hand. This limited demand is a vital part of the explanation for the absence of printing in the Ottoman Empire for several centuries after Gutenberg. It stood in stark contrast to the state of affairs in western and central Europe before the dawn of printing, where a rise in the use of written texts of many kinds had been felt from the late twelfth century onward. City merchants and artisans who used business records, university students who needed school texts, lawyers in need of law books, officials serving in state and city administration, members of the nobility who collected books for their prestige – all needed an enhanced production of texts. The demand was first addressed by expanding copying ventures, an increasingly thriving trade in the century before printing, whose members became numerous enough to be organized in guilds in some places. By the time printing was adopted in Europe, a considerable consumer market was already in place there, waiting for its products.[42] This kind of public demand had no parallel in the Middle East, certainly not on a comparable scale.[43]

[41] Messick; Proudfoot, "Mass Producing," 171–74. Why lithography was used so sparingly in the Ottoman Arab countries is a matter for further inquiry. Muslim-owned lithographic presses operated in Egypt alongside typographical ones since around the mid-nineteenth century, but not so in Lebanon and Syria, where the mostly Christian printers tended to follow the European model of typography. For recent probes into this issue in the Egyptian context, see Schwartz, 244–76; Suit, esp. chapter 1 (discussing the use of lithography in the context of printing the Qur'ān).

[42] Febvre and Martin, 170–80; Eisenstein, *Printing Press*, chapter 3.

[43] The possible rise in demand for books in urban Egypt and Syria during the sixteenth to eighteenth century, noted by Nelly Hanna, *In Praise* (see Chapter 2), if true, must have been markedly more limited than the European surge in demand earlier on.

To this, one may add the intuitive religious suspicion of innovations, especially, again, those of alien origin. The suspicion often proved to be surmountable, but it was a hurdle all the same (needless to say, such distrust of things foreign was hardly a unique Middle Eastern trait). Muslim societies had overcome such misgivings when a foreign novelty appeared to be profitable, as in the cases of paper and firearms. But when the new device was deemed unnecessary and unappealing, the fact that it came from the outside and reflected alien norms was an additional cause for distaste.[44]

Another context in which the issue should be examined is political. That the government and religious leaders were wary of embracing a device that could prove problematic in the long run is probably true. But there is an important complement to this political argument, which becomes apparent when we examine the matter in conjunction with the European precedent. When printing spread in Europe, it posed a threat to the authority of kings and other potentates, a potential threat at first and very real threat later on. Printing also posed a threat to the public standing of the Catholic Church, which became all too manifest with the Protestant Reformation if not earlier. Both the rulers and the Church invested efforts in trying to check or at least control the proliferation of printing and its products, but with limited success. Mighty forces were at play in pushing the new technology forward. Alongside the demand from below by students, merchants, and others was the initiative of entrepreneurial burghers with money and time who were driven by the economic promise of the expanding market, as well as religious groups seeking means to curb Church power. These actors had an essential interest in printing and publishing and served as a powerful dynamo in advancing them, skirting the impediments placed by the various authorities and eventually winning the day. Historic developments in early modern western and central Europe permitted more freedom of action for such enterprising subjects and citizens.

The contemporary Ottoman Empire was different: A highly centralized system, it was effectively run on the universally accepted principle of subject obedience to authority. It was a well-functioning machine, whose success was plainly proven in encounters with its foes between the fifteenth and late seventeenth centuries. Such a reality was not conducive to the emergence of entrepreneurial initiatives that would advance autonomous projects from below, let alone projects with potentially disruptive implications for the state, as could be seen in the case of Europe. The aversion to printing by sultans and *ʿulamāʾ* had its parallels in western

[44] Proudfoot, "Mass Producing," 178–79.

and central Europe; the public political norms that rendered their control effective did not.[45]

All of these factors combined would explain the basic apathy which the Ottoman state and the societies under its sway displayed toward printing prior to the nineteenth century. It was distrust from above along with – and perhaps more importantly – lack of interest from below. Until the nineteenth century, Middle Eastern societies had no use for machines that multiplied written texts at high speed. They were not convinced by the European-printed samples they saw, which to them were inferior to locally made manuscripts, and were distrustful of their alien origin. The attitude toward Western technology in premodern China has been depicted as a "superior indifference to Western things."[46] The portrayal seems equally apt in the case of Ottoman subjects, who were certainly indifferent and quite probably felt superior to Europe. Even if there had been independent endeavors in this regard, the political order and social conventions would have stifled them.

It is easy to see that the old explanations (to which many still subscribe) and the one laid out here are grounded in the same basic assumption: that the differences between Middle Eastern and European attitudes to printing from the mid-fifteenth to the early nineteenth century reflected substantial cultural and philosophical disparities. The difference between the two sets of explanations is largely one of accent. The common accounts, which attribute the absence of Ottoman printing to state and *ʿulamāʾ* prohibition that reflected concern about their own standing and an overall aversion to innovation, imply a kind of intrinsic cultural dogmatism that yielded an unenlightened Ottoman society. Alternatively, it could be more beneficial to look at the cultural preferences of that society, vindicated as they were by a fairly smooth functioning of the sociopolitical and religious order and by a victorious empire during the two or three centuries after Gutenberg. From this perspective, the choice not to adopt the foreign, unneeded technology would seem perfectly sensible.

Finally, let us remind ourselves that all of this is no more than an attempt to explain an absence, and as such must be regarded as tentative. So long as no direct evidence comes to light that explicitly elucidates this absence, we will have to make do with such provisional explanations. Direct testimonies on the matter may not be found in

[45] Landes, 6–8, points to premodern China as an analogous case, where the centralized state "was always stepping in to interfere with private enterprise – to take over certain activities, to prohibit and inhibit others," something that stifled scientific and technological advancement.

[46] Landes, 18.

the future. For a society that operated by what seemed to be a winning formula, there was little need to explain why a superfluous device was not adopted. Only when the empire's lot began to change in later times did the Ottoman view of printing start changing as well. Only then did its guardians and their subjects find it advisable to consider the foreign technique more seriously.

1 The Formative Phase of Arab Printing

A Historical Overview

As the eighteenth century turned into the nineteenth, the Ottoman and Arab benign disregard for printing began to crack and give way to a different attitude. The new century would witness a gradual and eventually extensive Arab adoption of printing, the birth of a publishing industry, and the emergence of massive reading in Arab societies, changes that would further accelerate in the following century.

These developments were central pillars in the historic movement known as the Arab *nahḍa*, a term that will appear repeatedly in this and later chapters. Before proceeding further, it would be worthwhile to take a brief look at this notion and its relation to our subject. "The Arab *nahḍa*" is a loose construct with a range of meanings. Used flatly with no additional specification, it is taken as a name for the vigorous "awakening," or "revival," of intellectual and literary activity that took place in certain Ottoman–Arab provinces during the latter decades of Ottoman rule. Among its prominent marks were an increase in literary and linguistic creativity and an excited journalistic enterprise. Opening up new intellectual vistas, this enterprise engaged members of the society's educated classes in a vivid written discourse on questions of modernity and cultural identity and encouraged the spread of learning and literacy. "*Nahḍa*" is also used in a different, essentially political sense to denote the vocal quest for national liberation, political rights, and individual freedom that ensued, or rather emanated from, the cultural ferment of that period. There is no clear division between the cultural and the political; usually they are closely intertwined. Even when considering themes that appear to be purely cultural, political implications are always there. Such, for instance, are questions concerning the role of foreign (as distinct from local) actors in generating the changes, or the share of non-Muslim minority members (vs. that of Muslims) in advancing them, which are essential to the cultural exploration but also bear obvious political allusions. The same is true when the *nahḍa*'s historic time framework, especially its inception, is considered: Did it start at the beginning of the nineteenth century, or even earlier (and hence was the fruit of a local-inner endeavor), or after mid-century (and hence was largely a product of foreign initiatives)?[1] Like all historic developments, especially those with major sociocultural implications, the Arab *nahḍa* had been portended in various ways long before its coming into full blossoming. Selecting a point of departure that would best serve its exploration is thus the historian's choice.

This study, it is important to clarify, is not intended as a study of the *nahḍa*. Although the *nahḍa* will repeatedly be invoked here as a framework of reference, the probe will be addressed, more narrowly, only to certain aspects of it, namely, the advent of printing, publishing, and massive reading. These were indispensable changes in facilitating the *nahḍa*. Other major aspects of it, even in its strictly cultural sense, are not a part of the discussion here. Thus I will not consider the contents of intellectual thought and the public discourse on broad issues such as modernity and communal identity. Nor will I examine the emergence of cultural fora, or political ones for that matter, such as associations and parties. The story here starts when printing in Arabic and the use of printed materials on a massive scale begins: In the early 1820s in Egypt and, more dynamically, after mid-century in Lebanon. Examining the *nahḍa* from this specific angle is meant to cast a new light on it as a broad cultural development and to allow a more balanced appreciation of its unfolding.

As we have seen, Ottoman societies had been exposed to printing prior to 1800, to an extent which at first glance might seem considerable. This included printing by Jews, Greeks, Armenians, and Christian Arabs; the Zākhir and Müteferrika enterprises; and the ongoing importation of Arabic and Turkish printed books from Europe. Sultan Ahmet III's *firman* from 1727 inspired some more activity, in Istanbul and Syria, which yielded a few dozen titles in small editions until the end of that century. To these we might add the famous French printing project in Egypt, from 1798 to 1801: The machines Bonaparte brought there produced a steady stream of proclamations in Arabic and French that were publicly circulated, two regular French periodicals for the occupying troops, and more.[2] On the whole, then, the region did have some initial experience with the technology and its products. Still, none of these initiatives or even all of them together may be said to have started a new era in this regard in the Ottoman Middle East. Printing had not become a tool of state administration, nor had it affected popular practices,

[1] A recent discussion of this question appears in Patel, 12–35. Patel dismisses the assumption that the *nahḍa* was a late-nineteenth-century phenomenon and argues that it was well under way already before Napoleon's 1798 invasion of Egypt. See also Visser, 48–51.

[2] Al-Ṣāwī; Schwartz, 121–31.

communications, or access to knowledge on any significant scale. Had we traveled back in time to the year 1800, or even a decade or two later, and landed in Istanbul or any Arab provincial town, we would have been unable to locate printing as a tool of much weight. All Arab printing activities up to that point amounted to a set of unrelated episodes which foretold no necessary continuity. The Zākhir, Müteferrika, and Bonaparte ventures were scattered instances of a start with no substantial continuation. At that early stage, the general circumstances of the empire and its Arab territories were not conducive to turning printing into the agent of change it would later become.

Historic changes during the eighteenth and nineteenth centuries, notably – though not solely – a shift in the international balance of powers, altered Ottoman military, political, and cultural attitudes, including the view of printing. The old "superior indifference" to all things Western came to be coupled with, and then replaced by, attentiveness and receptivity. The change was seen on two planes: on the state level from above and on the popular level from below. During the eighteenth century, the Ottoman government was signaling its growing readiness to listen to external voices and to explore technological and organizational innovations. By the end of the century, its leadership was engaged in early attempts to restructure traditional systems along novel lines. This ushered in the extensive Ottoman reforms of the empire's last century, a major drama whose details are well known. Having explicitly sanctioned printing in Arabic script, the government in Istanbul gradually came to appreciate the potential benefits of the device for its own administration and to employ it more regularly. A similar initiative was launched independently in one of its provinces, Egypt, whose resourceful ruler introduced printing along with many other changes. Both in Istanbul and in Cairo, the nineteenth century was a period of government-initiated reforms, from army to education, from industry to architecture, in a bid to bolster the state in the face of mounting foreign and domestic pressures. The adoption of printing with its apparent plusses was a part of these efforts.

The initiative was not limited to the government. The changes of the time and the reforms designed to address them generated activity from below that was largely motivated by a public need for information and guidance. Navigating the changing waters required a new compass, as the old means of conveying news and views were becoming inadequate. This thirst for orientation, it was becoming increasingly clear, could best be met in print. Both rulers and their subjects were thus abandoning the old disinterest in printing.

This chapter presents an overview of the emergence of mass printing and publishing in the Arabic-speaking Ottoman provinces during the late nineteenth and early twentieth centuries. Similar changes took place simultaneously in the Turkish-speaking parts, which are not included in the present exploration.[3] In both places, printing gradually became a routine tool of state bureaucracy and the community's political, social, and cultural life. The first potentate to take action was the governor of Ottoman Egypt, whose enterprise was the most significant printing project in the region during the first half of the century. Modest steps were also taken elsewhere, mostly by Christians in the Lebanon area encouraged by missionaries, which would gain momentum after mid-century. These two schemes evolved independently of each other and reached similar regional importance by the third quarter of the century. Egypt and Lebanon were the region's leading centers of book and journal production, and it was there too that a set of diffusion channels for the printed products as well as mass reading audiences first emerged, with smaller offshoots in other provinces. Historic changes toward the end of the century triggered a massive emigration of Lebanese to Egypt, including many educated and creative individuals who had been exposed to or involved in the world of publishing in their land of origin. This development produced an Egyptian–Lebanese confluence of intellectual enterprise, which largely enhanced overall production. Egypt became the capital of Arabic publishing and would remain so until long after the end of the period explored here.

Change Top-Down: Mehmet ᶜAlī's Print Shops

Mehmet (Muḥammad) ᶜAlī, a typical Ottoman potentate, governed the province of Egypt for nearly half a century (r. 1805–1848). His farsighted reforms changed Egypt's realities in more ways than one and sowed the seeds for more changes to come. Introducing printing to the country was one such move, initially designed to upgrade the performance of his state apparatus and army and to sustain his ambitious schooling endeavor. Printing facilitated the mass production of school texts, aided the translation of hundreds of books for the use of state cadres, and expedited communication among the different administrative units. Inspiring private publishing ventures was apparently an unintended outcome of the Pasha's printing project, which, along with the new schooling scheme, also laid the foundations for the future emergence of a reading public. Whether or not Mehmet ᶜAlī's enterprise should be regarded as the starting point of the region's Arabic printing industry is an open question:

[3] For a concise summary of changes in the empire's Turkish-speaking parts after 1800, see Neumann.

On one hand, it may be argued, his projects had no direct sequel and hence cannot be considered a true beginning; on the other, however, they did provide some indispensable footings for subsequent changes.

Although this study is concerned with the emergence of printing as a social and cultural development rather than with state schemes, an outline account of the story must begin with Mehmet ᶜAlī's initiative. The story of his press has been repeatedly told in detail,[4] and we can make do with briefly laying out its main contours. Curious about foreign printed works, Mehmet ᶜAlī ordered the acquisition of many of them ("he set up collecting [European] books with the keenness of a bibliomaniac," one observer noted), including European newspapers which were read out to him.[5] He acknowledged the benefits of printing elaborated in Sultan Ahmet III's *firman* a century earlier; but, unlike the sultan, he also moved to do something about it. In 1815, he sent the Syrian-Christian Niqūlā Masābkī (or Musābikī) – a former employee at the French press in Cairo – to Milan to practice the printer's craft and purchase printing machines. Four years later, upon Masābkī's return with the necessary skills and gear, Mehmet ᶜAlī ordered the building of a press in Būlāq, a northern suburb of Cairo. The Būlāq press machines began rolling in late 1820 or early 1821 and the first printed book came out in 1822. During the following decade, another thirteen presses were set up in government offices and army headquarters in Cairo and Alexandria. By the end of Mehmet ᶜAlī's tenure, these shops had turned out hundreds of books, mostly in Arabic and Turkish, along with innumerable public notices, administrative circulars, and diplomatic documents. They also published several periodical state bulletins, an utter novelty, including the first Arabic newspaper, *al-Waqāʾiᶜ al-Miṣriyya* ("Egyptian Events"), which was launched in 1828. Mehmet ᶜAlī is reported to have ascribed much importance to his presses, regarded them as a mark of progress, and boasted about them to his foreign guests.[6]

Two prominent features of the Pasha's printing project were its exterior source of inspiration and its having been instituted from above. The foreign origins were plainly visible: The model for emulation, the technical knowhow, the practical training, and the equipment itself all were of European origin. So were the original versions of many of the printed books, which were translated from Western languages into Arabic

[4] The most comprehensive study on the subject is Riḍwān. See also ᶜAbduh, *Taʾrīkh al-waqāʾiᶜ*, 20–52; Heyworth-Dunne, "Printing"; and Ṣābāt, 135–65.

[5] Heyworth-Dunne, "Printing," 327–29 (quotation from p. 328); ᶜAbduh, *Aᶜlām*, 12, quoting contemporary documents.

[6] Nuṣayr, 401–16; Ayalon, *The Press*, 14–18; Green, 215–16. *Al-Waqāʾiᶜ al-Miṣriyya* was preceded by an embryonic and short-lived executive periodic circular, *Jūrnāl al-Khidīwī*.

and Turkish. Among the scores of translated works were many that dealt, in unprecedented detail, with the history, geography, politics, and culture of non-Muslim countries, in Europe and elsewhere (symbolically, the first book printed in Būlāq was *Dizionario Italiano e Arabo*). In that, the press was akin to many of the Pasha's other projects, launched as they were with foreign assistance and tools. The other conspicuous feature of the venture was its being a top-down scheme, with the ruler as initiator and his state presses printing nearly everything in the country.[7] The government defined printing objectives and marked the intended audience. The bulk of publications were produced to serve state-designated needs: school texts, military manuals, guidebooks for the various reform units, and a host of dispatches to the different executive departments. The official bulletin was the epitome of this approach: a periodic compilation of mostly administrative notices, designed to keep the officialdom updated, with a modest domestic circulation of 600 copies per issue.[8]

An important study on the subject is Egyptian bibliographer ᶜĀyida Ibrāhīm Nuṣayr's work on nineteenth-century book publishing in Egypt, which is a detailed survey of the system's functioning and its products. Nuṣayr has traced a remarkable yield of 867 titles printed in Mehmet ᶜAlī's Egypt, with an estimated total print run of 724,500 copies. This was a weighty output, manyfold bigger than the total number of books printed anywhere in the Ottoman Empire prior to the nineteenth century, including Müteferrika's production. The great majority of these were educational textbooks and practical guides for the different state units. There were also works – about a quarter of the total – that dealt with issues of potential interest to a broader readership, including locally written tracts on religious subjects, history, literature, and language; and translations of European works, as already noted.[9] But state publishing under the Pasha was primarily designed for a select circle of consumers, mostly officials and graduates of the new government schools. Save for a small group of educated men, the general populace, vastly illiterate, was left out of it. Public enlightenment of the kind that would concern *nahḍa* leaders later on in the century was scarcely considered in Mehmet ᶜAlī's Egypt. Inevitably, the ruler's priorities and the people's minuscule level of education constrained the public impact of his enterprise. It would take decades of schooling for more substantial segments of the general public to become involved in the cultural awakening.

[7] Private printing also started during that time; see below.

[8] Ayalon, *The Press*, 14–16.

[9] Nuṣayr, 153–58, 401–16. There seems to be an error in data calculation on pp. 414–15 and, if so, the total number of all titles should be 877, not 867. Impressive in scope and detail, Nuṣayr's study is not entirely error free and is less than comprehensive.

An important development borne by the state initiative was the birth, in the early or mid-1830s, of private printing in Egypt. Private individuals began to take advantage of the option offered by the Būlāq press, to print their own selected works under contract (*iltizām*) with it. As Kathryn Schwartz has recently shown, this was an extension of the manuscript-age practice of hiring a copyist to produce or reproduce a text, with the state now serving as production agent.[10] In addition, private printing shops also appeared during this period alongside the state-run ones; Nuṣayr has traced seven of them, which by her count printed as many as ninety-six titles between them until mid-century.[11] Such undertakings, though few and subject to close government control, portended the onset of printing from below, a mode that would gain momentum later on and would become the backbone of the Arab literary awakening. Like the ruler's initiatives, these endeavors by his subjects represented a shift in the attitude to printing.

Egyptian printing, as well as most other state reforms, began to slow down in the early 1840s, for different historic reasons. Fewer books than before came out of the presses during this decade and the official newspaper dwindled to erratic appearance.[12] A visitor to the country at the end of that decade would quite likely get the impression that printing activity there had been relegated to history. Reduced activity marked not just the latter years of Mehmet ᶜAlī's rule but also the tenure of his next three successors. In yet another shift, in the mid-1860s, a renewed publishing endeavor would begin again, soon to gather powerful momentum.

With a hindsight that was unavailable to the visitor of the late 1840s, we may appreciate the Pasha's vital role in laying the foundations for Egypt's future printing industry: securing its place in the centralized state; introducing the machinery; training a cadre of printers in both the state and private plants; and – through his schooling projects – facilitating the naissance of a market of literate consumers. Mehmet ᶜAlī also created the first precedent of a periodical publication and running it for years, however irregularly. Finally, an aspect of his enterprise which anticipated a prominent feature of the *nahḍa* was setting Egypt as a regional center of publishing activity. Egyptian printing became reputed in the neighboring provinces, and already in the 1830s we hear of a demand for Egyptian-printed books in Syria and Palestine, books that were supplied in hundreds

[10] Schwartz, 199–206, 231–32. For the traditional routine of hiring copyists, see Chapter 2.
[11] Nuṣayr, 408–14. See also Hsu, 3–4, whose survey is more limited than Nuṣayr's.
[12] By Nuṣayr's count, 216 titles were printed during the first half of the 1840s (1841–1845) and only 172 during its second half (1846–1850); Nuṣayr, 78–79. For the fate of *al-Waqāʾiᶜ al-Miṣriyya* at the end of Mehmet ᶜAlī's rule and afterward, see ᶜAbduh, *Taṭawwur*, 38–41.

of copies.[13] The seeds sown in this period went in Mehmet ᶜAlī's closing years into hibernation, to flower a quarter-of-a-century later under the rule of his grandson. Meanwhile, a new phase in this history would start in Beirut and Mount Lebanon.

Enterprise from Below in Beirut and Mount Lebanon

With no extraordinary governor of the Egyptian Pasha's caliber, other Ottoman–Arab provinces experienced no comparable initiative from above in their printing history. But there were other creative actors, whose efforts eventually yielded similar results: foreigners, primarily Christian missionaries, who used printing in their proselytizing endeavor; and local entrepreneurs, some of them pupils of missionaries, who viewed the new medium as a promising lever for advancing their own and their society's interests. Already in the seventeenth and eighteenth centuries, a bout of literary creativeness had taken place in Aleppo under evangelist inspiration, making that city perhaps the most important locus of Arab cultural activity then. The printer ᶜAbdāllāh Zākhir, for one, was among the city's prominent products.[14] In the history of Arab printing, however, it was not Aleppo but rather Beirut, along with other towns of Mount Lebanon – an area to which I shall henceforth refer, conveniently if somewhat anachronistically, as "Lebanon" – that would become the regional center of activity. In the second half of the nineteenth century, Lebanon emerged as a publishing and cultural hub of the entire region.

Around the middle of that century, the lands of the eastern Mediterranean were becoming a theater of accelerated action by international and local interests. The changes their activities triggered in every sphere had a direct bearing on the developments that will concern us here and we will examine their impact in due course. One mark of this enhanced activity was the growing presence of Western agents, who brought with them new ideas, techniques, implements, and sociocultural norms. European evangelists were followed by consuls, traders, army and navy men, engineers, consultants, tourists, and adventurers. Here we are mainly interested in the first group of these foreigners, the missionaries. How central their role was in introducing printing and publishing to the region is a matter of controversy among scholars: While many historians tend to regard them as key inspirers of modern educational and cultural

[13] Tibawi, *American Interests*, 69–71; Tibawi, *Arabic and Islamic Themes*, 305–6. Tibawi traced lists containing as many as 1,600 copies of printed works that were ordered from Egypt by educated people in towns in Syria and Palestine.

[14] Patel, 37–49; Kaḥḥāla, 18–34. Other luminaries of this early intellectual awakening were Isṭifān al-Duwayhī, Jirmānūs Farḥāt, and Niqūlā al-Ṣā'igh. See also Marcus, 240–45.

change, including the entry of printing, others play down that role and underscore instead the contribution of local actors in these developments.[15] Obviously, the issue is one of appraisal rather than accurate calculation. For our purposes, it is not necessary to decide either way; suffice it to say that the roles played by foreign and local actors were both indispensable. This will become amply clear later on.

Religious propagandists – Anglicans, American Protestants, French Jesuits, Russian Orthodox, and some others – arrived in the region in order to spread their faith. An essential vehicle for that was education, by which the message was imparted to the local inhabitants via the young generation (we shall later meet a few prominent graduates of their schools). Another channel was circulating pious books and tracts, a practice employed by evangelists in Muslim countries and elsewhere from the late sixteenth century onward.[16] It was also used in Ottoman territories, where the government, tolerantly if not quite enthusiastically, permitted their circulation.[17] In the more technologically advanced nineteenth century, however, there were important new features to this endeavor. For one thing, in addition to being bearers of a sacred message, religious propagandists were also children of post-Napoleonic France and the post-Revolutionary United States. As agents of the changing West, they brought with them a host of new ideas and standards beside the pious call. For another, for the first time since the début of Arabic printing in Europe, Western propagandists now brought printing equipment to the area itself and began producing their publications there, rather than importing the printed works from abroad.

The first to bring in such machinery were evangelists of the Anglican Church Missionary Society (CMS), who set up their post not in an Arabic-speaking province but on the Isle of Malta, in 1815. The island was selected due to its pivotal geographic position and its having been under British rule since 1800. The CMS instituted a printing press there, believing that it would serve its mission better than importing printed literature, but also that it was "desirable to encourage Printing Establishments among the People of the Mediterranean" by erecting a model in their neighborhood.[18] Printing gear and Arabic fonts were brought from

[15] Abd al-Latif Tibawi was a sharp critic of the view that ascribed a major role to the missionaries; see his *Arabic and Islamic Themes*, 304–14. See also, more recently, Hanssen, 163–64. The historiographic debate on the missionary role is discussed in Sedra, 34–38.

[16] Roper, *Arabic Printing in Malta*, 42–104; Yaron Ayalon, "Richelieu."

[17] An oft-quoted Ottoman decree from 1588 permitted the circulation in the empire of "printed books and pamphlets in Arabic, Persian, and Turkish"; English translation in Atiyeh, 283.

[18] Mission head William Jowett, quoted in Roper, *Arabic Printing in Malta*, 108.

London and the press began turning out Arabic books in 1826. Over one hundred book editions, mostly in Arabic and Turkish, were printed there until 1842, including religious works, school texts in various fields, and even translations of English literary works. There were also several journals.[19] Unlike Mehmet ᶜAlī, the Malta printers were eager to spread their works to a circle of readers as wide as possible throughout the area. They therefore produced large quantities of them: More than 150,000 copies of Arabic and Turkish books and 6,800 newspaper copies from Malta are estimated to have been distributed in the Arab regions during these years, most of them in Lebanon and Egypt and the rest in Syria, Palestine, Iraq, the Maghreb, and even the Hijaz.[20] These were remarkable figures for the time.

Until the mid-1830s, the Malta press and that of Mehmet ᶜAlī were the only two sources of Arabic printed texts in the region. At that point, a third actor appeared on the stage, the Boston-based Presbyterian mission, better known as the ABCFM (American Board of Commissioners for Foreign Missions). ABCFM agents came to Malta at the same time as their CMS counterparts with a plan to establish an Arabic press there and with the necessary equipment, but for various reasons failed to carry out their plan. In 1834, they moved with their machines to Beirut, and in the following year began producing books in Arabic.[21] Difficulties – unfit fonts, the absence of trained printers – slowed down their work at first and limited it to short religious treatises and school books. In the mid-1840s, following a machinery upgrade and personnel changes, they embarked on a more energetic activity which made "the American Press," as it came to be known, a celebrated institution in Beirut. Another group of missionaries to start printing there before mid-century were French Jesuits, who had been proselytizing in Lebanon for the previous two centuries. Challenged by the Protestant initiative, they set up their own lithographic press there in 1848 and began producing mostly Catholic religious tracts.[22] They soon became the American mission's main rivals in the race for religious-cultural influence in the country. European evangelists also established presses elsewhere in the neighborhood: in Jerusalem (Franciscans in 1846, Anglicans in 1848), Mosul (Dominicans in 1857), and other places later on.[23] But none of these became as prolific

19 A detailed list in Roper, *Arabic Printing in Malta*, 330–48. See also Roper, "Arabic Books."

20 Roper, *Arabic Printing in Malta*, 270–302.

21 The ABCFM brought printing machinery to Malta, but managed to print only in Italian, Greek, and later Armenian. Roper, "Beginnings," 50–57. Regarding their Beirut enterprise, there is some uncertainty as to whether the first printed book was in 1835 or 1836; Roper, "Beginnings," 63. See also Auji, 26–36.

22 Shaykhū, 56ff.

23 Petrozzi, 64–69; Shaykhū, 171–82.

and influential as the presses of Beirut, which after mid-century was emerging as the capital of Arabic printing.

The missionaries found a fertile ground for their work and a pool of eager local partners in Lebanon. A non-Muslim island in a Muslim ocean, Lebanese Christians displayed the resourcefulness of a minority on the defensive and openness to the call coming from beyond their immediate surroundings. Some Christian groups had had ties with their European coreligionists for centuries: the Maronites and Greek-Catholics (Melkites) with Rome and France, the Greek-Orthodox with Russia, ties that would become tighter in the nineteenth century. Rivalries among communities and splinter groups often marred the country's public atmosphere, but also had a positive result: They prompted them to uplift their education level.

Another ingredient in the Lebanese readiness for cultural change, beside the intuitive openness to Europe and the competition among Christians, was a legacy of literary creativity which by mid-century was already several decades old. Since the late eighteenth century, educated Christians were engaging in a diligent study of the Arabic language and in chronicle writing. Some of them were graduates of the Maronite seminary at ᶜAyn Waraqa (founded 1789), an institution that imparted broad-base education, high-level articulation, and knowledge of languages. Amir Bashīr II, the ruler of Mount Lebanon for over half a century (r. 1788–1840), gathered in his Bayt al-Dīn court several of these gifted writers, among them men who may be regarded as precursors of the *nahḍa*: Nāṣīf al-Yāzijī, Buṭrus Karāma, Niqūlā Turk, and Ṭannūs al-Shidyāq.[24] In the early part of the century, their literary activity stirred intellectual ferment in Lebanon. It was a modest activity at that stage; but it would prepare the ground for the engagement with the Western agents and turning it into an "Arab awakening."

By mid-century, Beirut had become a place of spirited cultural activity, with an evident promise for more. A literary-scientific society, *al-jamᶜiyya al-sūriyya li-iktisāb al-ᶜulūm wa'l-funūn*, was founded jointly by American missionaries and local Christians in 1847. For the next five years, its members met regularly for lectures and discussions of issues in arts and sciences. It also had a library with several hundred volumes in several languages.[25] Private presses were popping up in the city, printing books of prose and poetry by local authors; and new bookshops opened for selling

[24] Makdisi, *Culture of Sectarianism*, 38–42; Makdisi, *Artillery*, 76–79; Zachs, *Making*, 28–38; Krymskii, 397–98; Kamāl al-Yāzijī, 43–74.

[25] Makdisi, *Artillery*, 194–96; Zachs, *Making*, 138–45. In 1852, the society published a selection of lectures delivered in its meetings; see *al-Jamᶜiyya al-sūriyya*. An account on the state of the society's library in 1847 appears on p. 120.

them along with titles imported from Egypt and Europe.[26] Periodical publications too became a part of the scene. When an émigré from Aleppo launched a newspaper in Istanbul in the mid-1850s – the very first private Arabic paper anywhere – copies of it reached Lebanon, as did, most likely, copies of other foreign journals in several languages.[27] Public appetite for this kind of publications led to the birth, in January 1858, of a local Arabic newspaper in the city itself, Khalīl al-Khūrī's *Ḥadīqat al-Akhbār*, which would become a durable product that would last into the twentieth century. Before too long, it was followed by a host of other journals that became popular conduits of new ideas and platforms for readers' exchanges. The ease with which one could now have their thoughts widely circulated further encouraged written productivity. Progress in education, to which the missions and the local communities were equally keen to contribute, was another essential facet of the changing cultural reality. By the mid-1870s, Beirut was a scene of lively writing, printing, publishing, and journalistic activity, with expanding marketing and diffusion mechanisms and a growing readership. At that point, the city already had some ten private presses that had issued scores of books, both locally authored and translated, in thousands of copies; some twenty newspapers and journals; and over ten bookshops selling local and imported works.[28] Unique in the region in these regards, Lebanon became a mecca for readers of Arabic from Fez to Baghdad and beyond the Middle East.

Center and Periphery

As literary endeavor was gaining momentum in Lebanon, Egypt was leaving its interval of cultural idleness behind and moving on to an era of energetic activity under Mehmet ᶜAlī's grandson. Khedive Ismāᶜīl (r. 1863–1879), an avid modernizer with a penchant for means of communication, labored to upgrade them in his realm so as to develop the country and bolster his rule. He built roads, railways, and ports, introduced telegraph, initiated postal services and news agencies, revitalized the official state bulletin, and authorized the opening of private presses and – for the first time – private newspapers by his subjects. He also gave

[26] See the 1859 advert for Fatḥāllāh Tājir's bookshop in Beirut, announcing the sale of imported books from Cairo and Paris and noting that it had been in this business "for a long time"; *Ḥadīqat al-Akhbār*, 8 September 1859, 4. See further in Chapter 4.

[27] The first private Arabic paper, Rizqāllāh Ḥassūn's *Mir'āt al-Aḥwāl*, appeared in Istanbul during the Crimean War (1854 or 1855) and lasted for about a year. According to Ḥassūn, copies of it were sent to Syria and Lebanon. Ayalon, "Hassun and Shidyaq."

[28] Shaykhū, 43–128; Ṣābāt, 56–61; Ṭarrāzī, *Ta'rīkh al-ṣiḥāfa*, Vol. 4, 4–7, 106–7; Ayalon, "Arab Booksellers," 86.

a considerable boost to state schooling. In this atmosphere of government enterprise, Egypt could again make strides in printing and publishing by relying on its own educated class, graduates of the schooling system set up by Mehmet ᶜAlī. This renewed momentum coincided with another historic development which gave it a further lift: a mass influx of skilled Syrians and Lebanese, who left their country in big numbers during the last third of the nineteenth century due to unfavorable political, social, and economic circumstances. Those who had previously engaged in publishing, or wished to do so, had an additional reason to leave: the rigid regime of Sultan ᶜAbdülhamid II (r. 1876–1909), with its policy of silencing and punishment which stifled written expression. Syrian and Lebanese immigrants, overwhelmingly Christian, went mostly to North and South America and to France. They also came in big numbers to Egypt, which was now emerging as a land of opportunities. For Syrians and Lebanese, moving there had the advantage of changing location without leaving their cultural and linguistic element.[29]

Educated and enterprising, the newcomers soon became the yeast in the Egyptian dough. They wrote, printed, and published Arabic books and journals and inspired a written discourse among learned readers across the region. They also played a central role in developing the channels necessary for circulating the printed products – bookshops, distribution agencies, advertising – and made up a sizeable segment of the consuming audience. Simultaneously, educated Egyptians took an increasing part in this endeavor alongside the newcomers. By the year 1900, Egyptians and Lebanese had founded over 100 printing presses in Egypt; had published no fewer than 7,700 books in over six million copies during the previous three decades; and had issued as many as 372 newspapers during the same time.[30] Further boosted by the onset of a culturally tolerant British occupation in 1882, the Egyptian–Lebanese convergence created a regional literary center of gravity on the banks of the Nile that will remain the heart of Arab intellectual creativity well beyond World War I.

Meanwhile, in the other Arabic-speaking provinces of Syria, Palestine, Iraq, and the Arabian Peninsula, political conditions constricted activity in this field and kept it at a scanty minimum. A stringent censorship by the suspicious Hamidian regime checked creativity in these parts for over three decades. In Lebanon, printed production that had begun prior to ᶜAbdülhamid's tenure was emasculated under his rule, prompting many

[29] Philipp, *The Syrians*, 78–85 and passim.

[30] Data on presses from Nuṣayr, 401–49, and on books calculated from figures in Nuṣayr, 79–80, 94–97. For newspapers, see Ṭarrāzī, *Ta'rīkh al-ṣiḥāfa*, Vol. 4, 162–78, 214–22, 274–88, 324–26.

writers to leave, as we have seen, and imposing restraint and fright on those who chose to stay. Elsewhere, where no such activity had been under way, the distrustful government prevented its emergence almost completely. Here and there printers were permitted to operate on a modest scale, or operated without a license; here and there, again, timid and poor-quality newspapers or books and pamphlets with innocuous substance were allowed to appear and circulate. Printing and publishing in these places began in earnest only after the 1908 Young Turk Revolution had changed the rules of the game and heralded a more liberal era. Only then did a surge of animated publishing activity occur in the cities of the Fertile Crescent and the Arabian Peninsula, just a few years before World War I. In Lebanon, the publishing endeavor which had been devitalized under ʿAbdülhamid likewise resumed its vitality then, with greater vigor. But nowhere in these new loci of publishing, nor yet in Lebanon, could the activity match, in scope or quality, the products that were coming out of Egypt, with its pool of talent and decades of experience.

It is important to note, however, that the provinces where big-scale publishing began only after 1908 had been affected by the adoption of printing in the region long before that time. Playing the largely passive role of consumers, the mostly urban educated classes in these other places were exposed to the sounds coming out of Egypt and Lebanon, which gradually altered their cultural world to an appreciable measure. Arabic-speaking societies had long represented one potential market for anything written in that language. Now, upon the appearance of printed works in the region, members of these classes started reaching out to the new products. We have already noted the demand for Egyptian-printed books in Syria and Palestine as early as the 1830s. Residents of other provinces purchased and read Egyptian and Lebanese books and journals, built up collections, and often responded to what they had read by sending letters to journal editors, circumventing the suspicious Ottoman censors when necessary and possible. Egyptian and Lebanese publishers, for their part, worked to distribute their products in the region's faraway places, appointed circulation agents in remote locations, and delivered books and journals to shops there. A network of lively written exchanges emerged, with a dual spring of production and a set of arteries extending from there to the region's remotest corners.

The advent of publishing, then, involved more changes than just the birth of a printing industry. At the opposite end of the production machinery, the consumer public was undergoing a shift in size and makeup, turning from a minuscule elite faction into an ever-bigger and more varied crowd. With their surroundings changing in front of their eyes, speakers of Arabic, turning into readers of Arabic, came to adopt the habit of resorting to written knowledge for contending with the new dilemmas. Past misgivings about printing were gradually abandoned not only by the rulers and members of the religious elite but also by the public at large. This was one of the *nahḍa*'s most significant achievements, arguably the single most important one. It was a chicken-and-egg process: The availability and growing utility of printed texts encouraged the acquisition of reading skills; and the expansion of the reading market, in turn, promoted more production. As the nineteenth century drew to a close, the number of Arab readers everywhere was on the ascent, more so in urban areas than in the countryside, more so near the centers of production than away from them. An important aspect of the changes was the development of modern diffusion arrangements that allowed the flow of the massive printed output from publishers to their clients. They comprised various mediatory mechanisms, from book and newspaper selling facilities, through mail delivery arrangements, to public-reading services and modern advertising ventures. Such tools, old, upgraded, or entirely new, represented vital threads of the cultural change fabric.

By the end of the Ottoman era, the segment of Arabic-speaking society exposed to books was several-fold bigger than half a century earlier, and growing. Exposure to journals and newspapers was even wider, at times becoming something of a popular addiction. As ever in such historic processes, the ubiquity of printed works and the public interest in them grew faster than people's acquisition of independent reading skills, an inevitable gap that was typical of the transition phase. To bridge across it, the society fell back on the familiar practice of vocal group reading, which markedly increased popular access to the texts most in demand, primarily newspapers. Printing also influenced people's daily life in various other ways. A host of printed items of everyday use from money bills to train tickets came to alter the routine of a society that hitherto had touched written items far more sparingly. These colorful aspects of the printing-inspired transformation will be probed in the chapters that follow.

2 Printers and Publishers

Two printed works lie close to each other in the Arabic book section of Firestone library at Princeton University: Buṭrus al-Bustānī's *Quṭr al-muḥīṭ* (Beirut, 1869) and Abū al-Hudā al-Ṣayyādī's *al-Ḥaqq al-mubīn fī abhāt al-ḥāsidīn* (Cairo, 1892). They are on adjoining shelves apparently because they were cataloged around the same time. Both were published during the early decades of private Arab printing and share certain physical and technical features typical of the time. There are also differences – in size, contents, and purpose – which make them rather dissimilar. Bustānī's book, a modern dictionary of the Arabic language, comprises two thick volumes, 2,452 pages in all, a work of great scholarly erudition designed for the educated. Ṣayyādī's is a ten-leaf opuscule, simple and concise, which obviously addressed a popular readership. Both are characteristic *nahḍa* products, each typifying a specific genre within a colorful range of printed works, varying in the routine of their making, material quality, objectives, and, likely, ways of consumption. The Bustānī and Ṣayyādī items may not represent two opposite ends of this range, but they are distinct enough from each other to be considered separately.

In the first part of this chapter, I examine private Arab printing and publishing of the kind embodied in the Bustānī work. This was an extension of the time-honored book-making tradition now continued on a much larger scale by other means, with new products alongside the old. The entry of a new device for a quick making of written texts attracted to the field people who had not usually engaged in writing before, surely not on a massive scale. This important aspect of the change – the popularization of printing – will be considered in the chapter's second part. This chapter deals with printers and publishers, two distinct occupations that were both new to the region. There were printers who were not involved in publishing and publishers who did not print. Many engaged in both.

Before considering the shift ushered in by the two groups, the scene that had preceded it should be laid out in general outlines. Books, book making, and book collecting represented an important facet of the region's cultural history. Accounts on early Muslim state libraries, most famously those of the Abbasids, the Cordoba Umayyads, and the Fatimids, feature dramatic data on their size and contents. These and some other libraries are said to have comprised hundreds of thousands of volumes, or more. Mosque collections and those of certain private scholars are likewise reported to have been especially vast.[1] Such fantastic figures and the venerating tone in which they are usually depicted suggest high esteem for writing and scholarship: Books were objects one would be proud to own and display, and the possession of many of them lent their owner much prestige, especially among other book owners. These legendary-size collections are said to have depleted and disintegrated in later times and little is heard of them after the thirteenth century. The next five centuries are often described in the literature – including works by Arab scholars – as an unhappy era in the stature of the Arabic book. Political instability, military turmoil, fires, floods and other natural calamities, poor maintenance, and the growing force of religious dogma at the expense of creativity, all have been mentioned as factors that contributed to this presumed deterioration.[2]

This image of depreciating post-classical Islamic book stocks has been questioned lately by Konrad Hirschler. In *The Written Word in the Medieval Arabic Lands*, Hirschler has offered a different view of the situation: not a sweeping decline but an institutional change, which included the restructuring of collections and redistribution of literary treasures. While the big libraries of the past diminished or disappeared, he has suggested, the collections of local mosques and *madrasa*s that usually relied on Waqf endowments were gradually increasing and multiplying throughout the region. The process had begun as early as the thirteenth century. Private collections were expanding too, their contents often ending on the shelves of the mosque or *madrasa* libraries to which they were bequeathed. Hirschler has argued that the growth of these libraries, and an increasing thematic diversity that typified especially the private collections, compensated at least in part for the loss of the big state and mosque libraries. These libraries also had the additional advantage of facilitating a greater public access to books and thus contributed to a growth in the number of readers.[3]

Another recent study, Nelly Hanna's *In Praise of Books*, has argued that between the sixteenth and eighteenth centuries a substantial surge in book production and consumption occurred in Egypt and apparently also in Syria. The change affected mainly the social sector she has

[1] Kohlberg, 71–74; Hirschler, 126–30.
[2] E.g., Sibāʿī, Chapter 6; Kurd ʿAlī, 196–200.
[3] Hirschler, 124–63.

identified as the middle class: traders, small business owners, commerce middlemen, artisans, and craftsmen, as well as middle- and low-ranking *ᶜulamāʾ*. Economic developments and an expansion in education altered the life routine of these groups, allowing them more leisure time and changing their cultural habits. One expression of this was a rising demand for books among them. Another development, a simultaneous decline in paper prices, reduced production costs so that books became a commodity more members of that class could afford. Hanna's evidence suggests a considerable increase in the number of books copied in Egypt during the two centuries prior to the entry of printing. This was reflected in the bigger number of volumes in private collections, of which we know from court probate lists, as well as in the growing numbers of copyists who, by some sources, were now organized in guilds.[4] During this period of expansion, alongside books that met traditional standards of format and accuracy were also cheap editions of lower-quality products, inexpensive items on various subjects, notably prayer books and ṣūfī tracts. Such a decline in quality was the inevitable result of rising demand and the increasing number of less professional copyists. More books, in a wider range of subjects, quality, and prices, came to be possessed by expanding groups of people in the middle social ranks.[5]

Hanna's study focuses on Egypt, especially Cairo, and her analysis is extended to Syria on the basis of available evidence on a few big cities there. Other parts of the region – smaller towns and rural places in Egypt, Syria, and other Arabic-speaking provinces – are yet to be explored for such possible developments. Similar shifts may or may not have occurred in those smaller places, although it is conceivable that some of the increased production in the big cities percolated to the other towns, maybe also to remoter parts of the region such as Palestine and Iraq. Yet, even if we take Hanna's findings only for the sixteenth to eighteenth centuries alone, along with Hirschler's sensible assumption on the ongoing growth of local collections that had begun earlier, the impression is of an activity whose scope was not shrinking – perhaps it was even increasing – before the arrival of printing. Manuscript production, book trade, and book diffusion all might have been in a process of expanding. We have no way as yet to assess the pace and scale of that process, and more research of these issues is required; but "decline" might well be an unfitting term for describing that scene.

A key figure at the heart of this process was the *warrāq*, literally "paper dealer" or "stationer" (also known as *ṣaḥḥāf*), the forerunner of the

[4] The copyists' organization in guilds is in some doubt; see Hanna, *In Praise*, 89; Schwartz, 107.

[5] Hanna, *In Praise*, especially Chapter 4. See also Schwartz, 106–12; Heyberger; Establet and Pascual.

printers and publishers of later times. This was a respectable calling, for which we have more or less constant evidence since the ninth century. Sometimes the *warrāq* was also a copyist (*nassāḥ*); at other times, he would collaborate with copyists and scribes. Before printing, the *warrāq* performed the manifold role of stationer, book maker, and bookseller, often also editor, binder, and publisher, producing new texts or, more commonly, replicating existing ones. *Warrāqīn* were members of the educated class. They worked in the service of rulers, scholars, and whoever wished to have a book copy made for him. Familiar throughout the region, their stalls or booths were often clustered in specific sections of the city bazaars, typically known as *sūq al-warrāqīn*. A routine way to increase one's book collection was to order a volume from one of them, who would reproduce it from an existing copy or search for it through his business ties. Educated people would sometimes copy books for themselves from public or private libraries, and at other times would call on the *warrāq* to do the job.[6] In times of increasing demand, as during the period just before the entry of printing explored by Nelly Hanna, people with limited training would sometimes join the circles of book copyists as a way of supplementing their income: teachers, students, lower *ᶜulamā'*, and even traders and artisans who could write.[7] Printing and the emergence of publishing would eventually render the copyists redundant. But, as in late fifteenth- and early sixteenth-century Europe, this would happen only very slowly and gradually. Long after the period examined here, *warrāqīn* and *nassāḥīn* would continue to make a living by offering their services in city alleys and the areas around mosques and public libraries.[8]

Authors as Publishers

Leaders of the Arab literary "awakening" are remembered mostly for their intellectual feat and sociocultural views. In their books and journals, they recovered old cultural treasures, articulated new thoughts, and preached novel ideas from nationalism to women's liberation. Had they lived in an earlier century, their writings would have reached the shelves of private or public book collections as pieces, or masterpieces, of the scholarly canon, known mostly to the community's learned. Buṭrus al-Bustānī (1819–1883), for example, would have remained in historical memory as, say, another Jāḥiẓ or Suyūṭī.

[6] Pedersen, 43–53; Qāsimī, Vol. 2, 269–70. See also the colorful description of this routine in preprinting Cairo, in Schwartz, 97–115.
[7] Hanna, *In Praise*, 89.
[8] Pedersen, 53.

But this was the age of printing and mass diffusion. Prominent thinkers and writers of the *nahḍa* also played a leading role in erecting the material infrastructure that sustained their intellectual output and made it accessible to the public. Some of them indeed practiced the whole range of activities typical of the printing age: not only authoring and translating but also printing, publishing, advertising, and selling books. This was often the case when an author-publisher had a newspaper or journal as his pivotal project. Issuing a periodical entailed constant dealing with printing, marketing, and vending, as well as continuous exchanges with readers. In studies on the *nahḍa*, this aspect of the work of leading thinkers has usually been eclipsed by a discussion of their ideas and the public discourse they evoked. But, as these men knew well, the effect of these ideas and discourse hinged on production quality and the scope of dissemination. The role of these intellectuals in making written texts available to the public was arguably as crucial as the thoughts they propagated.

Take Bustānī, again. His fame in modern Arab history rests on his being "dedicated to the discussion and spread of ideas," as Albert Hourani has noted.[9] Between "discussion" and "spread," far more attention has been given to the former, although Bustānī's contribution to the latter was just as indispensable. His written output was impressive: two groundbreaking Arabic dictionaries (of which *Quṭr al-muḥīṭ* was one); a multivolume universal encyclopedia; several works on language, history, and other subjects; a rendition into Arabic of Daniel Defoe's *Robinson Crusoe*; a leading biweekly journal, which he ran with his son for some sixteen years; and two other papers he issued for shorter periods. He is remembered, as well, as an innovative educator and an energetic exponent of patriotic ideas.[10] Bustānī was exposed to printing and acquired training in it as a young man in his twenties, working as a translator for the American Protestant mission in Beirut and as a copyist at the mission press. In the late 1840s and during the 1850s, he edited and printed several educational and other works there, and in 1860–1861 he wrote, printed, and distributed eleven issues of the passionate patriotic broadsheet, *Nafīr Sūriyā* ("Syria's clarion").[11] Bustānī ascribed great importance to this technology and its enlightening potential. In his famous 1859 *Khiṭāb*, he lamented his society's neglect of printing and the resultant dearth of Arabic books and tried to impress his audience that "presses, if properly employed for printing things of cultural value to the public, could enrich the Arabs with books and libraries in a short time," and

[9] Hourani, 113–14.

[10] Khūrī, *al-Muʿallim*; Abu Manneh, "The Christians"; Tibawi, "American Missionaries"; Hourani; Patel, 202–06.

[11] Detailed discussion in Sheehi and Jandora. Also Tibawi, "American Missionaries," 158–61, 170–71.

"disseminate knowledge and civilization (*tamaddun*) in this country in a quick moment."[12] Bustānī acted upon this commendation. In 1868, in partnership with Khalīl Sarkīs – to whom we shall return shortly – he established one of the earliest private presses in Beirut, *maṭbaᶜat al-maᶜārif* ("educational press"). Among other works, it printed Bustānī's Arabic dictionaries *Muḥīṭ al-muḥīṭ* and *Quṭr al-muḥīṭ* (the latter being an abridgement of the former), the first eight volumes of his encyclopedia *Dā'irat al-maᶜārif*, and the three journals he published with members of his family: *al-Jinān* ("Gardens"), the most important and durable of the three; *al-Janna* ("Garden" or "Paradise"; both from 1870); and *al-Junayna* ("Little Garden," from 1871). It also printed works by others who bought the press's services. Bustānī and his colleagues adopted the periodical format as a vehicle for informing the public on domestic and foreign political developments, enlightening it with historic works and entertaining it with literary pieces. He also devised creative methods of reaching out to the readers: He was a pioneer in introducing subscription arrangements not just for journals but also for books, in appointing remote distribution agents, and in formulating a workable routine for them, after much trial and error. During the formative years, especially in the 1870s, hardly an issue of *al-Jinān* was devoid of notices to the readers, agents, or distributors regarding delivery arrangements, fee collection, and other operational matters, all bearing the marks of the experimental stage. Bustānī and his partner Sarkīs also used their press as a book distribution depot. *Maṭbaᶜat al-maᶜārif* carried local and imported books and regularly announced their sale in Bustānī's *al-Jinān*.[13] We shall repeatedly see Bustānī's fingerprints in such operational innovations in the following chapters.

Aḥmad Fāris al-Shidyāq (1805–1887) is another example of a prominent intellectual who was also a pioneer in various aspects of publishing. His eminence in historical memory, like Bustānī's, comes mostly from his writings: the fifty-odd works on Arabic language, literature, poetry, and more, which he penned or translated; and his journal *al-Jawā'ib*, one of the most influential Arabic newspapers of its time. He is also noted in the annals for his curiously checkered career, his eccentric personality, and his many quarrels with contemporaries.[14] But Shidyāq's contribution to his society's cultural modernization was no less important in what he himself called "the lofty craft" (*al-ṣināᶜa al-jalīla*),[15] printing. Having

[12] Bustānī's "speech on the state of Arab culture," *al-Jamᶜiyya al-sūriyya*, 115.
[13] To pick an example, *al-Jinān*, 5 (1874), issue 6, front and back cover, advertised over 100 books on sale at *maṭbaᶜat al-maᶜārif*. For further discussion, see Chapter 4.
[14] Shidyāq is the hero of quite a few biographical studies. A credible survey of his career and historic role is ᶜImād al-Ṣulḥ. See also Roper, "Fāris al-Shidyāq."
[15] Al-Ḥammād, 11–12.

grown in the old scribal tradition and being a professional scribe himself, Shidyāq was, as Geoffrey Roper has shown, "well aware that the revival of Arabic literature and culture depended on bypassing [that tradition]."[16] He was trained in printing in his twenties, while working for the CMS press in Malta. His subsequent career took him to Cairo, Paris, Cambridge, London, and Tunis, and everywhere his activities were closely connected to publishing projects. In 1859 or 1860, he settled in Istanbul, and after a stint as chief corrector (*ra'īs al-muṣaḥḥiḥīn*) of the Imperial Press, he launched his paper, *al-Jawā'ib* – one of the earliest Arabic journals – which he published for twenty-three years (1861–1884). He set up a print shop for the paper, *maṭbaʿat al-Jawā'ib*, and turned it into a major publishing enterprise: *Maṭbaʿat al-Jawā'ib* printed scores of Arabic books during Shidyāq's lifetime, by him and others; advertised them in journals and in catalogs his press issued; and marketed them across the region through its own network of agents. Printing, advertising, marketing – in all of these, Shidyāq, like Bustānī, broke new grounds in the region and set an example that would be extensively followed.[17] Once an old-school scribe, Shidyāq became a leading maker and distributor of printed Arabic works, his career and personal pursuits embodying the cultural shifts that affected his society.

I could go on exploring Bustānī and Shidyāq still more closely and using the career of either or both of them as a window to the historic role of the Arab scholar-printers. But it should be more interesting and profitable to obtain that glance from the career of a less celebrated figure of that time: Khalīl Sarkīs, a publisher and author who is not remembered as one of his society's literary luminaries, but was certainly a key figure in the region's printing history. His life story offers a fine prism for inspecting the *nahḍa*'s most delicate components that relate to printing and publishing.

Khalīl Sarkīs (1842–1915) is not known to have left an autobiography or memoirs, nor are his personal papers known to be extant. Nor, again, have compilers of nineteenth-century biographies of eminent Arabs deemed him important enough to be included in their anthologies. His story comes down to us through numerous references by his colleagues and, indirectly, through casual personal comments in his own works.[18] Sarkīs was born in Lebanon, at a time when cultural change was just

[16] Roper, "Fāris al-Shidyāq," 210–12. Roper's is a rather singular exploration of Shidyāq's role as a printer, publisher, and book disseminator.

[17] ʿImād al-Ṣulḥ, 98–103; al-Ḥammād. See also Chapter 4.

[18] *Yūbīl lisān al-ḥāl* is rich in accounts of Sarkīs's life and accomplishments. Also Ṭarrāzī, *Ta'rīkh al-ṣiḥāfa*, Vol. 2, 129–38. The following discussion of Sarkīs is a modified version of a section in Ayalon, "Private Publishing," 564–67.

dawning. As a pupil at the American missionary school in Beirut, we are told, he was fascinated by the nearby mission's press and used to spend time there as a helping hand and later as an apprentice. Having graduated, he joined the press full time and acquired expertise, especially in molding and casting letters. The mid-century years, a fateful period for Lebanon, was also a time when new horizons were opening to the gifted and creative. In 1868, at the age of twenty-six, Sarkīs went into partnership with Buṭrus al-Bustānī, by then at the peak of his repute, and the two opened a press, *maṭbaᶜat al-maᶜārif.*

The nine-clause contract (*itifāqiyya*) that set the rules for their collaboration is an interesting document worth looking into. The partners agreed to open a business comprising a printing press, a letter-casting plant, and a book-selling outlet. Each of them was to invest 15,000 qurush in it, a considerable sum then. Sarkīs was to act as full-time director with a monthly salary of 450 qurush, in charge of obtaining supplies, managing the press's routine functioning, and handling the necessary paperwork, including accounts. Bustānī, the busier of the two, was charged with proofreading (*taṣlīḥ*) of all books, and his approval was required for every printing. Books, the contract stipulated, were to have set prices, with a price list affixed to the press's door; the only permitted deviation from them would be a 10 percent discount (*skūntū*), at the discretion of either partner. Discussing the choice of books to be printed, the contract mentioned only two kinds, indicating the scope of work that could be envisioned at that early time: books authored or translated by either of the two partners; and "old books" (*al-kutub al-qadīma*), to wit, those existing in manuscript, on any subject. Notably, no reference was made to new works by contemporary writers who would wish to have them printed in *maṭbaᶜat al-maᶜārif.*[19] The partnership became a family business sometime later, when Sarkīs married Bustānī's daughter Louisa.

Maṭbaᶜat al-maᶜārif was not the first private press in Beirut. It was preceded by three printing shops owned by Christian institutions[20] and by half a dozen private presses that had opened during the previous decade.[21] A central project of the Sarkīs-Bustānī business was publishing the three Bustānī family journals. But printing them did not keep *maṭbaᶜat al-maᶜārif*

[19] Text in *Yubīl lisān al-ḥāl*, 5–8.

[20] *Maṭbaᶜat al-qadīs jūrjiyūs*, from the mid-eighteenth century; the American missionary press, *al-maṭbaᶜa al-amīrikiyya*, from 1834; and the Jesuit press, *al-maṭbaᶜa al-kathūlīkiyya*, from 1848. Shaykhū, 43–93.

[21] Shaykhū, 93–113. The important ones were *al-maṭbaᶜa al-sūriyya* (1857) of Khalīl al-Khūrī, owner of the newspaper *Ḥadīqat al-Akhbār*, and *al-maṭbaᶜa al-ᶜumūmiyya* (1861) of Yūsuf al-Shalfūn, which printed several journals and quite a few books (we shall meet Shalfūn again in Chapter 5).

fully busy, not even with some additional jobs which it performed for other businesses around. The partners thus turned to what other printers in Beirut had been doing for a while – and what members of the trade had been doing ever since Johannes Gutenberg: publishing books.

An incomplete list of books[22] printed in *maṭbaᶜat al-maᶜārif* during its seven years under Sarkīs's management (1868–1875) contains twenty-three titles (plus a few with an unclear publication date). A yield on this scale was consonant with the general level of output during that early phase of printing: It was close to the thirty titles turned out during the same period by the more veteran printer Yūsuf al-Shalfūn in his *al-maṭbaᶜa al-ᶜumūmiyya*, and apparently more than the output of every other press in Beirut then.[23] Among them were works by the two partners themselves: Bustānī's Arabic dictionaries, and a book by Sarkīs entitled *Ta'rīkh ūrshalīm* ("History of Jerusalem"). There were also several school texts, works on history, poetry collections, and an edition of al-Ḥarīrī's classic *Maqāmāt*. In general categories, this was a portent for much of what *nahḍa* publishers would produce in later years.

But Sarkīs aspired for more. In 1875, he quit the partnership with his celebrated father-in-law, leaving the press to Bustānī.[24] He then started a new press all on his own, on the upper level of the Ayyās family *wakāla* in Beirut's Zuqāq al-Blāṭ quarter, sometimes described as the cradle of the Lebanese *nahḍa*.[25] He named it *al-maṭbaᶜa al-adabiyya* or *Imprimerie des Belles-Lettres*. The outset was modest: a few rudimentary printing machines and a hand-operated letter-casting device. Designing new Arabic letters was Sarkīs's personal hobby, which would buy him repute as a master printer throughout the region (there was even a font bearing his name, the "Sarkīs" font).[26] As in his previous project, he also opened a book-vending wing next to his shop. His press offered printing services to anyone wishing to duplicate anything – books, journals, commercial documents, and various ephemera. Assessing that the key to success was publishing a newspaper as the business mainstay, Sarkīs applied for and was granted a license for it. In October 1877, he launched his semiweekly *Lisān al-Ḥāl*, which would become one of the country's leading newspapers and remain

[22] Shaykhū, 113–15.
[23] Ibid., 93–113. A search of the bibliographic database Worldcat (www.worldcat.org, accessed 10 February 2015), covering some 10,000 libraries worldwide, turned out only 140 items printed in Arabic in Beirut during these years. Obviously, the holdings of contemporary libraries are not necessarily a credible indication of the actual production, but they may indicate general scale. If so, it supports the assumption that the Sarkīs–Bustānī endeavor was among the bigger presses there at the time.
[24] *Maṭbaᶜat al-maᶜārif* was operated by the Bustānīs into the 1880s.
[25] Hanssen, 163ff.
[26] Ṭarrāzī, *Ta'rīkh al-ṣiḥāfa*, Vol. 2, 129–31.

so for a full century.[27] This debut took place as rough times for freedom of speech and publishing were commencing in the Empire. The ever-distrustful Sultan ᶜAbdülhamid II, who came to power in 1876, employed censorship and punishment to muzzle exponents of new ideas, scaring many of them away. Choosing to stay in Beirut rather than join his emigrating compatriots, Sarkīs became subject to frequent government harassment. He was punished with the humiliating corporal *falaqa* and his press was set on fire, apparently by state agents.[28] Resilient and circumspect, he managed to keep afloat and even prosper, constantly modernizing his business equipment to the professional cutting edge of the time. *Al-maṭbaᶜa al-adabiyya* grew into a manifold enterprise with some fifty workers around the turn of the century. It published Sarkīs's newspaper (*Lisān al-Ḥāl* became a daily in 1895), printed several journals owned by other enterprising individuals,[29] and sold printing, binding, and letter-casting services to others. It also turned out hundreds of books, which were sold in the press's bookshop, *al-maktaba al-adabiyya*.

Speaking to a celebrating audience on the occasion of the *Lisān*'s twenty-fifth anniversary, in 1902, Sarkīs reviewed the production scope of his press. During a period of (unspecified) eighteen years, he revealed, *al-maṭbaᶜa al-adabiyya* had printed 650 works on "literary, scholarly, religious, agricultural and industrial" matters with a total print-run of 1,290,000 copies, in addition to journals and various other items.[30] A list elaborating this striking output is not extant, and our knowledge on what the press actually printed is therefore bound to remain partial. A search of several major data compilations[31] has turned out over 400 different entries printed by Sarkīs during his lifetime, over 300 of which had been produced prior to his 1902 speech. This is a sizeable slice of Sarkīs's claimed output; given the likelihood that many entries, especially smaller

[27] Details in Ṭarrāzī, *Ta'rīkh al-ṣiḥāfa*, Vol. 2, 27–33, and Ghālib.

[28] *Falaqa* or bastinado – flogging the soles of the feet – was a common penalty for offenders of every kind in the empire. Sarkīs's press was burnt in September 1895; see *Lisān al-Ḥāl*, 19 September 1895, where Sarkīs gives a detailed description of the press and its equipment that were eaten by the fire.

[29] Among other, *al-maṭbaᶜa al-adabiyya* printed the Druze monthly *al-Ṣafā'* (1886), the religious weekly *al-Manār* (1898; not to be confused with Rashīd Riḍā's journal of that name, Cairo from 1898), the scholarly monthly *al-Kawthar* (1909), and the literary quarterly *al-Mawrid al-Ṣāfī* (1910).

[30] Ṭarrāzī, *Ta'rīkh al-ṣiḥāfa*, Vol. 2, 133. Sarkīs may have counted multiple printings or editions of the same work as multiple items.

[31] Worldcat (www.worldcat.org, accessed 10 February 2015), a search for "*al-maṭbaᶜa al-adabiyya*"; Dār al-Kutub, *Fihris*, Vols. 3–7 (covering history, literature, language, geography, agriculture, trade, crafts, and "general knowledge"); Yūsuf Ilyān Sarkīs, *Muᶜjam*; and Shaykhū. None of these is complete in any sense, but together they seem to cover a considerable bulk of the period's production.

works, were lost before being registered in any list, it seems to lend credence to his claim of 650 printed works. This known part of his production already places him as one of Lebanon's most industrious printers of his time, if not the biggest. And if ᶜĀyida Nuṣayr's findings for Egypt are trusted, *al-maṭbaᶜa al-adabiyya* in Beirut was more productive than any private press in Egypt as well, at least until 1900.[32]

The career of Khalīl Sarkīs embodied a central theme in the early phase of private Arab printing: the printer as publisher. In the process of turning a handwritten text into a mass-printed work, running the press machines was one of several stages, some of them as novel as printing itself. The works had to be edited and copyedited, bound, advertised, and distributed on a big scale. Securing a publishing license, another innovation of the time, was also the publisher's responsibility. Periodical publications demanded still more action and a more dynamic production pace. A resourceful owner could turn a printing and binding shop into a successful publishing house; Khalīl Sarkīs, well-educated and shrewd, was an archetypal printer-publisher of the *nahḍa* and a successful one at that. He brought with him a desire to edify his society, a motivation shared by other learned Arabs of the time, and a desire for profit, a default motivation of everyone joining the trade. If we are to judge by the large sums he invested in his partnership with Bustānī and then in setting up his own press, he must have brought with him substantial financial resources as well, which was somewhat less typical. Facing a multiple challenge – at once assimilating a new product and creating the market for it – Sarkīs demonstrated superb acumen that made him a central brick in the edifice of modern Arab written culture.

Let us take a closer look at Sarkīs's modus operandi. We have no first-hand data on his plant's working routine, the performance and pay of his laborers, and Sarkīs's own daily schedule, of the kind that we have for early printers in Europe.[33] But small details on the title pages of books issued by his press, and recurrent bits of information in his newspaper, allow us to reconstruct much of the scene. Many of the books he produced were familiar items on the shelf of Arabic classics, and these would be readily available to him at the local manuscript sellers (*warrāqīn*), in public and private libraries, perhaps even his own or his family's collections. *Alf layla wa-layla*, *Kalīla wa-dimna*, the epics of *ᶜAntara bin shaddād*, *Sayf bin dhī yazan*, and *Banī hilāl*, Ḥarīrī's *Maqāmāt*, al-Suyūṭī's *Miftāḥ al-ᶜulūm*,

[32] According to Nuṣayr's survey, 434–43, Egypt's busiest private press until 1900 was *al-maṭbaᶜa al-sharafiyya*, with a total turnout of 332 titles from 1859 to 1900 – an average annual production lower than that of Sarkīs, even when counting only his documented products.

[33] Febvre and Martin, 129–36.

Ma^carrī's *Saqṭ al-zand*, and Ibn Khaldūn's *Muqaddima* were all items Sarkīs picked from the rich pool of classics, found them worthy and potentially profitable, and fed them into his production line. Texts could also be "borrowed" from editions previously printed in Europe or Egypt; such was the case with the "Thousand and One Nights," which Sarkīs seems to have pirated from the 1835 Būlāq edition and published in 1881–1883, in four volumes.[34] At times he personally chose the texts to be printed and edited them for publication, a task befitting his skills. Explaining his motivation for writing *Ta'rīkh ūrshalīm*, Sarkīs noted that there had been no book in Arabic on the history of Jerusalem, so he decided to produce one by gathering (*jam*ᶜ) data scattered in various works:

> I have based my narrative on reliable evidence, taken (*ma'khūdha*) from religious books and history books which contain information on this city ... Once I had completed authoring (*ta'līf*) it by borrowing (*naql*ᵃⁿ) from the most dependable works on the subject, I edited it and compared my text to the works on which I had relied, so as to avoid error. I gave it my utmost attention.[35]

At other times he published writings of his own authorship: accounts of his trip to Istanbul, Europe, and America, and of Emperor Wilhelm II's 1898 visit to Palestine and Syria (both previously serialized in his newspaper); a tract on manners and ethics; a cookbook, with hundreds of recipes "in styles of the East and West"; and a six-volume set of school readers.[36]

But *al-maṭba*ᶜ*a al-adabiyya* was more than a one-man operation. As in the busier presses during the early decades of printing in Europe, many of the books printed in Sarkīs's shop were joint products that involved more contributors than one, as their front pages reveal. They tell us of editors, copyeditors, underwriters, right-holders, and others, including people who were not members of the regular press team. For example, the title page of a *dīwān* by the tenth-century poet Abū Firās al-Ḥamdānī, which *al-maṭba*ᶜ*a al-adabiyya* printed in 1900, mentions Nakhla Qalfāṭ, a well-known Beirut writer, as having "expounded some of its expressions and

[34] Burton, Vol. 1, xx. Burton, the celebrated translator of the "Nights" into English, panned Sarkīs for having taken the book "entirely" from the Egyptian edition and "converting it to Christianity." He depicted Sarkīs's edition as a "melancholy specimen of the Nights ... beginning without Bismillah, continued with scrupulous castration and ending in ennui and disappointment." If this description was close to the mark, it might give us an idea of Sarkīs's methods in executing some of his products.

[35] Sarkīs, *Ta'rīkh ūrshalīm*, 2.

[36] *Riḥlat mudīr al-lisān khalīl sarkīs ilā al-īstāna wa-ūrūbbā wa-āmīrikā* (1893); *Riḥlat al-imbarāṭūr ghilyawm al-thānī malik brūsyā wa-imbarāṭūr almāniyā wa'l-imbarāṭūrah fikṭūriyā fi filasṭīn wa-sūriyā sanat 1898* (1898); *Kitāb al-*ᶜ*ādāt fī al-ziyārāt wa'l-walā'im wa'l-a*ᶜ*rās wa'l-ma*ᶜ*ātim wa-ādāb al-maḥāfil wa-ghayrihā mimma huwwa jār*ⁱⁿ *wa-muṭalla*ᶜ ᶜ*alayhi* ᶜ*inda al-shu*ᶜ*ūb al-mutamaddina* (1909); *Tadhkirat al-khawātīn wa-ustādh al-ṭabbākhīn* (1885; an abridged edition, *Mukhtaṣar ustādh al-ṭabbākhīn*, appeared in 1905); *Salāsil al-qirā'a*, 6 vols. (1901–1906).

Khalīl Sarkīs in his old age
Fīlīb dī Ṭarrāzī, *Ta'rīkh al-ṣiḥāfa al-ᶜarabiyya*, Vol. 2 (Beirut: al-maṭbaᶜa al-adabiyya, 1914), p. 130.

interpreted some of its verses"; Qalfāṭ, that is, served as literary editor. He also financed the book's publication along with one Jamīl Ramaḍān and retained the rights of republishing it.[37] Similarly, in an edition of the classic *Kalīla wa-dimna*, which Sarkīs published in 1888, Khalīl al-Yāzijī is identified as the one who had "edited, corrected and annotated it"

[37] *Dīwān abī firās al-ḥamdānī. Qad ḥalla baᶜḍ alfāẓihi wa-sharaḥa maᶜnā baᶜḍ abyātihi … Nakhla Qalfāṭ. Iᶜādat ṭabᶜihi maḥfūẓa lahu. Ṭubiᶜa bi-nafaqatihi wa-nafaqat jamīl ramaḍān.* The title page also provides details on the government license to print it and on the book's price. See image on p. 65 below.

(*naqqaḥahu wa-ḍabaṭahu wa-ᶜalaqa ḥawāshayhi*).[38] And Ibrāhīm al-Yāzijī, a writer in his own right, was involved as copyeditor (*muṣaḥḥiḥ*) in the publication of his father Nāṣīf al-Yāzijī's *dīwān* and prepared an abridgement of another work by his father.[39] The precise division of labor between those involved in each project is a matter of speculation (we will return to these functions and their significance later on in this chapter). With these and others like them taking part in production, it is easy to imagine *al-maṭbaᶜa al-adabiyya* as a meeting place for writers and intellectuals who would have their works published there. Sarkīs would host them in his elegant office, which contemporary pictures show to have been comfortably furnished, with overflowing bookshelves lined up against the walls. Teams of typesetters, correctors, and binders would occupy the spacious production halls in another section of the press.[40] Sarkīs's own routine must have been rather intensive, including correspondence with business partners, potential authors, agents in remote places, and government officials; overseeing the casting plant and printing operations; writing; editing; and above all producing *Lisān al-Ḥāl*, his newspaper. Running the paper, especially after it became a daily, must have been his central concern; it was a far more ambitious undertaking than book publishing, an undertaking whose elaborate examination is a matter for another study.[41]

Like his professional colleagues elsewhere, Sarkīs sought to keep his machines as busy as possible. This was especially vital in the early years, when the consumer market was still in its infancy. To that end, he turned to producing small and inexpensive works, skinny booklets in small format – typically single stories or small poetry compilations – that would easily sell and increase his income. Such, for instance, was a story from the twelfth-century epos *Majnūn laylā*, which he published as an eighty-four-page chapbook; a twelfth-century collection of aphorisms printed in thirty-two pages; a thirteenth-century *dīwān* printed in forty-eight pages; and a fifteenth-century Islamic preaching tract, published as a thirty-two-page pamphlet, all of them in small format.[42] He also printed a host of nonliterary items which businesses and private individuals ordered from his press, from commercial forms to *cartes de visite*, and an annual

38 *Kalīla wa-dimna* (al-maṭbaᶜa al-adabiyya, 1888).

39 Nāṣīf al-Yāzijī, *Dīwān, muṣaḥḥaḥa bi-qalam al-ᶜalāma al-fāḍil al-shaykh ibrāhīm al-yāzijī* (al-maṭbaᶜa al-adabiyya, 1898); Nāṣīf al-Yāzijī, *Kitāb al-jumāna fī sharḥ al-khizāna, mukhtaṣar bi-qalam waladihi al-shaykh ibrāhīm al-yāzijī* (al-maṭbaᶜa al-adabiyya, 1889).

40 Pictures in Ṭarrāzī, *Ta'rīkh al-ṣiḥāfa*, Vol. 2, 28, 132, 136.

41 See Ayalon, *The Press*, chapters 7 and 9. For *Lisān al-Ḥāl*, see Ghālib.

42 *Qiṣṣat qays ibn al-mulawwaḥ al-ᶜāmirī al-maᶜrūf bi-majnūn laylā* (1882); Aḥmad al-Rifāᶜī, *Ḥikam* (1883); Ibrāhīm ibn Sahl al-Isrā'īlī, *Dīwān* (1885); Rajab ibn Muḥammad al-Bayrūtī, *Kitāb al-ajwiba al-jāliyya fī al-ᶜaqā'id al-dīniyya* (1890).

calendar that became a hallmark of his press, *al-rūznāmah al-sūriyya*.[43] Like other press owners, again, he sold printing services to those who wished to publish their written works: literary pieces, poetry, religious tracts, and even journals as we have seen. This was another form of publishing, which I shall discuss in the next chapter. As a publisher who possessed his own press, let alone his own newspaper, Sarkīs had a considerable edge over most of his competitors of that early phase.

Other prominent *nahḍa* figures, some of them more famous than Sarkīs, were similarly involved in building the logistic foundations for the cultural change. Khalīl al-Khūrī, Yaᶜqūb Ṣarrūf, Fāris Nimr, Jurjī Zaydān, ᶜAbd al-Qādir al-Qabbānī, Ibrāhīm al-Yāzijī, and several other writers engaged in printing, publishing, and advancing diffusion conduits. They, like Bustānī, Shidyāq, and Sarkīs, were all owners of important Arabic journals, a novelty that served as a cornerstone of their endeavors. A quest for profit and, often though not always, a commitment to enlightenment were key motivations behind their activity. To bring light to their society, they had to lay the power grid, erect electricity poles, and put the bulbs in place.

Pausing for a moment to take a comparative glance, we may see that in their life stories and initiatives these frontrunners of Arab printing had much in common with the leading printers of post-Gutenberg Europe: Aldus Manutius in Venice, Jodocus Badius (Bade) and members of the Estienne family in Paris, Johann Froben and Johann Amerbach in Basel, Christophe Plantin in Antwerp, William Caxton in Westminster, and several other master publishers of the time, who translated the technological invention of movable letters into a literary momentum. They themselves were products of the humanistic and creative cultural spirit of their time – true "Renaissance men," as Elizabeth Eisenstein has described them[44]: experts in Greek and Latin culture (Aldus, Badius, the Estiennes), or in the literature of the Church Fathers (Froben, Amerbach, Plantin), who appreciated the scholarly value of the works they chose to publish. They were authors, translators, and artists, who collaborated with other writers and turned their shops into workshops of intellectual creativity. Always closely involved in the work routine of their presses, they promoted the technical and esthetic upgrading of their products no less than their contents. Some of them were more business-minded than scholarly inclined; the Englishman Caxton is perhaps a good

[43] E.g., sample in *Lisān al-Ḥāl*, 2 December 1889, 4, and description in *Lisān al-Ḥāl*, 16 December 1913, 4. The paper published ads for the press itself regularly; e.g., 23 June 1879, 4.

[44] Eisenstein, "The Early Printer."

example, although he too was a prolific translator, active author, and editor.[45]

Like their European vocational forerunners, the makers of the Arab *nahḍa* were at once the choosers, producers, and distributors of printed texts. Some of them were also renowned thinkers and scholars. Others, less prolific, contributed to the mass circulation of old and new writings more than to Arabic scholarship itself. Many of the early European publishers, it has been observed, "had neither the time nor perhaps the inclination to produce personal work"; rather, their impact on the society's culture resulted from collaboration with other intellectuals, bringing their works to light and encouraging them to produce more.[46] This last description would seem to fit Khalīl Sarkīs, who was more of a businessman than a philosopher. But the role he and his likes played in inducing the change was as vital as that of his more celebrated contemporaries.

Cultural, technological, and organizational dissimilarities distinguish the European early publishing experience from that of the Arabs several centuries later. For example, in the popular attitude to the practice, Arab societies seem to have displayed more suspicion of, and less zeal for, printed products than their Western predecessors, something that posed a serious hurdle to the Middle East advancement of the practice, as we shall see later on. Still, the many similarities between the two cases are at least as visible and meaningful as the variances. Like early European book makers, their Arab counterparts had to mold their own production routine and diffusion networks and to build their own markets. Large pools of classic texts existed in both periods and places, and new works were being written all the time. In both cases, it was up to the printer's intuition and feel for the public taste to choose publishable pieces that would serve the public's interests, and his. If a learned man, he would turn to the great works of his society's written heritage – Plato, or Ibn Khaldūn – counting on their age-old value to guarantee circulation and profit. Otherwise, he would rely on his business instinct to select recently authored works to the same ends. He would print them in whole, in part, as sections in anthologies, or in all of these forms and reprint them repeatedly as commercially desirable. The Alduses and Caxtons and the Bustānīs and Sarkīses were always personally involved in the processes of printing, copyediting, and binding; in advertising the printed works, in their own journal if they had one, or in that of a colleague if they did not; and in distributing them through a bookshop that could be their own or a neighbor's. The more

[45] Lowry; Barolini; Clair, esp. 57–133; Febvre and Martin, 143–59; Blake, 1–18.
[46] Febvre and Martin, 149.

ambitious printer-publishers would also publicize their products away from their province or region and recruit agents to circulate them there.

Publishing Popularized

Abū al-Hudā al-Ṣayyādī, whose work lies next to Bustānī's on the Princeton library shelf, likewise employed printing to circulate his educational message among the Arabic (and Turkish) reading communities. Ṣayyādī (1850–1909), a religious activist and writer, is mostly remembered as a propagandist in the service of Sultan ᶜAbdülhamid II's pan-Islamic initiatives and a ṣūfī leader (shaykh of the Rifāᶜīyya *ṭarīqa*). We now know that his religious line was still more intricate than that and his career rather convoluted.[47] To us, the important side of the Ṣayyādī story is his ingenious application of printing to make simple didactic items that were readily accessible to his intended audience. Not a printer or publisher himself, he was aided by his numerous followers, among them some printers and booksellers. When he began issuing books, in the early 1880s, printing was already an expanding trade in parts of the Ottoman Empire, and its potential for spreading messages of any kind – not just pious works or high scholarship – was becoming increasingly evident. Ṣayyādī proved to be a master in exploiting this potential. By one count, no fewer than 212 books and booklets are attributable to him, a great many of them in the slim format of *al-Ḥaqq al-mubīn*, referred to earlier in this chapter. Published between ca. 1880 and 1908 in Istanbul, Beirut, and Cairo, they usually dealt with the history, rituals, and teaching of his ṣūfī *ṭarīqa*, with other *ṭarīqa*s, and with other pious matters. Many more similar works are ascribed to his disciples.[48] Ṣayyādī and his plentiful publishing enterprise represented the crucial, but scantily acknowledged, changes which printing introduced on every conceivable level to Middle Eastern social and cultural functioning and life routine.

Many thousands of Arabic books and booklets and some 1,500 journals appeared in the Middle East up to World War I, the great majority of them in Egypt and Lebanon. Only a tiny segment of these was works by leading contemporary thinkers and old classics selected for printing by the big publishers. The majority was produced by private individuals and small entrepreneurs, who sought to pronounce an idea or hoped to make

[47] Eich, "Forgotten Salafī"; Eich, "Abū l-Hudā." Both articles are based on Eich's 2003 doctoral dissertation. See also Abu Manneh, "Sultan Abdülhamid."

[48] The figure of Ṣayyādī's publications is quoted from Abu Manneh, "Sultan Abdülhamid," 140. The number might be exaggerated; see Eich, "Forgotten Salafī," 79. For the contents of these publications, see Eich, "Forgotten Salafī," 79ff.

a profit. Once the potential of printing had been recognized and the technology had become available, it became an appealing means for amplifying one's voice and circulating opinions. The range of subjects and genres was infinite, from literary and poetic works to political and religious treatises, and from bulky volumes to skinny pamphlets. It was a gushing flow of printers and printed materials. Like bloggers today, just about everyone could have his voice heard and his message travel over vast areas.

Printing expanded rapidly during this period. In her survey of nineteenth-century Egyptian publishing, ᶜĀyida Nuṣayr has identified sixty-five private presses that were established there during the second half of the century (as against a mere five in the first); of these, thirty-four opened during the two decades ending in 1900.[49] Egyptian presses continued to proliferate more briskly after the turn of the century. The Egyptian National Library catalog mentions at least fifty Egyptian presses in operation from 1900 to 1914 that are not included in Nuṣayr's survey of the pre-1900 period.[50] To these, we should add the print shops owned by the big journals, especially daily newspapers, for which possession of a press was a must: *Wādī al-Nīl*, *al-Ahrām*, *al-Maḥrūsa*, *al-Iᶜlām*, *al-Muqaṭṭam*, *al-Mu'ayyad*, *al-Liwā'*, *al-Jarīda*, *al-Hilāl*, and several others. Many of these also printed books, sometimes scores of them.[51] Elsewhere in the region presses emerged at a slower pace, but by 1914 dozens of them were already scattered all over the region – in Beirut and several towns of Mount Lebanon, Damascus, Aleppo, Tripoli, Baghdad, Mosul, Jerusalem and Jaffa, and a few other places.[52] Our knowledge of these presses comes primarily from the books and journals they printed, but we should bear in mind that more presses existed which printed items other than books and newspapers. On the whole, then, it was an increasingly thriving vocation.

The economics of operating a press is crucial for recovering a clear picture of the activity in that field. The data at hand for that period, however, allow us to reconstruct little more than a general outline of it.[53]

49 Nuṣayr, 408–11, 434–46. Nuṣayr's lists, however, seem to be less than complete. Searching the Egyptian National Library catalog, I came across quite a few presses not mentioned in her study; Dār al-Kutub al-Miṣriyya, *Fihris*, Vols. 3–7.

50 Dār al-Kutub al-Miṣriyya, *Fihris*, Vol. 3. Fifty such presses are mentioned in that volume alone, out of the catalog's seven.

51 Nuṣayr, 431–34. Nuṣayr has traced 380 books that were printed by the presses of twelve Egyptian journals until 1900; e.g., the press of *Wādī al-Nīl* printed 79 books from 1867 to 1883 and that of *al-Iᶜlām* 52 from 1885 to 1900.

52 Worldcat (www.worldcat.org/ accessed 10 February 2015); Yūsuf Ilyān Sarkīs; Shaykhū; Ṣābāt.

53 Elsewhere I have tried to examine this question in the context of setting up and managing Arabic newspapers in the late nineteenth and early twentieth centuries; Ayalon, *The Press*, 195–202.

Acquiring high-quality typographic gear was costly in the late nineteenth century (lithographic equipment would be less expensive),[54] and adding binding and other equipment, or hiring a team of workers, entailed further expenses. As we have seen in the joint Sarkīs–Bustānī endeavor, setting up such a project involved an initial investment of hundreds of pounds, which in the Ottoman Arab provinces then was equal to a person's average income in a decade, or more.[55] Only a handful of press owners in the region were sufficiently well-off to set up a plant of a size and production capacity equal to *maṭbaᶜat al-maᶜārif* of Sarkīs and Bustānī or *al-maṭbaᶜa al-adabiyya* of Sarkīs. Among these were, apparently, several print shops in Egypt, notably *al-maṭbaᶜa al-sharqiyya*, *al-maṭbaᶜa al-ᶜuthmāniyya*, and *al-maṭbaᶜa al-kastīliyya*, which put out over 200 books each during the second half of the nineteenth century.[56] So were also the presses of the leading journals, some of which were organized as share companies with considerable capital.

But the great majority of Arab presses were small businesses, often one-man ventures designed for limited-scale production. These were nameless rank-and-file operators of the *nahḍa*. Small presses were started by men who expected to make a living by selling a service that was in growing demand: printing other people's books, pamphlets, or journals and serving businesses that chose to use printed paperwork. They would rent a small place, obtain second-hand rudimentary machines or (in Egypt) lithographic equipment, and conduct most of the work singlehandedly or with an assistant or two. At first glance, the rapid proliferation of such small shops may suggest that entering the trade was a smart investment in the late nineteenth-century Middle East. But there are indications that, without substantial financial means or unusual business acumen, one would have a hard time surviving economically, let alone prosper in that vocation. While setting up a modest press and running it on a shoestring budget meant low production costs, the gains one could expect if successful may not have been very high either. Government agencies, commercial firms, and private individuals who sought printing services for their official paperwork or various personal needs made up a fairly small consumer market, which could not sustain more than a few presses in each province.

[54] Schwartz, 274–75.

[55] See ibid. By one assessment, on the eve of World War I, the annual average per capita income in the Ottoman Arab provinces was around 42–50 US dollars, which was equivalent to 8.5–10 Egyptian pounds. Large segments of the society, such as peasants and unskilled workers, had a markedly smaller income. See Issawi, *Fertile Crescent*, 34; Issawi, "Asymmetrical Development," 383. The Egyptian pound was roughly equivalent to the English pound and slightly higher than the Ottoman pound.

[56] Nuṣayr, 434–36. Nuṣayr has traced over 300 books published by each of the first two presses.

The book and journal market, while gradually expanding, was still small and unfriendly during that formative period. Most of the presses known to us printed only a handful of books or booklets; some have come to our attention thanks to a single product. Thus, of the sixty-five private presses in Egypt recorded in Nuṣayr's lists for the period 1850–1900, over half printed less than five books each during their lifetime, and nineteen of them are known to have printed only one title.[57] Those who got involved in printing a journal or newspaper could scarcely do much better, with their business being affected by the childhood diseases of the early Arabic press. The list of such ephemeral papers is almost endless – papers which, as one observer noted in 1914, "eke out a miserable existence … they appear, disappear and appear again spasmodically."[58] By and large, then, while data on the economic viability of Arab presses are scant, the clear impression one gets from available descriptions is of a precarious occupation. Except for the few big and prospering endeavors, printing shops during the *nahḍa* were usually humble institutions with poor equipment, pitiable physical conditions, and small yield. Often they were also short-lived.

Let us, once more, take a closer look at one typical case, a man whose career embodied this category in more ways than one: Jūrjī Ḥabīb Ḥanāniyā, one of the earliest printer-publishers in Palestine toward the end of the nineteenth century. We will recall that Palestine, like other places in the Fertile Crescent besides Lebanon, was in the periphery of Arab printing activity prior to 1908. By the last third of the century, several missionary and local Christian presses – Franciscan, Anglican, Armenian, and Greek Orthodox – were in operation there, all in Jerusalem, printing in Arabic and other languages; and a few Jewish shops were printing in Hebrew.[59] We also hear of four private Arab presses in Jerusalem, apparently small and short-lived, about which we know nothing beyond the names of their owners.[60] Their activity on the whole was very limited; despite their fewness, Ḥanāniyā would later note, there was "no adequate work for all of them."[61]

[57] Nuṣayr, 441–44. Again, these lists may not be complete but they do seem to give a sense of scale.

[58] Lord Kitchener, describing the Egyptian press; quoted in Baron, *Women's Awakening*, 74.

[59] Sulaymān, 74–84; Yāghī, 77–80; Gordon, 85–86; Halevi, Introduction, pp. *tet-vav* to *mem-zayin* (15–47). At least two of the Jewish presses are said to have been equipped with Arabic characters.

[60] Details in Yehoshuᶜa, 7–13; Sulaymān, 81–82. On p. 77 Sulaymān quotes a reference in an official Ottoman publication to similar activities taking place elsewhere in Palestine, noting he had found no evidence to corroborate it. Frequent discrepancies between the existing studies suggest that the early history of printing in Palestine still awaits a systematic exploration.

[61] Quoted in Yehoshuᶜa, 12.

Jūrjī Ḥabīb Ḥanāniyā (1864–1920)[62] was born to a deep-rooted Jerusalemite Greek Orthodox family. He was educated at Bishop Samuel Gobat's Protestant School on Mount Zion and was said to have mastered "seven-and-a-half languages": Arabic, Turkish, Greek, French, English, German, Russian, and "a little Hebrew." Once out of school, sometime in the late 1870s, he apparently took up employment in one of the city's presses and acquired a knack for the craft. In 1894, still working for another printer, he applied for a license to open his own press. Under the Hamidian government, this was usually a protracted procedure. While waiting for the authorities to grant his request, he moved ahead clandestinely to start his business anyway. By his account, he acquired Latin and Russian letters "of the latest style and attractive design," bought slots of printing time from presses in town, and began performing seasonal printing jobs for tourists around Easter, for three months a year. Sometime later he proceeded to a more daring endeavor. He obtained Arabic characters and a small leg-operated machine "for printing small things" (receipt-books, commercial forms, envelopes, and the like) and began to print stealthily for private customers, working in his home at night and as a press employee during the day. The government prohibited printing in Arabic, and it did not take the authorities long to expose Ḥanāniyā's venture. But as he also provided services to some local Ottoman officials, he managed to get away with it and continued with his work. In 1898, his four-year-old application for a license was eventually granted, and he opened his own press at the ᶜAlwān market (*suwayqa*) in the Armenian quarter of the Old City.[63]

What did it mean to become a small-scale printer in an Arab provincial town then? An observer in 1889 suggested that comparing printing in the Middle East with that of contemporary Europe called to mind the contrast "between prehistoric man and the telephone age, between the Tower of Babel and the Eiffel Tower."[64] A printing shop was usually a simple place with a small room or two and a couple of basic machines for different kinds of works. Spare parts for the often-breaking pieces had

[62] Most of the information about Ḥanāniyā comes from Yehoshuᶜa, 40–50 and passim, whose study is based on accounts by Ḥanāniyā himself and members of his family; from Jūrjī Ḥanāniyā's granddaughter, Mary Hanania, "Jurji Habib Hanania"; and from Sulaymān. Yehoshuᶜa (47) gives Ḥanāniyā's year of birth as 1857. Mary Hanania (57) notes that her grandfather was fifty-six years old upon his death in 1920, i.e., he was born in 1864. Various details in his biography make this last date somewhat more likely.

[63] Ḥanāniyā in the first issue of *al-Quds*, 18 September 1908, reproduced in Yehoshuᶜa, 42–43. There is some uncertainty regarding the precise location of this press – see Yehoshuᶜa, 45, and the document quoted on p. 49.

[64] Eliezer Ben Yehuda in *ha-Tzvi*, referring to the situation in Jerusalem; quoted in Gordon, 86, note 11.

to be brought from Europe, like the machines themselves, which was a lengthy operation. Much of the work was conducted manually and slowly by the press owner, sometimes assisted by a hired hand who would help in setting the type, cutting and folding paper, and running the machines. Typesetting was the part that required the most skill, a proficiency usually acquired on the job. It was hard work, taxing the body and especially the eyes, both because the equipment was difficult to operate and due to poor conditions: insufficient light and ventilation, with harmful materials such as lead all over the place.[65]

Having received his license, Ḥanāniyā began working legally in broad daylight. Assessing that a printing shop alone might not be adequate for earning a living under the existing circumstances, he approached local officials once again and applied for a permit to issue a newspaper in Arabic, "for serving the state and the country." He must have been optimistic about a swift handling of his request, for he ordered from Europe a modern, gasoline-operated machine for printing newspapers.[66] But the waiting this time was even longer than before – as long as eight years – and the bureaucratic troubles more oppressive. Not only was the license slow to arrive, but also the authorities took control of his newly acquired machinery and his staff, in 1902, in order to print the local official bulletin, *al-Quds al-Sharīf/Quds-i Sharīf* during the next two years. This caused Ḥanāniyā considerable loss of revenues, because the constant presence of officials in his press scared away other clients. The license for a newspaper was granted only after the change of regime in Istanbul, in 1908. Six weeks later he launched his semiweekly, "scientific, literary, communal newspaper" *al-Quds*, one of the country's earliest Arabic journals.[67]

Ḥanāniyā's decision to publish a journal was a smart move, given the country's slowly changing cultural realities. There was a rising demand for news and for an open public discussion of the transforming environment. Books, by contrast, were still a merchandise of small demand. In the animated outburst of journalism throughout the Fertile Crescent following the Young Turk Revolution, fifteen papers appeared in Palestine within the last five months of 1908 alone, most of them of cultural-literary contents.[68] Ḥanāniyā could now put the machines he had bought to a use of his own choice, rather than the authorities', and try to prosper. The excitement that reverberated all over the Arab provinces in the summer of 1908 was reflected in the

[65] Gordon, 86–88. See also descriptions in Yehoshuᶜa, 45–46; Crabitès, 1051; Mūsā, *al-Ṣiḥāfa*, 20.
[66] For the technology of presses imported to Palestine during that period, see Gordon, 100–01.
[67] Ḥanāniyā, reproduced in Yehoshuᶜa, 42–44.
[68] Details in Khūrī, *Ṣiḥāfa*, 7–15.

masthead of his paper, which featured three stars carrying the words *ḥurriyya, musāwāt, ikhā'*, an emotional allusion to the ternary battle cry of the French Revolution. Similar expressions of hope appeared in many other journals around the region.[69]

Issuing a newspaper would turn a printer into a publisher. Putting out the paper was in itself an act of publishing, but quite a few press owners who focused on journal publishing also used their machinery and the time left in between issues to publish books. Ḥanāniyā had engaged in publishing books years before he launched *al-Quds*: In the opening article of his newspaper in 1908, relating the story of his fluctuating business career until that point, he reported that from the opening of his press until then he had printed "281 books (*kitāb*) in different languages, including 83 Arabic books, in addition to circulars (*dafātir*) of all the local government departments."[70] This number, if true, would mark an impressive yield for a single press in a small town such as Jerusalem at the time. We have no supportive evidence for this claimed output. A search in the Worldcat database of holdings in many thousands of libraries has turned out a mere six items in Arabic and one in Turkish that were printed in *maṭbaᶜat jūrjī ḥabīb ḥanāniyā* until 1908.[71] Some of these are skinny booklets of fewer than 100 pages. It is possible that other items printed in Arabic were small-size pamphlets, ephemeral leaflets, and perhaps single-sheet products rather than full-fledged books, which would explain why they did not survive. Ḥanāniyā continued to produce books after starting his newspaper – we know of at least three of those[72] – but at that stage the newspaper must have taken up most of his publishing energy. The few books known to us which he published both before and after 1908 include tracts on language and literature, a brief account of a voyage to the Holy Land, and the catalog of the Khālidiyya Library in Jerusalem. The eighty-seven-page Khālidiyya catalog (1900), for example, is an esthetic work, printed in an agreeable and clear font and generally error-free. It also betrays some of the deficiencies of the equipment available at the time: broken letters here and there and paint stains throughout the text.

Was Ḥanāniyā's share in producing these items limited to printing them only, or did he also contribute to their selection, editing, binding, and distribution, which would make him a publisher in a fuller sense? We have no way of knowing. Some of the items are identified as having

69 Ayalon, *The Press*, 65–68.
70 Quoted in Yehoshuᶜa, 43.
71 Accessed 10 February 2015.
72 All three are small, 60- to 70-page works on language by Muḥammad Salīm ibn Quṭayna, printed in 1911 and 1912. The National Library in Jerusalem has copies of them in its collection.

been written by his contemporaries; others could have been authored in earlier periods and may have been retrieved by Ḥanāniyā himself from some collection, printed and published, which would make him an entrepreneurial publisher. Once he started *al-Quds*, however, he could surely be counted as such. He himself wrote parts of the paper, gathering news and other items from various sources and personally translating pieces from the foreign press. He also served as editor throughout the paper's lifetime, oversaw production, and took care of marketing.[73]

As printer and publisher in turn-of-the-century Palestine, Ḥanāniyā had to contend with considerable difficulties, not least on the economic front. While professing, like many of his colleagues, to have entered the trade in order to serve the homeland and "sow the seeds of amity," he was primarily eager to feed his four-children family. His debut was hardship-ridden, and he managed to survive only thanks to jobs he performed for officials, which apparently assured him of a regular if modest income; "this is what facilitated stability and persistence in the business," he later acknowledged.[74] Starting the newspaper at first improved the economic situation: Ḥanāniyā ran it successfully for four years and hired a team of workers that was big enough to "form a line when gathering to receive their weekly wages," and journalists who wrote for him. When needed, his wife Anīsa, an educated woman, also helped in running work at the press.[75] In the fifth year, however, Ḥanāniyā ran into troubles again, mostly due to difficulties in collecting subscription fees, a perennial problem of the Arabic press in its youth. His response was adventurous: He embarked on yet more ambitious projects, expecting them to bail him out of his predicament. In 1913, he acquired a modern printing machine and large quantities of paper and mortgaged his press against a loan from the Deutsche Palästina Bank to finance the new venture. This proved to have been a misguided move. Precarious as the business of publishing had been anyway in the small Arab provinces, the approaching global war made it even riskier. In mid-1914, Ḥanāniyā was announced bankrupt and hastily left Jerusalem for Alexandria, hoping to muster some assistance there. He stayed in Egypt till the end of World War I and beyond, cut off from his family and laboring hard to make ends meet in the only craft he knew. In 1920, he died there of heart failure.[76]

Ḥanāniyā's career, his creativity, struggles, and unceremonious fall, symbolized the experience of many who entered the new trade in the Arab provinces. Most of them were less successful than he, and their

[73] Mary Hanania, 63–69, including a summary of the paper's contents during its first year.
[74] Quoted in Yehoshuᶜa, 42.
[75] Mary Hanania, 54–55, 60.
[76] Mary Hanania, 55–57; Yehoshuᶜa, 48–50.

Jurjī Ḥabīb Ḥanāniyā with his family
Jerusalem Quarterly, 32 (autumn 2007), p. 54; from the collection of his granddaughter, Mary Hanania. Courtesy of the *Jerusalem Quarterly*.

professional careers were often shorter and less productive. A conspicuous feature of this business was transience. Those who entered it were undoubtedly more numerous than the ones known to us; we may safely assume that there were many more that engaged in printing or publishing for a while and abandoned it without leaving a trace. Of the others, we know primarily from the books or periodicals they issued, frequently no more than a single item. Often, all we have is their name or the name of their shop. Just as often we do not even have that.

More Entrepreneurs, Sponsors, and Contractors

Book title pages, colophons, and occasionally other parts hold valuable clues to their production history and the makers involved in it. Examined intently they often reveal aspects of the scene that have no trace in other sources. The simplest and most common front-page format is that which contains only the book's title, the author's name, and the name of the press with or without its address. In such cases, if the author is a contemporary (rather than historic) figure, the work is usually the product of his own initiative and of the press whose services he hired; or it could be a joint author-printer undertaking. To pick an example, a work by Syrian writer Rafīq al-ᶜAẓm, which was "printed in *maṭbaᶜat al-manār* on darb al-jamāmīz street, Cairo, 1321 [1903]," as its title page laconically indicates, was apparently a product of the author's collaboration with the Manār press owner, Rashīd Riḍā (who in this case happened to be al-ᶜAẓm's political partner then).[77] When the author is not a contemporary but a writer from the literary past, the book is usually the outcome of a printer/publisher initiative, representing intent to render the text publicly accessible and profit from it. Khalīl Sarkīs, we shall recall, printed quite a few works of this kind, from *Kalīla wa-dimna* to Ibn Khaldūn, whose front pages mentioned the author's name, work title, and Sarkīs's press. Such was the case with numerous items produced by smaller printers – from al-Ḥarīrī's twelfth-century *Maqāmāt*, which a little Cairo press issued in 1856, to the thirteenth-century epic of ᶜAntara bin Shaddād, published in Beirut in 1898 by another small press.[78] Similarly, printers who were Abū al-Hudā al-Ṣayyādī's followers published works from the old (mostly ṣūfī) heritage.[79]

As well as the author and printer, others who took part in the production in different roles are sometimes referred to on title pages. Frequently these are bookshop owners, whose diligence in initiating publishing during the *nahḍa* was second only to that of printers. Booksellers instigated the printing of works, so they could sell them in their own shops or distribute them otherwise. Such schemes did not necessarily require possession of printing equipment, and most of them indeed had none. Typically, a bookseller would locate a text with a promising vending

[77] Rafīq al-ᶜAẓm, *Ashhar mashāhīr al-islām fī al-ḥurūb wa'l-siyāsa*, Vol. 1 (Cairo: maṭbaᶜat al-manār, 1321 [1903]).

[78] *Maqāmāt al-ḥarīrī fī al-lugha al-ᶜarabiyya wa'l-funūn al-adabiyya* (Cairo: dār al-ṭibāᶜa al-bāhira, 1272 [1856]); *Dīwān al-shāᶜir al-mufliq wa'l-bāligh alladhī baḥr faḍlihi mughriq, abī al-ṭayyib aḥmad ibn al-ḥusayn al-shahīr bi'l-mutanabbī* (Cairo: maṭbaᶜat hindiyya, 1898); *Dīwān ᶜantar* (Beirut: maṭbaᶜat al-ādāb, 1898).

[79] E.g., a collection of fourteenth-century *qaṣīdas* by the ṣūfī ᶜAbd al-Raḥīm al-Buraᶜī, *Dīwān* (Cairo: al-maṭbaᶜa al-maymuniyya, 1324/1906). See also image on p. 93.

potential, obtain a license to publish it, enlist an editor and copyeditor if necessary, have the text printed and bound, and then advertise and sell it. This procedure would sometimes be recorded on the title page. The front cover of an 1889 book by Nāṣīf al-Yāzijī, published in Cairo, reveals that its making had been carried out by "The Egyptian Bookshop (*al-maktaba al-miṣriyya*), owned by ᶜAzīz Zand and his partners, where [the book] is sold." Zand, a Lebanese émigré to Egypt, owned a big bookshop in Cairo in the late 1880s.[80] In Tripoli (Syria), ᶜAbdāllāh al-Rifāᶜī, proprietor of a book dealership bearing his name, initiated and financed the printing of a work by Ḥikmat Sharīf. On the book's last two pages, Rifāᶜī listed seven other works by the same author which his shop had previously published, announced his possession of another seventeen Sharīf manuscripts, and called upon sponsors to fund their publication "through an arrangement with us."[81] And in Beirut, bookseller Ibrāhīm Ṣādir underwrote and published a book by Sulaymān Jāwīsh, with its title page properly noting its having been "printed at the expense of (*bi-nafaqat*) Ibrāhīm Ṣādir and his sons, owners of The Public Bookshop (*al-maktaba al-ᶜumūmiyya*) in Beirut in 1887."[82] Only a small minority of all booksellers were involved in such ventures.

The Egyptian Amīn Hindiyya was a prototypical bookseller-turned publisher. We first hear of him in the late 1880s, as a stationer and seller of books and journals in Cairo's Muski quarter (we will meet him again in that capacity when examining bookshops). Seeking to upgrade his business, he acquired printing gear, opened a print shop in another part of the city, and began turning out books. In 1898, he published the *rasā'il* of the tenth-century Abū al-Faḍl al-Hamadhānī ("*badīᶜ al-zamān*"), thereby commencing a prolific publishing career that would continue into the 1920s. The book, the front page notes, was the third printing of that opus. In the colophon, Hindiyya explained: "We have taken great care to closely follow two existing copies [of this work] that are credible and accurate to the utmost: one printed in the famous *al-Jawā'ib* press in Istanbul [1881], the other in the Jesuit press in Beirut and edited by the late scholar shaykh Ibrāhīm Effendi al-Aḥdab [1889]. We have exerted great efforts to adhere

80 Nāṣīf al-Yāzijī, *Fākihat al-nudamā' fī murāsalat al-udabā'* (Cairo: al-maktaba al-miṣriyya, 1889). Zand was a businessman and the author of at least two books; Ṭarrāzī, *Ta'rīkh al-ṣiḥāfa*, Vol. 2, 8; Vol. 3, 58.

81 Ḥikmat Sharīf, *Saᶜādat al-maᶜād fī mukhtaṣar sharḥ bānat suᶜād* (Tripoli: al-maktaba al-rifāᶜiyya, n.d.). The book seems to have been published sometime during the last Ottoman decade. The advert of Rifāᶜī's shop appears on pp. 23–24. We will revisit Rifāᶜī in Chapter 4.

82 Sulaymān Jāwīsh, *al-Tuḥfa al-saniyya fī ta'rīkh al-qusṭanṭiniyya* (Beirut: dār ṣādir, 1887). For further details on Ṣādir and other booksellers in Beirut and Cairo who engaged in publishing, see Khayyat, 62–67.

strictly to the original." The practice was standard: Anticipating demand for this already-published work, Hindiyya utilized extant editions to produce one of his own.[83] More aspects of the production routine were depicted in an advert posted in 1901 by Nakhla Qalfāṭ (himself an author and a translator) and Salīm Maydānī, who together ran a bookshop in Beirut called *al-maktaba al-kulliyya*.[84] Announcing the printing of a work by the eleventh-century linguist Ibn al-Sayyid al-Baṭalyawsī, they told future buyers how its publication was arranged:

> We have been looking for this book for a long time. A trip to Cairo created an opportunity to visit the Khedivial library, where we came across a [manuscript] exemplar of it. We copied it and brought it back to Beirut, aiming to serve the educated by printing it . . . We have asked our friend, the great scholar, meticulous linguist, poet, and prose-writer ᶜAbdāllāh al-Bustānī, professor of Qur'ān in the patriarchal [Jesuit] college in Beirut, to assume the task of editing [it] and overseeing its printing, which he accepted.[85]

Republishing a previously printed work, or locating a manuscript in a library, copying it, and bringing it to light with or without editing – that's how books were made by big publishers like Sarkīs and by the many smaller ones, such as Hindiyya, Qalfāṭ, and Maydānī.

There were more forms of involvement in book and journal publishing. Books often mention sponsors who funded production, the common formula being "*ṭubiᶜa bi-nafaqat*...," that is, "printing funded by..." usually with no further elaboration. Thus, a collection of poetry (*Dīwān*) by the fourteenth-century poet Ṣafyī al-Dīn al-Ḥillī was published in Beirut in 1893, "*bi-nafaqat nakhla qalfāṭ*"; an Arabic translation of Shakespeare's *Othello* was printed in Cairo in 1899, "at the expense of Murqus Jirjis"; and *al-ᶜAlam al-shāmikh*, a work by the seventeenth-century scholar Ṣāliḥ al-Maqbalī, was "printed at the expense of a group of Hijazis and Syrians" in 1910.[86] Often,

83 *Rasā'il abī al-faḍl badīᶜ al-zamān al-hamadhānī* (Cairo: maṭbaᶜat hindiyya, 1898), title page and p. 332. The Worldcat database (accessed 17 September 2015) contains seventy-four books in Arabic and Turkish published in his press from 1898 to 1928. Hindiyya is also noted as the author of *kitāb al-aḥkām al-sharᶜiyya fī al-aḥwāl al-shakhṣiyya ᶜalā madhhab al-imām abī ḥanīfa al-nuᶜmān* (Cairo: maṭbaᶜat hindiyya, 1900). It is unclear whether or not he continued to engage in book selling after becoming a publisher. See also Chapter 4.

84 Qalfāṭ was the author of at least three books. In 1880, he was mentioned as the owner of another bookshop, *al-maktaba al-sūriyya* (*al-Muqtaṭaf*, May 1880, inside front-cover), and in 1901 as Maydānī's partner in *al-maktaba al-kulliyya* (*Lisān al-Ḥāl*, 7 October 1901, 4). See also Ṭarrāzī, *Ta'rīkh al-ṣiḥāfa*, Vol. 2, 63–65. I have found no information on Maydānī.

85 *Lisān al-Ḥāl*, 7 October 1901, 4. The announcement also provided details on places of distribution, prices, etc.

86 Ṣafyī al-Dīn al-Ḥillī, *Dīwān* (Beirut: maṭbaᶜat al-ādāb, 1893); *Riwāyat ūtillū* (Cairo: maṭbaᶜat al-tawfīq, 1899); Ṣāliḥ al-Maqbalī, *al-ᶜAlam al-shāmikh* (Cairo, 1328 [1910]).

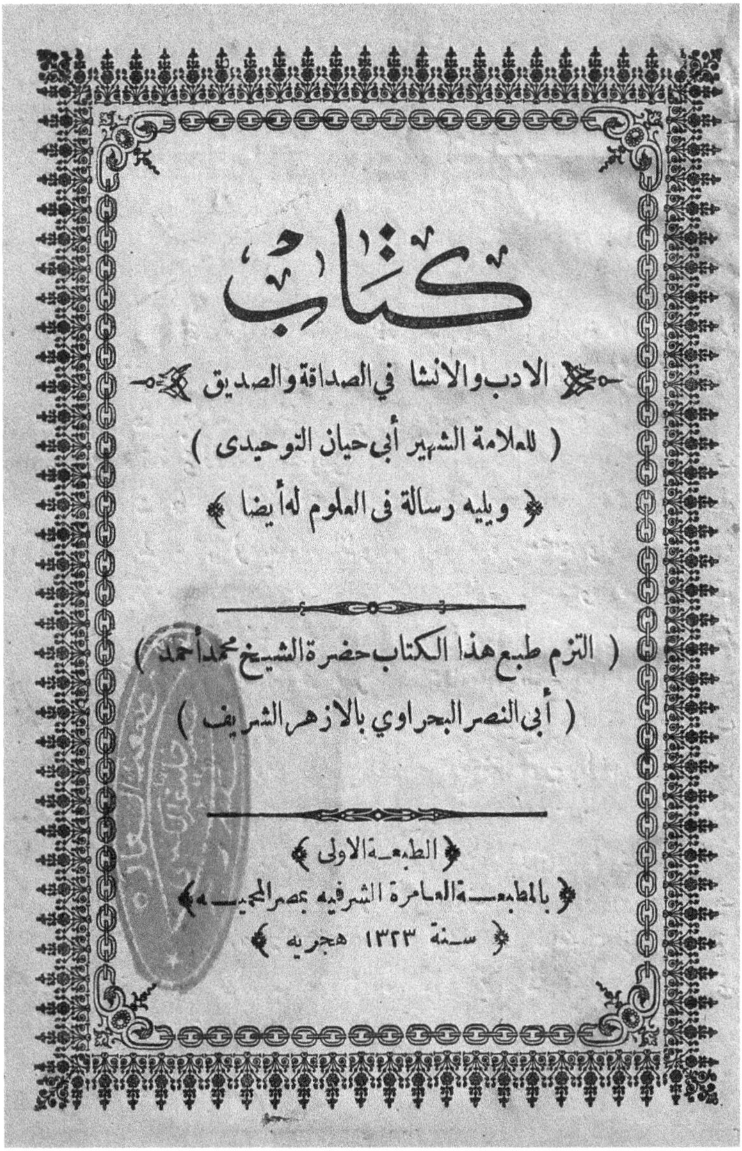

كتاب

الادب والانشا في الصداقة والصديق

(للعلامة الشهير أبي حيان التوحيدى)

ويليه رسالة فى العلوم له أيضا

(التزم طبع هذا الكتاب حضرة الشيخ محمد أحمد)

(أبي النصر البحراوي بالازهر الشريف)

الطبعة الاولى

بالمطبعة العامرة الشرفيه بمصر المحميه

سنة ١٣٢٣ هجريه

Al-Tawḥīdī, *Kitāb al-adab wal-inshā'*

Cairo: al-maṭbaʿa al-sharafiyya, 1905. 198pp. Muḥammad Aḥmad al-Baḥrāwī of al-Azhar is identified as the books *multazim*.

these were obscure persons of whom we know almost nothing, nor is their share in the process quite clear. The motivation behind such private ventures is rarely stated, but we may assume that it was akin to that of printers and booksellers: a wish to reclaim a valuable text from oblivion and put it at the public's disposal, along with a desire to profit from the investment. Usually it was both.

One other kind of publishing routine was through contract struck between an entrepreneur and a press. Typically an Egyptian practice, it first appeared in Cairo of the 1830s where private individuals were allowed and even induced to print works of their choice at the Būlāq press under a contract known as *iltizām*.[87] Contractors, or *multazim*s, were mostly affluent people who could afford the relatively high cost the press normally charged or book dealers who expected to turn a profit from selling the printed works. The *multazim* was usually given an exclusive concession to print a specified text, and his name was announced on the book's front page, alongside those of the author, printer, and occasional underwriters. Such deals, at first involving the state press, were later extended to private print shops as well. Thus, a play-script authored by one Ismāᶜīl ᶜĀṣim and printed in Cairo's *al-maṭbaᶜa al-ᶜabbāsiyya* identified ᶜAlī ᶜĀṣim (a relative of the author?) as "*multazim al-ṭabᶜ*"; three plays written by Najīb al-Ḥaddād were printed in Alexandria "under the *iltizām* of Aḥmad Rifāᶜī"; and the front page of a work by the eleventh-century scholar al-Tawḥīdī, produced in a privately owned Cairo press, identified Muḥammad Aḥmad Abī al-Naṣr al-Baḥrāwī as the man who "*iltazam* this book's printing" (see image on p. 61).[88]

Printing arrangements of this kind sometimes involved safeguarding the *multazim*'s publishing "rights." Statements such as "the rights of printing [or: reprinting] are reserved for him" (*ḥuqūq al-ṭabᶜ maḥfūẓa lahu*) or similar formulae appear in book title pages and colophons published in the region throughout the period.[89] The occurrence of such statements is too haphazard to allow a sound notion of these "rights," and more research is needed before we can be sure of their precise intent and practical effect. In their phrasing, these notices seem to evoke the idea

[87] Nuṣayr, 408–10, 443; Schwartz, 199–206.

[88] Ismāᶜīl ᶜĀṣim, *Riwāyat ḥusn al-ᶜawāqib* (Cairo: al-maṭbaᶜa al-ᶜabbāsiyya, 1894); Najīb al-Ḥaddād, *Riwāyat al-ṭabīb al-maghṣūb, Riwāyat ḥilm al-mulūk, and Riwāyat al-sayyid* (all published in Alexandria: maṭbaᶜat jurjī gharzūzī, 1904); Abū Ḥayān al-Tawḥīdī, *al-Adab wa'l-inshā' fī al-ṣadāqa wa'l-ṣadīq* (Cairo: al-maṭbaᶜa al-sharafiyya, 1905).

[89] E.g., title pages of Nāṣīf al-Yāzijī, *Dīwān* (Beirut: al-maṭbaᶜa al-adabiyya, 1898); Abū Firās al-Ḥamdānī, *Dīwān* (Beirut: al-maṭbaᶜa al-adabiyya, 1900); *Riwāyat ūtillū* (Cairo: maṭbaᶜat al-tawfīq, 1899); ᶜAlī Fikrī, *Ādāb al-fatāt* (Cairo: maṭbaᶜat hindiyya, 1911); Qusṭanṭīn Ilyās Khūrī, *al-Hadiyya al-sharqiyya li-ṭalabat al-lugha al-inklīziyya* (Beirut: Author's printing, 1883). More examples in Khayyat, 60; Schwartz, 303–04.

of copyright, to wit, state legal protection of a writer's or publisher's exclusive entitlement to benefit from the text and reproduce it. Provisions for copyright did exist in Ottoman and Egyptian laws ever since the late 1850s, apparently inspired by European models; but the impression one gets from the scanty evidence at hand is that not much public heed was paid to them. The "approach to the legality of reproducing a text was informed by their manuscript tradition," one scholar has suggested; that is, the old lax norms of replicating any text at anyone's will were carried over into the printing era.[90] Thus, when a Cairo publisher with "reprinting rights" for a work warned that "whoever dares to print it would be legally prosecuted and made to pay compensations,"[91] this was likely a wishful warning. Though a familiar legal principle in the region then, the systematic application of copyright would take place long beyond the era explored here.

Along with enterprising individuals, scientific societies and share companies were set up to engage in publishing. It seems to have been a marginal phenomenon, whose contribution to Arab publishing at the time was small. In Egypt, four scientific literary societies and three share companies that published books during the second half of the nineteenth century have been traced. According to Nuṣayr's count, their total published output was 133 titles, or less than 1.5 percent of the country's overall printed output during that period.[92] In Beirut, a share company for "publishing useful Arabic books and selling them at a low cost" was formed in the 1860s under the name *al-ᶜumda al-adabiyya*. It advertised itself repeatedly in the local press but with scanty practical results.[93] There might have been more such efforts here and there, but on the whole, the role of these actors was trivial. Private publishing was predominantly in the hands of individuals, big and small.

Publishing was an exacting occupation during the formative phase. There were obstacles of many sorts – economic, cultural, and political. Introducing a new consumer good of any kind into the market is ever

[90] Schwartz, 302–06. Schwartz presents the general contours of the copyright scene in Egypt during this time. Elaborating this sensible but rather basic picture should entail more archival searching.

[91] Abū Ḥāmid al-Ghazālī, *al-Risāla al-laduniyya* (Cairo: maṭbaᶜat kurdistān al-ᶜilmiyya, 1328/1910), title page. See also image on p. 64

[92] The most active of these, *jamᶜiyyat al-maᶜārif*, published 47 titles until 1900; details in Nuṣayr, 422–30; Rāfiᶜī, *ᶜAṣr ismāᶜīl*, Vol. 2, 245–46. Schwartz, 261–66, has identified printers who worked in groups (she labels them "consortiums") to produce lithograph books and chapbooks in Cairo during the 1850s and 1860s.

[93] *Ḥadīqat al-Akhbār*, 31 May 1860, 3; 17 April 1866, 3; 21 May 1867, 3. The title page of al-Mutanabbī's *Dīwān*, printed in Beirut in 1860, indicates that "its printing was funded by *al-ᶜumda al-adabiyya*." The company itself reported two other titles it published, in 1866 and 1867 (*Ḥadīqat al-Akhbār*, 17 April 1866 and 21 May 1867).

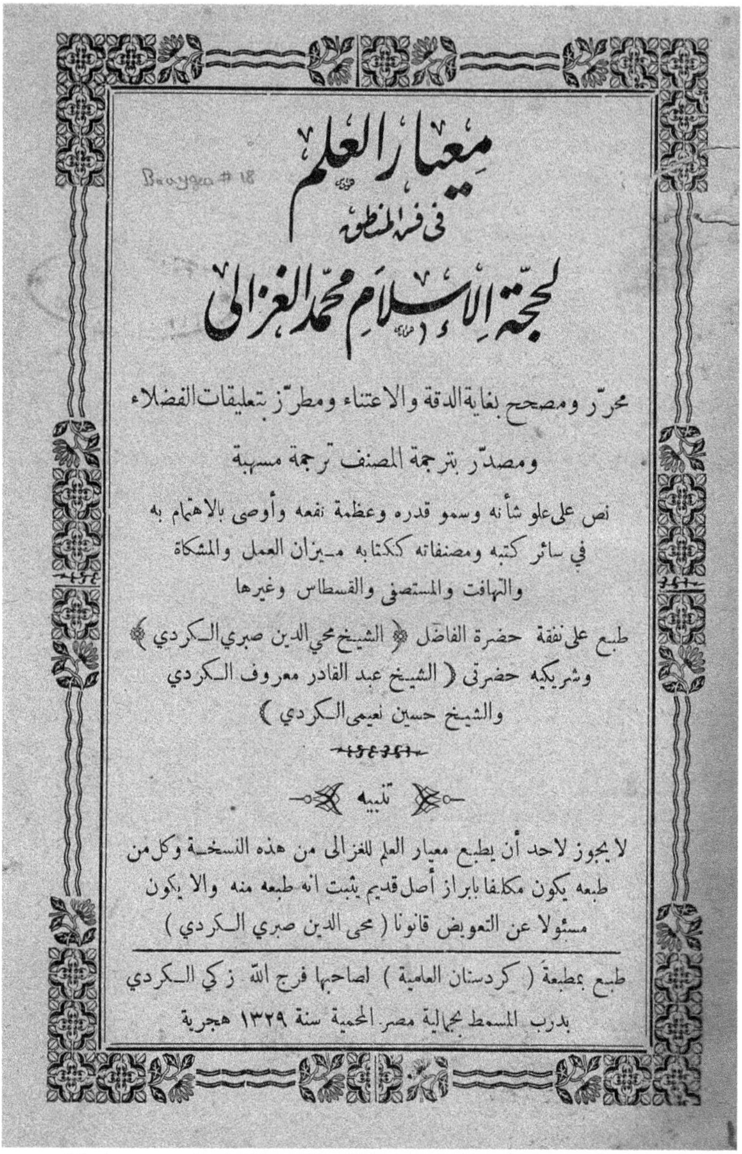

معيار العلم

في فن المنطق

لحجة الإسلام محمد الغزالي

محرر ومصحح بغاية الدقة والاعتناء ومطرز بتعليقات الفضلاء

ومصدر بترجمة المصنف ترجمة مسهبة

نص على علو شأنه وسمو قدره وعظمة نفعه وأوصى بالاهتمام به

في سائر كتبه ومصنفاته ككتابه ميزان العمل والمشكاة

والتهافت والمستصفى والقسطاس وغيرها

طبع على نفقة حضرة الفاضل (الشيخ محي الدين صبري الكردي)

وشريكيه حضرتي (الشيخ عبد القادر معروف الكردي

والشيخ حسين نعيمي الكردي)

تنبيه

لا يجوز لاحد أن يطبع معيار العلم للغزالي من هذه النسخة وكل من

طبعه يكون مكلفا بابراز أصل قديم يثبت انه طبعه منه والا يكون

مسئولا عن التعويض قانونا (محي الدين صبري الكردي)

طبع بمطبعة (كردستان العلمية) لصاحبها فرج الله زكي الكردي

بدرب المسمط بجمالية مصر المحمية سنة ١٣٢٩ هجرية

Muḥammad al-Ghazālī, *Miʿyār al-ʿilm fī fann al-manṭiq* (Cairo: maṭbaʿat kurdistān al-ʿilmiyya, 1911), 200pp. "Edited and corrected with utmost precision and care and adorned with annotations by eminent scholars . . . Printed at the expense (*nafaqat*) of the honorable shaykh Muḥyī al-Dīn Ṣabrī al-Kurdī and his partners . . . It is forbidden for anyone to print Ghazālī's *Miʿyār al-ʿilm* from this copy. Anyone printing it would be required to produce an[other] original source proving it was copied from it or be legally subject to compensations . . . Printed in maṭbaʿat kurdistān al-ʿilmiyya owned by Farajāllāh Zakī al-Kurdī on al-masmaṭ street in Jamaliyya Cairo."

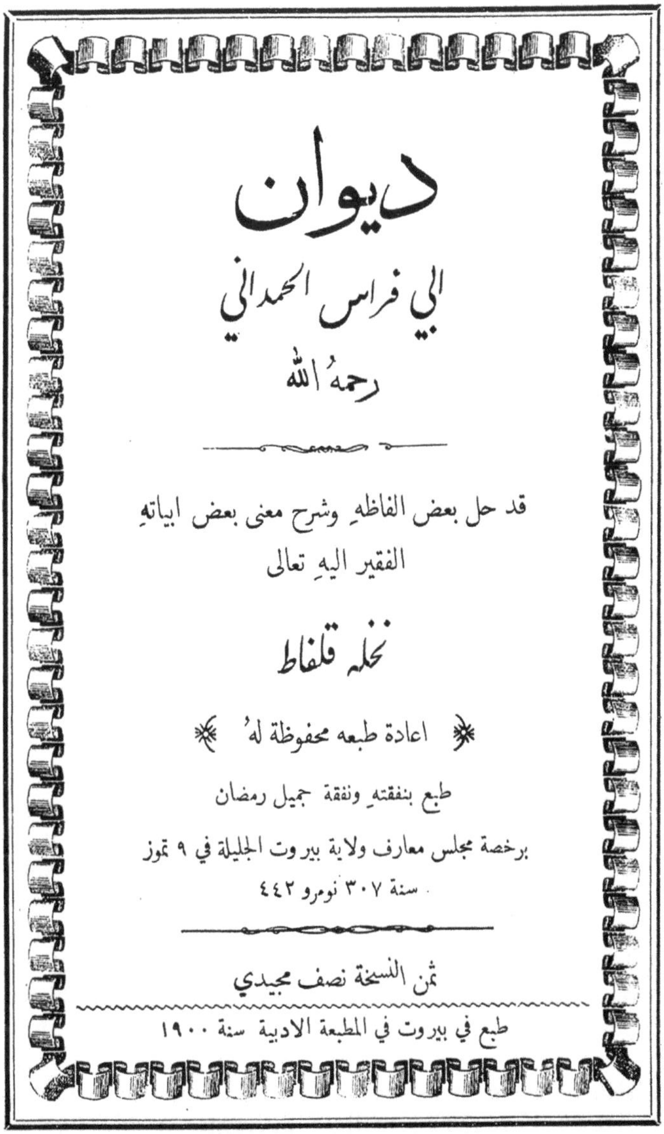

ديوان

ابي فراس الحمداني

رحمه الله

قد حل بعض الفاظه وشرح معنى بعض ابياته

الفقير اليه تعالى

نخله قلفاط

اعادة طبعه محفوظة له

طبع بنفقته ونفقة جميل رمضان

برخصة مجلس معارف ولاية بيروت الجليلة في ٩ تموز

سنة ٣٠٧ نومرو ٤٤٢

ثمن النسخة نصف مجيدي

طبع في بيروت في المطبعة الادبية سنة ١٩٠٠

Dīwān Abī Firās al-Ḥamdānī

(Beirut: al-maṭbaᶜa al-adabiyya, 1900), 160pp. Elucidated by Nakhla Qalfāṭ, who underwrote its printing (*ṭubiᶜa bi-nafaqatihi)* together with Jamīl Ramaḍān, and to whom reprinting (right) is preserved (*maḥfūẓa*). Printed with permission of (*bi-rukhṣat*) the exalted education council of the province of Beirut, 9 Tammūz [1]307, number 442. Copy price is half-a-majīdī. Printed in Beirut in al-maṭbaᶜa al-adabiyya, 1900.

a challenge, and printed products represented an especially intricate one in the nineteenth-century Arab provinces. As we shall see in later chapters, the market for books and journals was initially constricted by pervasive illiteracy, indigence, and public apathy toward anything printed. Nor was there at first an adequate physical infrastructure for circulating the massive quantities. One had to be exceptionally quick-witted and highly driven to persist and prosper under such circumstances. Hurdles were also placed by the suspicious authorities, who were wary of the idea of their subjects employing such a potent amplifier. The rulers in Istanbul and Cairo, opening the doors for foreign influences and adopting new measures to modernize their states, were concerned about the potentially problematic repercussions of private publishing for the political order and sought to check its spreading. It was mostly items of political relevance, mainly newspapers and journals, which they distrusted.[94] But their control was all-encompassing, applied through restrictive legislation, selective licensing, prepublication censorship, harassment, and punishing, including corporal punishment, a policy that reached its notorious apogee in the Ottoman state under Sultan ᶜAbdülhamid II.[95]

Inspecting the whole range of means Ottoman and Egyptian authorities employed to control publication is at once impractical and unnecessary. We may, more narrowly, look at just one of these methods: licensing. Permission to print, known as *imtiyāz* or *rukhṣa*, became a requirement under the Ottoman Printing and Publication Law of 1857, which also applied to Egypt. Those wishing to obtain a permit to print had to get the approval of two state agencies: the Council of Education and the Ministry of Police. Front pages of books printed in Beirut sometimes carried the license number and even its date of issue, apparently a legal requisite though probably not a rigid one, as many books did not follow this routine. Publishers who did may have done so as a defensive measure, to demonstrate their compliance with the authorities' line. Such, for example, were the publishers of Ṣafyī al-Dīn al-Ḥillī's *Dīwān*, mentioned above, whose front cover noted its having been "printed by license of the exalted Council of Education of Beirut province, [granted] on 9 Tammūz 1307 [1893], number 441." Likewise, the front page of Khalīl Sarkīs's *Mukhtaṣar ustādh al-ṭabbākhīn* indicated it was printed by license of the same council, "number 15, dated 5 Mārt 1317 [1899]."[96] In Egypt, an official permission to

[94] For a discussion of this issue with regard to early Arab journalism, see Ayalon, *The Press*, 110–26.

[95] ᶜAbdülhamid's harsh measures have often been discussed, and ridiculed. For one vivid description, see *al-Hilāl*, 1 October 1908, 31–36.

[96] Ṣafyī al-Dīn al-Ḥillī, *Dīwān* (Beirut: maṭbaᶜat al-ādāb, 1893); Sarkīs, *Mukhtaṣar*. A similar indication appeared in a book published in Istanbul already in 1882: *Dīwān al-Buḥturī*,

print and issue books was required already during Mehmet ᶜAlī's tenure. The rule applied to all private publishing and seems to have been systematically implemented. But unlike in Lebanon, here it did not reflect in title-page indications, perhaps because in the highly centralized Egyptian state, unlicensed publishing was quite inconceivable.

Licensing was a block on the road to printing and publishing. It was more so with newspapers than with books and more so with matters pertinent to the political order than with harmless substance such as classic literature or cooking. Involving a prior examination of the work's contents and the applicant's agenda, it often ended in rejection and always protracted the process, sometimes to an absurd length, as we have seen in the case of Jurjī Ḥabīb Ḥanāniyā. Unlicensed publishing was impossible except clandestinely, or unless one wished to defy the government openly and pay the price for it. Obtaining a license, except for the most innocuous texts, was wearying enough to discourage all but the most resilient, especially, again, during Sultan ᶜAbdülhamid's long tenure. Rashīd Riḍā, who moved from Syria to the freedom of Egypt to publish a journal, observed that the state had a fairly clear policy of granting licenses; but its agents in the different localities "commonly twisted the rules by granting permits only to those who bribed them." Riḍā related how his partner, who came with him from Tripoli to Cairo and became manager (*mudīr*) of his journal *al-Manār*, had applied for a license to open a press and issue a newspaper while still in Tripoli:

> Once all legal procedures had been fulfilled with the Tripoli governorship, the district executive council issued a report affirming that he was entitled to a license. The required dues were levied from him, and the paperwork was sent up to the *wālī* of Beirut, who was to forward it to Istanbul. The *wālī* procrastinated for a long time, seeing no urgency in the matter. Eventually he ruled that there was no problem in permitting the printing press, but granting a newspaper license was out of the question, "because Tripoli already had one newspaper, and if another one were to appear this could fatigue the censor (*al-sinsūr*), who would thereafter be required to inspect two papers." Thus the compassion of his highness Rashīd Bey and his care for the Tripoli censor prevented the applicant from getting his modest wish.[97]

Licensing was just one item in the government's toolbox, and government control was only one kind of impediment in the printer's way. We will consider other difficulties in later chapters. The various obstacles

"printed by license (*rukhṣa*) of the exalted Ministry of Education; date of license 28 Rajab 1300 [1882], number 261" (Istanbul: maṭbaᶜat al-jawā'ib, 1300 [1882]).

97 *Al-Manār*, Vol. 1 (1898), 657–58. The manager was ᶜAbd al-Ḥamīd b. ᶜUbayd Effendi Murād; details in Ryad, 35–37. (Ryad is rectifying an error in my book, *The Press*, where I erroneously ascribed Murād's frustrating trials to Riḍā himself.)

did not prevent publishing, but they did weigh down on initiatives and discouraged those who might otherwise have entered the field. Consequently, the early Arab experience in printing and publishing was marked by the fleeting existence of most ventures in this area. A few of the presses grew into big projects, but the overwhelming majority of them were tiny and short-lived. Many publishers issued only a single book or booklet, or a handful of them, and then fell silent. The early history of Arabic journalism brightly mirrored this situation: The greater part of pre–World War I papers were ephemeral products that died young, sometimes after a single issue. Only a few of those who entered the field were tough enough to persist and lucky enough to thrive.

Fortunately, however, the efforts in this area, both the successful and the flimsy, were numerous enough to allow Arab publishing to survive beyond its delicate childhood. As it triumphed, printers and publishers, big and small, came to mold the world of written texts that were available to the public: their contents, variety, and formats. Printers, booksellers, and stationers assumed the role of putting written texts at the public's disposal, previously fulfilled by spiritual guides, jurists, and scholars. And business considerations became as central in the mass production of writings as were cultural, educational, and pious ones.

3 Books, Journals, *Cartes de Visite*

Perhaps the greatest achievement of Aldus Manutius (1449–1515), the most famous of early European printers, was the redeeming of old literary treasures. As a scholar of Greek linguistics and literature, Aldus's priority was to commit works of ancient Greek civilization to print and save them from oblivion. With the help of hired Cretan scribes, he issued Greek dictionaries and grammars; published the philosophy of Plato and Aristotle; printed literary pieces by Homer, Sophocles, and Aristophanes; brought out the histories of Herodotus and Thucydides; and printed other precious works, thus assuring their preservation. The Aldine Press also printed works in Latin and Italian, including ancient writings such as the letters of young Pliny and rhetoric of Quintilian, and literary works by renaissance luminaries such as Dante and Petrarch that had already been considered classics by then. As a secondary priority and on a more limited scale, his press printed writings by contemporaries, most famously Erasmus. To a first-generation printer, these were obvious choices: using the new technology first to bring old treasures to light, and second to make valuable contemporary writings accessible to the public. Business concerns underlay these priorities, above all the drive to produce texts that were in high demand as manuscripts, so as to assure profit. In the process, Aldus and his colleagues also labored to upgrade the appearance of books, setting the mold for their improved future format (some old basic attributes were preserved – the codex format, binding, use of illustrations, and some important aspects of text layout). They made old objects in a new dress: old and familiar in contents, similar but distinct in appearance, and all too novel in production pace, quantities, and attainability.[1]

Early Arab printers similarly relied in their pioneering endeavors on a rich literary heritage. Twelve hundred years of creativity yielded a vast pool of writings in the languages of Islam, in every field of human knowledge. Only a segment of it, an unknown share of the whole but a very

[1] Lowry, esp. 48–71, 180–216; Barolini, 1–90.

considerable corpus in itself, had remained as the Middle East was about to enter the age of printing; the rest had perished under rough circumstances. An extensive account of this remaining corpus is a task for another study, but it is possible here to point out its main categories, which will help us later in the chapter. Reflecting the cultural world of Arabic speakers and writers, primarily the Muslim majority, this surviving segment was marked by a distinct accent on religious themes: Qur'ānic exegesis, Hadith, Islamic law, prophetic biography and panegyric, homiletics, theological discourse and polemics, works on mysticism, and prayer recitation, as well as works in disciplines sometimes described as "auxiliary," such as Arabic language, grammar, and lexicography. Books in these subjects made up the better part of institutional and private collections most everywhere. Next to these were products of the scholarly tradition in Islamic societies: in science – medicine, mathematics, biology, alchemy, astronomy, and meteorology; in human disciplines – philosophy, logic, history and chronicles, and geography; and a colorful range of *adab* – eposes, poetry, and guidance in practical matter, from education to letter-writing and from etiquette to cooking. Public and private libraries in the early nineteenth-century Middle East contained items in all of these areas, original manuscripts or, more often, copies of them. Many works existed in more editions than one, and precious exemplars were coupled with their simpler, cheaper, sometimes partial duplicates. Some were large tomes or multivolume works of learning, others more modest books or booklets, most typically prayer books and ṣūfī tracts. Items of this last kind were especially widespread; one such text, the fifteenth-century ṣūfī prayer book *Dalā'il al-khayrāt*, is said to have been a real "bestseller" in Egypt on the eve of printing.[2] Also very popular were books of *adab*, notably the whole or parts of *Alf layla wa-layla* and al-Ḥarīrī's *Maqāmāt*. These were works in the languages of Islam, primarily Arabic, Turkish, and Persian, as well as items in idioms of the local ethnolinguistic minorities, such as Armenian, Syriac, and Coptic.

It is equally important to note what kinds of writings these pre-nineteenth-century collections did not contain. Most noticeable, they held no works in idioms not spoken in the region itself. Moreover, there were few works if any that dealt with the non-Islamic parts of the world – their geography, societies, histories, or cultures – and little in the various fields of knowledge that had evolved in Europe since the renaissance and

[2] Hanna, *In Praise*, 92–96. The book, apparently by the fifteenth-century ṣūfī shaykh Muḥammad bin Sulaymān al-Jazūlī, was copied again and again and was included in many private and public collections. It also appeared frequently in adverts of book sales during the latter part of the nineteenth century.

the advent of printing. The fruits of European scholarship on Eastern societies, their languages and history, did reach local libraries, but in minuscule quantities. Such external knowledge would begin to enter the region on a bigger scale only in the nineteenth century, with Mehmet ᶜAlī's book acquisition and translation projects and the enhanced missionary educational schemes. Middle Eastern book collections usually expanded at a slower pace than their European counterparts, both because they increased through copying while Europe was already printing and because they contained no periodical publications, the category of writings that had rapidly augmented European libraries from the seventeenth century onward.

Early Middle Eastern printers of the nineteenth century did not have to wait for gradual developments in technology, genre, and format. By that time, advanced tools and practices had become available in Europe, and Arab publishers could borrow and assimilate methods that in Aldus's time had been unknown. The choice they faced in applying the new technology was richer and more diverse than that which had been available to European printers of the fifteenth and sixteenth centuries: not only bringing to light works from the old literary legacy and current writings, but also producing publications hitherto unknown to their societies in type and pace. Printing could help preserve the local written heritage, as it had in Europe, but now it could also avail the society with new directions of thought and new tools for everyday use. This chapter examines the choices the early Arab printers had, focusing first on those which reflected continuity and then on innovations inspired by modern examples and needs.

Much More of the Familiar Same

The entry of modern technology, the appearance of new written products, the speed of their circulation, and the new public discourse they facilitated, all signified a major break with the past. These changes seemed especially dramatic because of the vibrant momentum with which they unfolded as compared to their evolutionary progress in Europe earlier on. But these sharp turns should not mask another important aspect of the change: continuity. Because printing came into the region along with many other novelties, we often tend to focus on its innovative impact while ignoring its role in upholding the long-standing routine of making books, especially of the old kind. Such a slanted view may not have occurred had the region adopted printing in the seventeenth or eighteenth century, before the many feverish shifts of the nineteenth. The new technology, we shall remember, was initially embraced by writers of

Arabic in order to keep up a traditional endeavor with better tools. And indeed, it allowed perpetuity of much of the former text-making activity, in contents, genres, and even form. Continuity was of a greater weight than we tend to acknowledge.

Continuity was most visible in the choice of works to be printed, many of which came from the old literary and scholarly heritage. Making classic works available to the public was a prime preference for pioneer publishers. Hitherto, book-collection owners had been "keeping their books behind closed iron doors," Buṭrus al-Bustānī complained in his celebrated 1859 *Khiṭāb*, referring to the state of affairs in Lebanon; "What is the use of so many books if nobody reads them?"[3] Just as ancient Greek treasures were saved from neglect by fifteenth- and sixteenth-century printers, Arabic books had to be salvaged from a similar fate by the new technology. The desire to contribute to that end was complemented by the assessment that reproducing them in large quantities made good business sense. The educated classes were interested in works from the traditional stock, highly regarded assets that lent their possessors some local prestige. Major works in every field, alongside more esoteric items, thus began to be pulled off dusty library shelves and fed to the printing machines.

Let us look at a few examples. Mehmet ᶜAlī's press in Būlāq, an icon of modernization, produced classic works such as al-Bayḍāwī's thirteenth-century Qur'ān exegesis (*Anwār al-tanzīl*, printed in 1836), the grammars of the fourteenth-century Ibn Hishām (*Shudhūr al-dhahab*, 1837) and fifteenth-century Khālid al-Azharī (*Sharḥ al-azharī*, 1837), Fīrūzābādī's celebrated fourteenth-century lexicon (*al-Qāmūs al-muḥīṭ*, 1835), and literary epics such as *Kalīla wa-dimna* (1836) and *Alf layla wa-layla* (1836). One survey of works printed in Mehmet ᶜAlī's shops has identified about a third of them as "classical."[4] Later on in the century, in Beirut, Khalīl Sarkīs's press turned out scores of such classic works in print beside the newer products. Among these were Abū al-ᶜAlā' al-Maᶜarrī's eleventh-century *Rasā'il* (1894); Ibn Mālik's thirteenth-century grammar, *al-Khulāṣa* (1888); Ibn Khaldūn's fourteenth-century *Muqaddima* (1900); al-Suyūṭī's sixteenth-century encyclopedia, *Miftāḥ al-ᶜulūm* (1899); poetry collections (*dīwāns*) of the ninth-century Abū Tammām Ḥabīb al-Ṭā'ī (1889), tenth-century Abū Firās al-Ḥamdānī (1900), and eleventh-century Abū al-ᶜAlā' al-Maᶜarrī (1884); literary pieces, such as

[3] *Al-Jamᶜiyya al-sūriyya*, 115.

[4] Hsu, especially 12–13; Perron. In Hsu's partial survey of Arabic books printed in Egypt from 1822 to 1851, 86 out of the 255 he traced had been written before 1800, which he classified as "classical" works. Another 86 "classical" books were published there in Turkish during that period.

al-Ḥarīrī's *Maqāmāt* (1888 and 1903), *Kalīla wa-dimna* (1888 and 1902), and *Alf layla wa-layla* (1880–1882); and the eposes of ᶜAntara bin Shaddād (1883–1885) and *Majnūn laylā* (1882).[5]

More publishers undertook to make the existing reservoir of texts accessible through printing, reproducing works by the luminaries of Arab and Islamic literary and scholarly tradition in every field. A glimpse in the catalog of any library with stocks of early Arabic printings readily reveals works in religion – al-Bukhārī's *Ṣaḥīḥ* (1862, 1878, 1883, 1896),[6] al-Tirmidhī's *Ṣaḥīḥ* (1875), and al-Zamakhsharī's *Kashshāf* (1865); in grammar and lexicography – Sībawayh's *Kitāb* (1898), Ibn Manẓūr's multivolume *Lisān al-ᶜarab* (1882–1891), and Suyūṭī's *al-Muzhir fī al-lugha* (1865, 1907); in history – Ibn al-ᶜArabī's *al-Futūḥāt al-makiyya* (1911), al-Maqrīzī's *Khiṭaṭ* (1853, 1906–1908), Ibn Iyās's *Badā'iᶜ al-zuhūr* (1878, 1886, 1891), and al-Suyūṭī's *Ta'rīkh al-khulafā'* (1887); in geography and travel – al-Masᶜūdī's *Murūj al-dhahab* (1885) and Ibn Baṭṭūṭa's *Riḥla* (1867, 1870, 1904); in law and philosophy – al-Māwardī's *al-Aḥkām al-sulṭāniyya* (1880), Ibn Rushd's *Falsafa* (1895), and al-Ghazālī's *Ikhyā' ᶜulūm al-dīn* (1866); and in classic literature and poetry – al-Iṣfahānī's *Kitāb al-aghānī* (1868, 1905), Ibn Qutayba's *al-Shiᶜr wa'l-shuᶜarā'* (Beirut, 1865, 1902), and al-Mutanabbī's *Dīwān* (Beirut, 1860, Cairo, 1898).[7] Many works were printed repeatedly, by the same or by different presses, sometimes in piratical impressions that exploited another printer's labors in editing a manuscript. Ibn Khaldūn's *Muqaddima*, for instance, appeared in at least eleven editions between 1857 and 1909 (seven in Cairo, four in Beirut).[8] Of *Kalīla wa-dimna*, no fewer than thirty-seven printings by state and private presses are verified for the period 1833–1914 (eighteen in Cairo, seventeen in Beirut, two in Mosul).[9] It was surpassed by the highly popular *Alf layla*, of which an incalculable number of (mostly partial) editions appeared throughout the region. Every self-respecting publisher would try to produce a better- or lesser-quality copy of the ever-popular "Nights," or select stories from it, extending the old pervasive routine of copying the work into the era of

[5] Worldcat, accessed 1 September 2013.
[6] Items mentioned from here to the end of this paragraph were published in Cairo, unless otherwise indicated.
[7] Worldcat, accessed 1 September 2015.
[8] We have full bibliographic data for the Cairo editions of 1857, 1867, 1893, 1904 (by three different publishers), and 1909, and for those printed in Beirut in 1867, 1879, 1886, and 1900. A few more seem to have been produced during this period, for which the publication data are incomplete. Worldcat, accessed 20 September 2015.
[9] Cairo: 1833, 1835, 1868, 1880, 1885 (by two publishers), 1887, 1889, 1896, 1900 (by three publishers), 1903, 1905, 1906, 1907, 1909, 1912; Beirut: 1868, 1878, 1882, 1884, 1888, 1889, 1890, 1896, 1899 (by two publishers), 1902, 1905, 1906, 1907, 1909, 1911, 1912; Mosul: 1883, 1897. Worldcat, accessed 20 September 2015.

printing.[10] Reproducing old works in print was not limited to the format of books. Early Arabic journals, a novelty in themselves, often serialized classic works of scholarship and *adab*. For example, the Beiruti *Ḥadīqat al-Akhbār* carried excerpts of Ibn Shāma's thirteenth-century history, *Kitāb al-rawḍatayn*, and the Cairo-based *Wādī al-Nīl* featured segments of Ibn Baṭṭūṭa's *Riḥla*.[11]

The long-winded string of examples in the last two paragraphs above is admittedly tedious. But such copiousness seems necessary for underscoring the massive drawing of early Arab publishers on past treasures, which is sometimes eclipsed by the striking novelties of the *nahḍa*. Cornerstone works of the literary legacy came up as obvious choices for printing once the new book-making technology became available. To the publisher, reproducing scholarly gems like Suyūṭī's and Ibn Khaldūn's, which would be the pride of the educated book collector, and printing pieces from *Alf layla*, which would easily sell to a popular audience, were sound investments. In that, early Arab printers did not differ from their predecessors in early modern Europe. Nor did they differ from publishers of the early Hebrew press in the fifteenth and sixteenth centuries: Major works of Jewish tradition dominated the lists of early printings – the Old Testament and Talmud, biblical exegesis, Jewish *halachic* law, rabbinical scholarship, Jewish philosophy, and more. Here, too, publishers' business concerns coincided nicely with the desire to sustain the old legacy.[12] Modern ideas were certainly attractive to Arab publishers, but preserving the old heritage by committing it to print was likewise a high priority.

Continuity typified more than the contents of printed works. It was also seen, especially in the early decades, in the adherence to old literary genres and forms even when the substance was new. That this should be so would seem obvious; after all, printing was meant to alter production mode, not genre and form. But it is useful to bear in mind that continuity, which went hand in hand with innovation, had more facets than one. Many of the early printed works on religion, language, chronicle, travel, literary prose, and poetry featured a rather smooth extension of traditional genres. Take works on Arabic grammar, such as Buṭrus al-Bustānī's didactic *Miftāḥ al-miṣbāḥ fī al-ṣarf wa'l-naḥw* (Beirut, 1867) or Fāris al-Shidyāq's commentary on the *Qāmūs* of Fīrūzābādī, *al-Jāsūs ʿalā*

[10] See Chapter 2, note 34.

[11] *Ḥadīqat al-Akhbār*, July 1858 and later; Ḥamza, Vol. 1, 154.

[12] Baruchson, 37–44. According to Baruchson's search, 78 percent of the Italian Hebrew *incunabula* focused on four subjects: Old Testament (34.5 percent of the total), Mishna and Talmud, liturgy, and *poskim* (rabbinical views on *halachic* questions). The tendency continued in the sixteenth century as well. These, the author notes, represented "a sure market of buyers."

al-qāmūs (Istanbul, 1882): While produced by a new technology, both adhered to the habitual philological tradition, employing the familiar methodology and mold of argumentation their predecessors had used in earlier times. Or take nineteenth-century travelogues: Describing places and phenomena never before depicted in Arabic, most of them echoed classic works of the *riḥla* genre. Rifāᶜa al-Ṭahṭāwī's celebrated *Takhlīṣ al-ibrīz* (Cairo, 1834) and Nakhla Ṣāliḥ's *Al-Kanz al-muḥabba' li'l-siyāḥa fī urūbbā* (Beirut, 1876) readily evoke the accounts of Ibn Jubayr and Ibn Baṭṭūṭa in their marveling at exotic places, strange peoples, and striking habits; in their comparative allusions to familiar places closer home; and in valuing them by their (and the readers') accustomed standards. So were guidebooks for practical matters such as agriculture, housekeeping, cooking, children edification, or medicine, which likewise displayed a march along a trodden path lined with familiar precedents. And so were tracts on religious issues, as we shall see below.

Continuity was also seen in form. Books in print were produced in a format akin to that of traditional writings, designed to carry their attractive features into the new era. One eye-catching facet of this was the enduring norm of rhyming book titles, an esthetic attribute that remained highly common during the period examined here and long beyond – from Ṭahṭāwī's edited *al-Kanz al-mukhtār fī kashf al-arāḍī wa'l-biḥār* (Cairo, 1834) to Yaᶜqūb Ṣannūᶜ's *Ḥusn al-ishāra fī musāmarāt abī naẓẓāra* (Cairo, 1900). Another was the embellishment of books, most famously but not exclusively those printed in Būlāq, in imitation of manuscripts: Adorned headings, decorated margins, and tapered colophons were all common in Arabic printed books of the early decades. So were commentaries on the text, or other related books, which were printed on the book's margins in their entirety in continuation of past practice. For example, an edition of Ibn al-Athīr's *al-Kāmil fī al-ta'rīkh*, printed in Cairo in 1885, had the text of Masᶜūdī's *Murūj al-dhahab* printed on its margins.[13] In this tendency to retain attractive manuscript features, early Arabic printings were reminiscent of the European *incunabula*.[14] Besides the habitual inclination to preserve the familiar forms, there was business logic behind clinging to them: If manuscripts were esteemed for their esthetic design and if their value was enhanced by

[13] ᶜIzz al-Dīn Ibn al-Athīr (thirteenth century), *al-Kāmil fī al-ta'rīkh*, Vol. 1, with Masᶜūdī's (tenth century) *Murūj al-dhahab wa-maᶜādin al-jawhar* on the margins (Cairo: idārat al-ṭibāᶜa al-munīriyya, 1303/1885).

[14] Dondi, 83–85; Finkelstein and McCleery, 47–48. These and other physical attributes of early Arabic printing are a matter for another study. They have been explored most recently by Hala Auji, in her thesis on the American Press in Syria. See Auji, with numerous illustrations. More illustrations appear in Hanebutt-Benz et al., plates 82, 84, 85, 94, 96a, 101, 102. See also Roper, "Arabic Books."

additional texts on the margins, their printed version should match them as closely as possible to generate public appeal.

Released from the shackles of slow-pace hand-copying, old works in a new dress reached public and private libraries much faster than hitherto. By the end of the nineteenth century, printed items in the traditional fields had come to make up sizable segments of these stocks, and often the bigger share. Such was the case in the Khālidiyya library in Jerusalem, an impressive family collection that was converted into a public library in 1900 (or shortly beforehand). At that time, its stock of books already included more printed items than manuscripts: ca. 1,100 out of a total of ca. 2,100. Printed books, gathered during the nineteenth century, now formed the bulk of the collection even in religious categories, such as Qur'ānic exegesis, prophetic panegyric, biographies, and Sufism (*taṣawwuf*), as well as in natural sciences, philosophy, history, and *ādāb*.[15] At that point, the Khālidiyya possessed quite a few printed works of which it also had manuscript copies, a mark of the transition phase that would continue to typify libraries later on.[16] Often printed copies complemented the modest stock of manuscripts and enriched its different categories. Thus, in lexicography, the library had six hand-copied items, among them most prominently copies of volumes 1, 6, and a part of 7 of the tenth-century linguist Jawharī's *Ṣiḥāḥ*. Printing now expanded this section of the library with another forty works, among them an abridged version of Jawharī's opus *Ṣiḥāḥ* (Cairo, 1894) and the important four-volume *Qāmūs* of Fīrūzābādī (Cairo, 1885). Similarly, the category of history, comprising 7 manuscripts, was now enriched with another 206 printed works of classic authors such as Masʿūdī, Suyūṭī, Ibn Khaldūn, and others.[17] We may carefully assume that the Khālidiyya mirrored the common trend in other collections in the region.

The perpetual growth of this stock reflected the educated class's enduring interest in works of the old legacy, regardless of their format. It also reflected an important aspect of book making and book collecting at that stage: the acceptance of printing as a legitimate way of producing traditional works, even those of sacred nature. We will recall the aversion to printed copies reported in earlier times and the preference for manuscript copies over their printed versions, for both esthetic and pious reasons.

[15] Al-Maktaba al-khālidiyya; Conrad, 199–201. The share of printed books as part of the entire collection obviously continued to grow in later years, and by 1917, it had apparently reached some two-thirds; Conrad, 205.

[16] E.g., *Tafsīr al-jalalayn*, Ms. from 1200 [1786], printed copy from 1884; Ibn al-Fāriḍ's thirteenth-century *Dīwān* in both manuscript and a Būlāq printed edition (dates not indicated). Al-Maktaba al-khālidiyya, 6, 49.

[17] Al-Maktaba al-khālidiyya, 44, 55–58; Conrad, 200–01.

Such a preference may or may not have prevailed in the seventeenth and eighteenth centuries; if it did, it was clearly on the wane in the nineteenth. This was clearly mirrored in the Khālidiyya's prestigious collection with its majority of printed books, which included many editions of old-time classics, sacred texts, and even a printed Qur'ān. Printed volumes stood on library shelves side by side with hand-copied ones, and they appeared together in the same, not separate, sections of the library catalog. Modern technology, an essential parameter of *tamaddun* ("becoming civilized"), seemed fit for reproducing traditional and even holy writings. Such texts could now be printed in the region itself under local supervision, with the ruling authorities themselves playing an active role in it. This was different from the situation in Antoine Galland's times, in the seventeenth century, when manual copies were favorably contrasted with printed Arabic works imported from presses in Rome or Paris that were of poor esthetic quality. No misgivings about printing in Arabic seriously constrained the reproduction of works from the classical heritage, or any other texts for that matter.

Were industrially produced Bukhārī or Masᶜūdī considered as credible as their handmade versions? And did they carry an equal degree of prestige? To the former question, the answer is surely yes. As bearers of texts, manuscripts and printed copies came to be equally acceptable and, in principle, were regarded as equally reliable. The answer to the latter, somewhat looser question is inevitably no. From the start, printed editions were regarded as being less precious than manuscripts, in particular original (as distinct from copied) manuscripts. If the plentiful availability of treasured Arabic classics was a happy circumstance for those wishing to possess their own copies, their increasing quantity brought down their prestige along with their prices. The mirror image of this withering value of books was a concurrent rise in the value of manuscripts, which became rare as their production was grinding to a halt. They, especially copies that were accurately and esthetically executed, became precious collectors' items and a source of much pride. They remained valuable as artifacts, while as retainers of contents, their value now was identical to that of their printed versions, which lay next to them on the same shelves.

Printed Innovations

Printed works with contents and physical features of the past were coupled by products that diverged from the old in both substance and form. Here the reservoir of models was not local-traditional but foreign. Exposure to the peoples north and west of the Mediterranean inspired a journey of active exploration of their ideas and practices. A spate of information on Western societies, unprecedented in scope and detail, came to mark a growing share of the printed Arabic yield. Examining these works for their contents and impact is unnecessary, since much of the rich scholarship on Arabic thought during the *nahḍa* is devoted exactly to that. The themes of this printed output need not detain us, then, and we can move on to examine, more profitably, innovations in product types and format.

An important path through which the foreign culture was accessed was translations of European works into Arabic. Rendering texts from other languages into Arabic was nothing new, of course, but works in European idioms, which had once been eagerly studied by Muslims, had not been translated into Arabic for nearly a millennium.[18] The changes of the nineteenth century prompted a renewal of this pursuit, first through the organized ventures of Mehmet ᶜAlī in Egypt and then, more intermittently, through those of others. Books were translated or adapted from French, English, Italian, and German, for practical purposes and to other ends. In her survey, ᶜĀyida Nuṣayr has identified 168 works published in Egypt until 1850 that were translated from European languages into Arabic. Most of them were on military, technological, and scientific subjects, whose practical utility was obvious. But some were in history, geography, the social sciences, philosophy, and literature.[19] Such, to pick an example, was Voltaire's *Histoire de Charles XII, Roi de Suède*, rendered in Arabic and printed in Cairo in 1841[20] – seemingly a nonpragmatic choice of text, though it could be of some utility to a ruler keen on learning from a skilful predecessor. Other works – on ancient Greek and Roman history, the European Middle Ages, the Holy Roman Emperor Charles V, the history of France and the French Revolution, Russia's Peter the Great, global geography, human manners and customs, and more – were similarly converted into Arabic, some as direct translations and others as compilations of unacknowledged European sources.[21] This activity continued after mid-century in Egypt and Lebanon, now also including adaptations of European fiction, such as Fénelon's *Les aventures de Télémaque*, Defoe's *Robinson Crusoe*, Dumas' *Le Comte de Monte-Cristo*, and Verne's *Cinq semaines en ballon*. The first of these was serialized in *Ḥadīqat al-Akhbār* from 1861 to 1867, following the publication of some

[18] Lewis, *Muslim Discovery*, 71–76.

[19] Nuṣayr, 243–90, especially the table on p. 276. Out of the 168 works, 160 were translated from French, 4 from English, and 4 from Italian. Hsu in his survey has identified 115 translations out of 255 Arabic books published in Egypt from 1822 to 1851 (original languages not indicated). Hsu, 13.

[20] *Maṭāliᶜ shumūs al-siyar fī waqāʾiᶜ karlūs al-thānī ᶜashar*, translated by Muḥammad Muṣṭfā Bayyāᶜ.

[21] Examples and discussion in Abu-Lughod, *Arab Rediscovery*, 28–65.

ten other translations, which thus adopted not just the foreign contents but also the foreign sequential format.[22] By the end of the period, we see translated detective stories (*al-kutub al-būlisiyya*), such as Sherlock Holmes and Sinclair, reaching places in the Egyptian countryside[23] and no doubt also elsewhere. On the whole, this was a drive to explore Europe geographically, politically, and culturally by adopting enlightening pieces that could also be enjoyed in their Arabic dress. Printed translations were a major vehicle in that explorative expedition.

Other Arabic works with foreign-inspired contents were not taken directly from the external inventory. Scarce in earlier times, Arab travel to Europe represented a nineteenth-century novelty in its focus and extensive scope. The new opening to Europe and changes in transport made such journeying increasingly feasible. Travel accounts, a familiar genre in the local literary tradition as we have seen, were given a considerable boost and a big twist in emphases. Travelers set out to explore new lands, and the sights and ideas encountered in them aroused enough thrill to justify reporting. Travel books by Arab businessmen, tourists, and scholars who went to Europe and occasionally to America (and even Japan) began to appear in the second third of the nineteenth century and by its end had amounted to over twenty. Beyond eyewitness testimonies, they carried information on the history, culture, and social manners of the visited places,[24] their authors airing both amazement and criticism at what they saw. Another old medium in a modern dress was encyclopedias, compendia of knowledge with a local tradition going back to Abbasid times. Two new encyclopedias appeared in print, both in Beirut and both remained incomplete. First was *Āthār al-adhār*, a four-volume geographic and historic universal reference work by Salīm Jibrā'īl al-Khūrī and Salīm Mikhā'īl Shiḥāda, which is not known to have gained much popularity.[25] The other, more ambitious and famous, was *Dā'irat al-maᶜārif*, "Compass of knowledge," launched by Buṭrus al-Bustānī in 1876 and continued by members of his family.

Dā'irat al-maᶜārif was an outstanding achievement of nineteenth-century Arab scholarship and publishing, and it would be worth our

[22] Nuṣayr, 276, has identified 422 translations into Arabic in Egypt during the second half of the nineteenth century, from French (255), English (161), Italian (4), and German (4). *Al-Jinān*, 1 April 1874, inside back cover, carried an advert for books sold by *maṭbaᶜat al-maᶜārif*, among them the first three literary translations mentioned here. For the serialization of Fénelon's *Télémaque* and other adaptations in *Ḥadīqat al-Akhbār*, see Bawardi, 177ff. See also Holt, 66–69.

[23] Quṭb, 110–14.

[24] Abu-Lughod, 66–85. An extensive but partial list of nineteenth-century Arab travelers appears on pp. 72–75.

[25] Beirut: al-maṭbaᶜa al-sūriyya, 1875–1877.

while to look at it briefly. The *Dā'ira* epitomized the efforts by *nahḍa* intellectual leaders to utilize the printing press for acquainting Arab readers with knowledge in a wide range of disciplines, old and new. Published in eleven large volumes, ca. 800 double-column pages each, it reached only to the Arabic letter *ᶜayn* where it was discontinued, thus covering roughly two-thirds of the Arabic alphabet. Encyclopedias were the invention of civilized nations, Bustānī explained in his opening remarks to volume 1. Representing a highly concentrated assemblage of wisdom, they rendered hundreds of books "superfluous." The Arabs, he noted, had begun to follow in the footsteps of these nations and had "made great strides on the road of civilization and progress"; but they still lagged behind in what concerned "modern knowledge" (*maᶜārif hadhā al-zamān*). *Dā'irat al-maᶜārif* was designed to serve as a shortcut to remedying that condition.[26] It covered extensive local-classical grounds; entries beginning with "ibn" and "abū" filled the equivalent of a whole volume,[27] and there were numerous other entries on the history, personalities, places, and literary production of the region and the Islamic world – from "Baghdād," through "Bayrūt," to "Dimashq" and from "Bukhārī," through "Ṣalāḥ al-Dīn," to "ᶜAbd al-Qādir al-Jazā'irī."[28] For our concerns here, however, the more interesting items are those that dealt with new matters which had not been discussed in Arabic before. Many articles, some of them quite substantial, addressed aspects of European and other civilizations in great detail. The seven-page article *jarīda* ("newspaper"), for example, surveyed the history of the periodical press from its ancient Roman antecedent (the *Acta Diurna*), through the early papers of sixteenth-century Venice, to European journalism in later centuries, and presented elaborate data on the British, Chinese, Indian, Japanese, American, and Australian press, as well as those of the Ottoman Empire and Syria. There was much intelligence on modern scientific and technological matters: physics, chemistry, zoology, botany, engineering, and more. An elaborate, thirty-page illustrated entry on the human brain (*dimāgh*) explained its physical and chemical makeup, functions, and diseases as known to modern medicine then. An entry on the telephone (*tilifūn*) was published in volume 6 in 1882, only six years after Bell's invention. And a more detailed one on telegraph (*tilighrāf*), by then a well-familiar technology, devoted ten pages with text and illustrations to explaining its mechanisms, physical principles, history, uses, and

26 *Dā'irat al-maᶜārif*, Vol. 1, 2.
27 About one-half of volume 1 (pp. 345–792) and one-half of volume 2 (pp. 1–389).
28 Ibid., Vol. 5, 229–31, 505–16, 744–53; Vol. 8, 1–29; Vol. 10, 749–61; Vol. 11, 616–21.

distribution.[29] *Dā'irat al-maᶜārif*, if we will, was a nutshell embodiment of the *nahḍa* quest for modernity.

Innovations in genre and format were as important as those in contents. By far the most consequential new product was the periodical press. Having taken decades, in some places even centuries, for journals and newspapers in Europe to evolve and reach their centrality, they were embraced in the Middle East as highly developed media and soon became pillars of public communication. Journals and newspapers were a major source, perhaps *the* major source, of intelligence on the world beyond the local confines. Here we are concerned with their being a novel form of writing. Nearly everything about newspapers was new: their sequential appearance, with each issue rendering the previous one obsolete; their physical traits – large format, no binding, portability, foldable shape; their page layout; and their being explicitly disposable, in departure from the customary deference to written texts. Another novelty, typical of journals more than of newspapers, was their serving as a platform for interactive exchanges between author/editor and readers and among the readers themselves. Periodical publications introduced a dynamic pulse of text making, thereby enhancing the pace of their consumption and making book collections (which kept bound volumes of them) grow faster than before. The scale and geographic compass of their circulation, too, were wider than those of other texts. These papers also assumed the role of public announcers and promoters of various services, activities, and goods, on a far wider scale than had hitherto been possible. And finally, periodicals, especially newspapers, prompted reading modes previously unknown in the region, as we shall see later on. In all of these, newspapers and journals marked a real shift in text making and consuming.

Like no Arabic text before, Arabic periodicals displayed intense curiosity about the societies beyond the region's perimeter and reviewed their affairs regularly (an endeavor sometimes depicted as "discovery" or "rediscovery"). Such active inquisitiveness would have been unimaginable in the times before Arabic printing. The papers did not only report the foreign developments, but also inspired public discussion of them, including sensitive issues such as civil freedom and political participation, which in the past had not been openly debated, certainly not by people outside the ruling circle. Journals and newspapers were not the only writings to discuss foreign societies or political questions, but they served

[29] Entries in *Dā'irat al-maᶜārif*: "Jarīda," Vol. 7, 441–47; "Dimāgh," Vol. 7, 737–66; "Tilifūn," Vol. 6, 201–02; "Tilighrāf," Vol. 6, 192–201. See also article "Dā'irat al-maᶜārif" in Vol. 7, esp. 589–93; Hourani; and Booth, *Classes*, 154–58. Elsewhere I examined the *Dā'ira*'s treatment of issues related to America, likewise a novel notion in the region, with entries on people, places, and historic events; Ayalon, "Arab Discovery," 13–15.

as an expedient platform for that and clearly led the way. Another new (and often overlooked) facet of newspaper practice was the regular dealing with simple daily matters: not just important concerns that warranted recording in chronicles or discussing in tracts, but also trifling topics, such as minor interpersonal episodes or a person's view of an event – matters that in the past had been seldom discussed in writing.

There were three main types of Arabic periodicals: government bulletins, journals of scientific or literary interest, and news-oriented papers. The first of these was the earliest kind to appear in the region – in Cairo in the late 1820s and in the Ottoman capital and several other Arab provinces from the early 1830s onward. Mehmet ᶜAlī who pioneered the idea, and the sultans who followed him, introduced these printed circulars as a control mechanism vis-à-vis their executive cadres, so as to "improve the performance of the honorable governors and other distinguished officials in charge of [public] affairs."[30] Such narrow orientation molded these bulletins as organs of limited purpose and substance. They reported state matters, personnel appointments, and administrative measures, and only seldom addressed other subjects, let alone events in other countries. Their material appearance was as dull as their contents. Often produced on simple paper with defective letters, they were marked, in the words of one observer, by a "total disregard of the Oriental idea of beautiful calligraphy."[31] Their readership was small, consisting mostly of state officials. Yet, their poor quality and small readership regardless, these papers continued to appear so long as the ruler deemed it beneficial. On the whole, they were of much lesser importance than private papers of the other two types and surely far less interesting.

The more significant papers were launched after mid-century by private individuals in Beirut, Cairo, Alexandria, and Istanbul. From 1870 onward, members of the educated class began to publish journals of weekly, biweekly, or monthly frequency. The *majalla*, as these journals came to be known, emerged as a vehicle for expounding scientific, literary, and historical knowledge drawn from the local legacy and from foreign sources. Unlike news-oriented papers, whose operation required an elaborate system of news gathering and rapid dissemination, the *majalla* was relatively easy to put together and distribute. Its maker could draw on locally available literary sources, imported publications, and his own thoughts and analysis; and there was less of a time-pressure in producing and circulating it. The leading Arab intellectuals of the time appreciated the promising potential of this device and turned it into a central vehicle

[30] *Al-Waqāʾiᶜ al-Miṣriyya*, 3 December 1828, 1, quoted in Jayyid, 31.
[31] Heyworth-Dunne, "Printing," 330.

of cultural discourse. Buṭrus al-Bustānī's *al-Jinān* (1870–1886), Yaʿqūb Ṣarrūf and Fāris Nimr's *al-Muqtaṭaf* (1876–1951), Jurjī Zaydān's *al-Hilāl* (1892–present), Muḥammad Rashīd Riḍā's *al-Manār* (1898–1935), and Lūīs Shaykhū's *al-Mashriq* (1898–present) were among the most influential journals of the time. The *majalla* contained an ocean of knowledge. To pick an example, the 15 April 1875 issue of the biweekly *al-Jinān* included, among other items, an editorial on current political issues; a report on a recent speech by the Pope; articles on prince Bismarck, his rivals, and his relations with Napoleon III; articles on Prussian–Italian relations and on Egypt; an essay on political economy and another on "wonders of the world"; an installment of a serialized survey of modern French history; and a chapter from the serialized novel *bint al-ʿaṣr*. Hardly any of these kinds of matters had been discussed in Arabic until then. Names such as Bismarck and Napoleon, once evoking, at best, obscure figures with odd names engaging in a remote game, were now becoming familiar and even locally relevant. Begun as enlightening media, Arabic *majalla*s later came to be utilized by men and movements with different agendas: political, sectarian, and religious. This last variety will be more closely considered below.

The last kind of periodicals was newspapers (*jarīda* or *ṣaḥīfa*), designed to address the growing demand for news. Relying on local informants for domestic news and on the foreign press for international coverage, early Arab newspapers – prominently *Ḥadīqat al-Akhbār* (Beirut, 1858), *al-Jawāʾib* (Istanbul, 1861), *Thamarāt al-Funūn* (Beirut, 1875), *al-Ahrām* (Alexandria, 1876), and *Lisān al-Ḥāl* (Beirut, 1877) – were first issued at a weekly or semi-weekly frequency and continued at that pace for a while. They disseminated information in Arabic with speed, regularity, and scope that were unprecedented and further increasing over time. The 22 May 1858 issue of the Beirut *Ḥadīqat al-Akhbār*, for instance, published an account of a banquet held in that town three days previously, apparently based on locally circulated information; a report on events in Damascus that had occurred five to nine days previously, recounted in a letter by a Damascus resident; news from Istanbul during the preceding three weeks; miscellaneous reports on different states in Europe from the previous six weeks, culled mainly from the European press; and economic data, three weeks old, on markets along the Mediterranean shores. The issue also carried a segment of a serialized report on a political episode in France that had unfolded during the previous several months. Such graded intervals mirrored the logistic limitations of the time. To produce fresher information, access to telegraph or news-agency reports was required, along with more efficient distribution means. These would come in during the last third of the century, first to Egypt and then elsewhere (see Chapter 4), and allow the appearance of daily newspapers, beginning in the 1880s. *Al-Ahrām* became a daily in 1881, and several other daily papers appeared in Cairo later in the decade, most importantly *al-Muqaṭṭam* and *al-Mu'ayyad* (both in 1889). In Beirut, *Lisān al-Ḥāl* moved from a semi-weekly to a daily frequency in 1895.

In the region's fast-changing environment, papers offering to make sense of the changes were a hot commodity. Starting a paper, especially a *majalla*, was a relatively simple challenge that required little beyond some writing skills and trifling resources (unlike sustaining one for long, which was quite a different matter).[32] The public demand for news and guidance and the relative ease of putting out a journal resulted in the appearance of innumerable periodicals, the great majority of them short-lived. Only a few became enduring and influential. Surveys of Arab journalism contain unending lists of paper titles from this period, many hundreds of them, most of which died at birth or shortly thereafter with little impact on their society.[33] Individually each of them is of small historical consequence. Taken together, however, they, like the more durable publications, attest to the increasing acceptance of printing as a potent tool that many sought to wield.

The periodical press is one of the most widely studied products of printing, in the Middle East and elsewhere. Another popular product, chapbooks, has been given far lesser attention. Chapbooks – simple looking, typically skinny, and small-format booklets on any subject – were another printing-age novelty in the Middle East (as they had been in Europe).[34] Before printing, small-size texts in Arabic were sometimes copied for personal use or popular circulation, from short stories (*qiṣaṣ*) to religious treatises.[35] With printing, however, the few turned into a great plenty. Usually made of one or two print-sheets cut to octavo size and folded into a booklet, they were easy to turn out and sell even in the poor market conditions then. As we have seen, Khalīl Sarkīs, a big printer who published major Arabic classics and a newspaper, also used his machinery to print small items of literature, poetry, and religious texts, designed for mass retailing at low prices. But one did not have to own a big press to issue chapbooks: Small printers, booksellers, and indeed any creative individual with humble resources could engage in putting out slight products of this kind, thereby adding considerably to the region's printed volume. Most often they included literary works, such as sections from classic epics,

[32] Ayalon, *The Press*, 195–202, discussing the material aspects of launching and running a paper.
[33] Ṭarrāzī, *Ta'rīkh al-ṣiḥāfa*, Vol. 4, 5–15, 107–15, 163–97, 215–27, 275–307, 325–31.
[34] See e.g., Altick, 27–28, 74–75.
[35] E.g., Hanna, *In Praise*, 94–98; Marzolph, 163; Schwartz, 264–65.

folk tales, poetry, and anecdotes, many of which had long circulated orally. To pick an example, again, *Qiṣṣat ḥiqār al-ḥakīm wa-huww wazīr al-malik sanḥārīb* was a popular story which the Beirut printer and bookseller Ibrāhīm Ṣādir issued in a thirty-six-page booklet at his "Public Bookshop" (*al-maktaba al-ᶜumūmiyya*) in 1903.[36] There were also small social and philosophical tracts, usually with an educational message; jocular items; and numerous pamphlets on religious issues. This last category, possibly the most plentiful type of this format, will be examined more closely in the last section of this chapter.

Other printed items have been explored to a still lesser extent. Some of them, of the kind Western libraries usually classify as printed "ephemera" – those "humble print products that only rarely survive the time of their usefulness"[37] – have hardly received any attention in the Middle East. But their role in the society's daily practices had not been immaterial, and, as pieces of written evidence, they may serve as unique historical sources for aspects of daily life.

Let us look at one illustrative category of such items: placards, and other variants of similar purpose such as broadsheets and handbills – printed bits that became standard tools of public communication and politics in the Middle East. In the region's tradition, verbal signs in the public domain had usually been in the form of stone inscriptions, typically in places of worship, cemeteries, and public building dedications; they had a spiritual or commemorative rather than functional purpose (in some historic periods, notably under the Mamluks, stone inscriptions had also been used for public announcements). Popular graffiti had also been seen occasionally, especially in times of political unrest. Printing allowed easy making and circulation of written announcements, proclaiming a cause or promoting a business. Here, again, Europe offered a precedent: Placards and handbills had been in extensive use there ever since the birth of printing, by the ruling authorities and by public and private groups.[38] Napoleon Bonaparte seems to have been the first to bring this medium to an Arabic-speaking country, having profitably used it earlier in his European war campaigns. The French used written proclamations as a tool of control during their three and a half years of occupation in Egypt.[39] Addressing a largely illiterate public in writing was of dubious effectiveness, and once the French had departed, the practice was abandoned until close to the end of the century, with few exceptions.

[36] See more examples and discussion in Khayyat, and Marzolph.
[37] Chartier, *Author's Hand*, 68. See also Harris (where newspapers are also counted as ephemera); Stallybrass; Preston and Preston, ix–xix.
[38] Martin, 295ff; Steele, ix–xviii; Jouhaud.
[39] Al-Ṣāwī, 36–42, 73, and appendix, reproducing many proclamations.

One such exceptional instance was Buṭrus al-Bustānī's famous periodic broadsheets, *Nafīr Sūriyā*, which he circulated in Beirut, in 1860–1861, calling for unity and patriotism (see Chapter 2). It was an uncommon initiative by an unusual individual, apparently with a scant effect and no immediate continuation. Printed proclamations appeared again in the towns of Lebanon and Syria in the early 1880s, distributed clandestinely by antigovernment Arab political groups, and once more on the eve of the Young Turk Revolution.[40] By then, the use of this medium was becoming more common. The circulation of stealthy broadsheets by opposition groups marked an important development. It revealed the access of private individuals to means of printing while evading the censorship that was imposed on the open press. Producing a multiple-copy handbill was simple: It required none of the complex apparatuses of gathering information, editing, or distribution which journals entailed, but only a printing machine, even a primitive one, which could be small enough to hide in one's home. The humblest device could turn out many copies, whose big number – rather than the printing quality or esthetic aspects – was its main plus. In the twentieth century, this kind of simple, fast, often secret notice would become very common, signaling the increasing popular access to printing. In the twenty-first century, it would be replaced by Internet blogs and Facebook.

Alongside broadsides and handbills, numerous transient products emerged in Arabic print, of the kind we usually tend to disregard because of their triviality. But they do deserve attention at least as pieces of historical evidence on individual and communal daily practices that came to be affected by modern technology. Such items began to appear in the region as the nineteenth century was entering its last third. In a notice in August 1866, the Beirut paper *Ḥadīqat al-Akhbār* offered the public a new service of its press, which would "from now on, print commercial papers (*awrāq al-tijāra*) . . . and various notices (*al-rasā'il al-mukhtalifa*)."[41] The advert did not elaborate further, and we may assume that the intended "commercial papers" included items such as letterhead sheets, business forms, logo envelopes, etc. At that early stage, the routine use of standard office forms in Arabic was still in the future, with a possible handful of exceptions. A decade later, an announcement in *al-Jinān* by a press that was about to start operating was more specific. The shop, the announcement read, would "print everything the honorable public needs, including notices (*iʿlānāt*), circulars (*al-shirkūlāriyāt*),

[40] Antonius, 80; Tauber, *Emergence*, 16–20, 238–41; Tauber, "Four Syrian"; Landau; Zaʿrūr, 70–71. See also Chapter 7 below.

[41] *Ḥadīqat al-Akhbār*, 7 August 1866, 3. This seems to have been the first such advert in the paper's eight years of publication until then.

notebooks (*dafātir*), insurance policy forms (*bawāliṣ*), and *cartes de visite* (*awrāq al-ziyārāt*), in simple or elaborate [format] to suit the customer's preference."[42] In subsequent years such products would regularly figure in promotion notices for printing presses, which would offer to turn out additional items, such as bank receipts (*ḥawālāt ᶜalā al-bank*),[43] invitation cards (*riqāᶜ daᶜwāt*),[44] coupons (*qasā'im*), bills of exchange (*kambiyālāt*), and lawyers' office needs, e.g., dossiers (*dusya*), folders (*ḥawāfiẓ*), and warrants of attorney (*tawākīl*).[45] The actual scope of the use of these items in state administration, business, and people's daily routine is a matter for another search. But their frequent advertising in the 1870s and more so in the 1880s suggests that by then they had become items that "the honorable public needs," in *al-Jinān*'s words. By 1895, Khalīl Sarkīs's big press, which produced a daily newspaper, journals, and books, also featured a special section for printing "all commercial needs (*iḥtiyājāt al-tujjār*), *cartes de visite* (*al-kārt fīzīt*) and maritime company stuffs."[46] The use of printed business and office forms, many of them still bearing alien names that betrayed their foreign origin, mirrored the emergence of new norms of running affairs.

Similarly, in the day-to-day routine of the urban higher social echelons, new practices were becoming customary, such as the use of visiting cards or sending wedding invitations and holiday greeting cards. In a guidebook on etiquette, published in 1911, Khalīl Sarkīs discussed at length the manner of utilizing written invitations, which "appropriately, should be sent printed." He dwelt on the social events that called for sending them – a dinner, a lecture, an engagement, wedding parties, etc. – and expounded the desired formulation, the proper timing for their dispatch, and the utility of the R.S.V.P.[47] By the time the book appeared, the use of such cards had been known in the region for several decades already, and Sarkīs's elaborate discussion of the rudiments of using them seemed to suggest that the circles of users were expanding and new ones were joining in, who still needed to be instructed. These external practices reached the region along with the machinery that permitted their application.

Pious Printing

In the colorful scene of old and new printed works, religious publications represented a distinct shade. Wearing a modern dress like all printed items, they harked back to old values in their message, phrasing, and

[42] *Al-Jinān*, 29 February 1876, inside and outside back cover.
[43] *Al-Muqtaṭaf*, March 1885, 384.
[44] *Al-Bayān*, 1 June 1898, back cover.
[45] Āṣāf-Naṣr, 236, an advert for *al-maṭbaᶜa al-ᶜumūmiyya*, 1889.
[46] *Lisān al-Ḥāl*, 19 September 1895, 1.
[47] Sarkīs, *ᶜĀdāt*, 125–29.

aim. They made up a category about which we know considerably less than we do about other kinds of publications. The dissonance between substance and form and the murkiness surrounding much of the religious printed materials seem to warrant a separate probe into pious publishing in the region.

In historic battles among religious movements in Europe, notably between the Catholic Church and its critics, the printing press was an important arena from its early years. The power of this tool was recognized by all, and much attention was given both to employing and to muzzling it. In the Middle East, where religious principles had much authority in private and public life, such encounters were of a far more limited scope. As already noted, the notion that Muslim religious leaders had thwarted the emergence of Arabic printing is somewhat shaky: The *ᶜulamā'* were apparently not the main force that checked its adoption in the region before the eighteenth century, surely not as an organized group. Some of them no doubt had reservations about it, but perhaps no more so than others who were not of their ranks. Nor did they represent a major obstacle to the subsequent expansion of printing. Conversely, ample evidence is available about *ᶜulamā'* promoters of the technology once it had been adopted.[48] When Arab presses began to proliferate and private journalism appeared, men of religion did sometimes criticize the press, but not in a sweeping way as a *bidᶜa*; rather, they lashed at it for certain abuses performed by some of its practitioners. *ᶜUlamā'* often had good things to say about printing and about the periodical press to which it gave birth. Thus, Muḥammad ᶜAbduh commended the Egyptian paper *al-Ahrām* as being "nourishment of the spirits" and "the tongue of heavenly secrets," and Rashīd Riḍā defined the roles of the press as "teaching, preaching, and 'promoting good and forbidding evil'," traditionally the tasks of the community's spiritual guides.[49] From 1803 in Istanbul, and from 1825 in Cairo, presses printed books on unmistakably religious topics: Qur'ānic exegesis, ḥadīth, dogmatics, Islamic law, mysticism, and more, in considerable numbers that made up a sizeable share of the general printed output.[50] This activity raised no noticeable opposition among men of religion.

The printing of books and booklets with explicit religious messages expanded in many directions during the rest of the nineteenth century and beyond. We shall return to that below, but first let us look at a more revealing development: the birth of religious journals, a product which,

[48] See Introduction, sources cited in note 24.
[49] Quoted in Skovgaard-Petersen, 78–79.
[50] Tentative but illuminating details in Schultze, 41–60; also Wilson, 42–45, 55ff, 84ff.

from a traditional perspective, seems a little odd. Shortly after the inception of the Arabic press, periodical organs expounding a religious call emerged in the region. First came a few Christian journals in Arabic, which echoed themes of missionary propaganda and interfaith rivalries, notably the Protestant *al-Nashra al-Shahriyya* (1866) and the Jesuit *al-Bashīr* (1870), both in Beirut. Islamic papers, appearing somewhat later, were inspired less by the local Christian example and more by the worrisome circulation in the region of modernity-oriented periodicals, whose impact was palpably increasing. The civic ideas these last journals were advancing were changing the habitual spirit of the public discourse. Sensing that the faith was being challenged, Muslim writers reckoned that utilizing print could be just as effective in shielding and even reviving it. Islamic journalism was thus born as a defensive measure against the mass spreading of nontraditional ideas, mostly by non-Muslims.

One of the earliest figures to engage in Islamic journalism, surely the most intriguing at the initial stage, was political-religious activist Sayyid Jamāl al-Dīn al-Afghānī (1839–1897). In the late 1870s, he managed to inspire a group of disciples in Egypt to set up political newspapers for fending off threats of the European imperialist onslaught. Going on exile to Paris, he launched his famous *al-ᶜUrwa al-Wuthqā* in March 1884 together with another illustrious Egyptian exile, Muḥammad ᶜAbduh. Eighteen issues of the journal appeared altogether, irregularly, until October of that year. Although short-lived, it is reported to have exercised immense influence in Islamic communities in the Middle East and way beyond it. Its passionate essays were devoted to "defending the rights of the people of the East in general, and the Muslims in particular, and to drawing the attention of the ignorant among them to that which is good for them."[51] *Al-ᶜUrwa al-Wuthqā* contained essays designed to edify the believer on the right way to practice the faith in view of the new challenges and to confront its modern-day enemies. Its main beat, however, was political and anti-imperialist, with messages that were laid out in unambiguous Islamic speech replete with Qur'ānic citations. Sayyid Jamāl al-Dīn and ᶜAbduh spoke of Islamic solidarity, communal unity, and the evils of tyranny. Most frequently, they lashed at the British for their occupation of Egypt and offensive against the Mahdi's Sudan. It was a unique voice among the modernist-secular Arabic publications of the time.

Al-ᶜUrwa al-Wuthqā blazed the way for pious journalists to use their papers for preaching religious ideas. Frequently this was done as part of a political battle in the name of Islam against its political adversaries. ᶜAlī Yūsuf's daily *al-Mu'ayyad* (Cairo, 1889) is a prominent example of such

[51] *al-ᶜUrwa al-Wuthqā*, 230.

a publication: An *ᶜālim* and devout believer, Yūsuf followed the path of *al-ᶜUrwa al-Wuthqā* in thrust and jargon, utilizing his paper as a weapon against the British occupation of his country and making it a popular daily in turn-of-the-century Egypt.[52] The next influential pious journal was Rashīd Riḍā's *al-Manār* (Cairo, 1898), a product with a somewhat different slant. Riḍā (1865–1935), a vocal proponent of Salafi thought during the first third of the twentieth century, published his journal not only to defend Islam against its foes and galvanize the community of the faithful but also to help the pious cope with their day-to-day dilemmas. To that end, he opened the pages of *al-Manār* for public exchanges on issues related to the faith that preoccupied the readers, and believers from Marrakesh to Indonesia took advantage of this service. Remarkably, *al-Manār* ran a section of *fatwā*s, religious-legal rulings in response to readers' queries on everyday matters, beginning from the journal's first volume. Riḍā presented his own views and those of *ᶜulamā'* with whom he consulted, based on the Qur'ān, Hadith, and Muslim jurists, quoting extensively from traditional sources. To pick an example, volume 7 (1906) of the journal dealt, among many other readers' inquiries, with a question from Java regarding the permissibility of listening to musical instruments; from Singapore, on the invocation of and communication with the dead; from Russia, on accepting Russian government money for Islamic education; and from Fayyūm (Egypt), on the true nature of paradise – and so on and so forth, queries that oftentimes spread over several pages, to which Riḍā's responses were as long, or longer.[53]

*Fatwā*s in print, and the option to discuss daily issues from a religious perspective across great geographic distances, put at the disposal of the community's pious section an apparatus as potent as the *nahḍa* secular press was for the nonreligious segments. Riḍā had no qualms about the appropriateness of using an imported technology to such ends. He did denounce excesses in print by irresponsible journalists who, he argued, disgraced the medium and the message[54]; but otherwise he regarded printed publications as expedient tools for his cultural-spiritual agenda. Engaging believers for thirty-seven years, *al-Manār* served as a model for numerous papers with like disposition in the twentieth century. Eventually, even the conservative al-Azhar would move to join the field so as not to leave it open to the enemies of Islam, by launching its own monthly journal, *Nūr al-Islām*, in 1930.[55]

52 Ṣāliḥ.
53 *Al-Manār* 1906, February, 35ff; March, 130ff; April, 205ff, 307ff. See discussion in Skovgaard-Petersen, 81–85. The section was called *fatāwā al-manār.*
54 E.g., *al-Manār*, Vol. 1 (1898), 659–61.
55 *Nūr al-Islām*, opening article of the first issue, Muḥarram 1349/May 1930.

Looking at the rainbow of Arabic journalistic products at the time, one gets the impression that papers like *al-Mu'ayyad*, *al-Manār* and several others that promoted a similar line represented a minority voice in the community's discourse (and a rather lackluster one at that). During the early decades of the Arabic press, and actually for a whole century since the onset of the *nahḍa*, papers fostering religious ideas or addressing religious questions seemed to be a secondary tributary in the general flow of periodical printed yield, whose main thrust – certainly its more vocal part – was secular in nature, modernist, and liberal. Needless to say, the relatively small number of religious periodicals did not necessarily indicate a limited popularity of religious faith; for, unlike modern liberal ideas, spiritual guidance to the faithful was imparted through other effective channels, not least through the familiar mosque sessions. Journals were a kind of ancillary conduit in the ongoing transmission of pious guidance. Outshined as they were by the many worldly minded papers, Muslim and Christian religious journals continued to appear on a modest scale and serve their more educated constituencies.

Religious books and especially booklets and pamphlets were far more widespread than periodicals. We have already seen that works from the traditional heritage were published by government and private presses from the very outset of printing. They continued to be produced regularly thereafter, with a clear pious slant, by religious groupings and individual printers. Such, to pick a random example, was Muḥammad Zuᶜaytir al-Nābulusī's *al-Qawl al-sadīd fī maᶜrifat al-tajwīd* (1312/1894), a thirty-eight-page tract on proper Qur'ān recitation. Such was also Ḥasan Ḥumaydān's 148-page theological treatise, *al-ᶜUqūd al-fākhira fīmā yunjī bi'l-ākhira* (1320/1902).[56] Hundreds of booklets like these appeared in the region during the studied period, their writing no doubt motivated by the attractive potential for wide circulation. An 1874 advert for books on sale in *maṭbaᶜat al-maᶜārif* (Beirut), featuring a total of 105 titles, had among them 19 in a category entitled "religious books" (*kutub dīniyya*).[57] And a catalog of a private bookshop in Cairo in 1887 presented a list of over 500 books in 16 categories, including some 90 on religious matters, ca. 60 Christian and ca. 30 Muslim (the rest were items in secular fields such as science, language, literature, and history).[58] The proportion of pious works portrayed in these examples may or may not have reflected

[56] Both printed in Beirut by *al-maktaba al-adabiyya*.

[57] *Al-Jinān*, February 1874, inside front cover. Both the shop and the journal promoting the sale were owned by Christians (Bustānī and Sarkīs), and most of these religious works were Christian texts, such as the Bible and tracts on the Messiah. Other categories included "scholarly books," "poetry," "literary prose," and "history books."

[58] Al-Maktaba al-Miṣriyya, 4–28.

the overall situation. But they do indicate that religious books made up a noteworthy share of the general yield from quite early on.

In reality, the share of religious items in the overall production was far bigger than its incidence in bookshop sales lists. Many printed items reached neither the shops nor press adverts. They were diffused through other outlets, often without leaving a trace in historical records, and their number must have been very large. Ephemeral pieces printed by various groupings, big and well-organized like the major ṣūfī *ṭarīqa*s or small and short-lived factions, often circulated mostly or only within the closed circles of their membership. It was a diverse literature: prayer books and litanies, prophetic biographical chapters and biographies of *ṭarīqa* shaykhs, tracts on principles and practices of the faith, treatises of popular spirituality, ṣūfī teachings, and so forth. Polemics, theological and otherwise, between different trends of the faith – modernist vs. conservative *ᶜulamā'* and *ᶜulamā'* vs. ṣūfīs – were also a part of this printing enterprise.[59] The Khatmiyya *ṭarīqa* in Egypt and northern Sudan produced its devotional writings in print as early as 1870, starting with a prayer book (*rātib*) that was put together by its leader, Muḥammad ᶜUthmān al-Mīrghanī and continuing with a host of similar items.[60] Abū al-Hudā al-Ṣayyādī and the *rifāᶜīyya ṭarīqa* which he headed printed many similar booklets in Egypt and Istanbul from the early 1880 onward, as we have noted in the previous chapter. So did smaller groups that popped up and disappeared, not before issuing some publications in print. A typical product of this kind would be a small-format, humble-quality, inexpensive edition that would be easy to circulate and carry, printed in letterset or (especially in Egypt) lithography. A curious and somewhat surprising example was proclamations (*manshūrāt*) and other statements by the Sudanese Mahdi, Muḥammad Aḥmad ibn ᶜAbdāllāh, the leader who professed to embody Islamic rigor in the late nineteenth century. They were printed in the mid-1880s by his heir, Khalīfa ᶜAbdāllāh, utilizing an Egyptian lithograph press captured during the Mahdi's conquest of Khartoum. These items were apparently printed in very few copies, fewer than the known hand-copied exemplars of them. The reason for this move remains obscure; it has been suggested that it could indicate recognition of printing as a sign of modernity, or as something that imparted legitimacy.[61] Be that as it may, the adoption of printing by a strictly backward-looking leader represented a unique variant in the polychromatic output of religious Arabic products, though not quite an atypical one.

[59] Delanoue, 261–339, and especially 273–74.
[60] O'Fahey, 136–41.
[61] Ibid., 142.

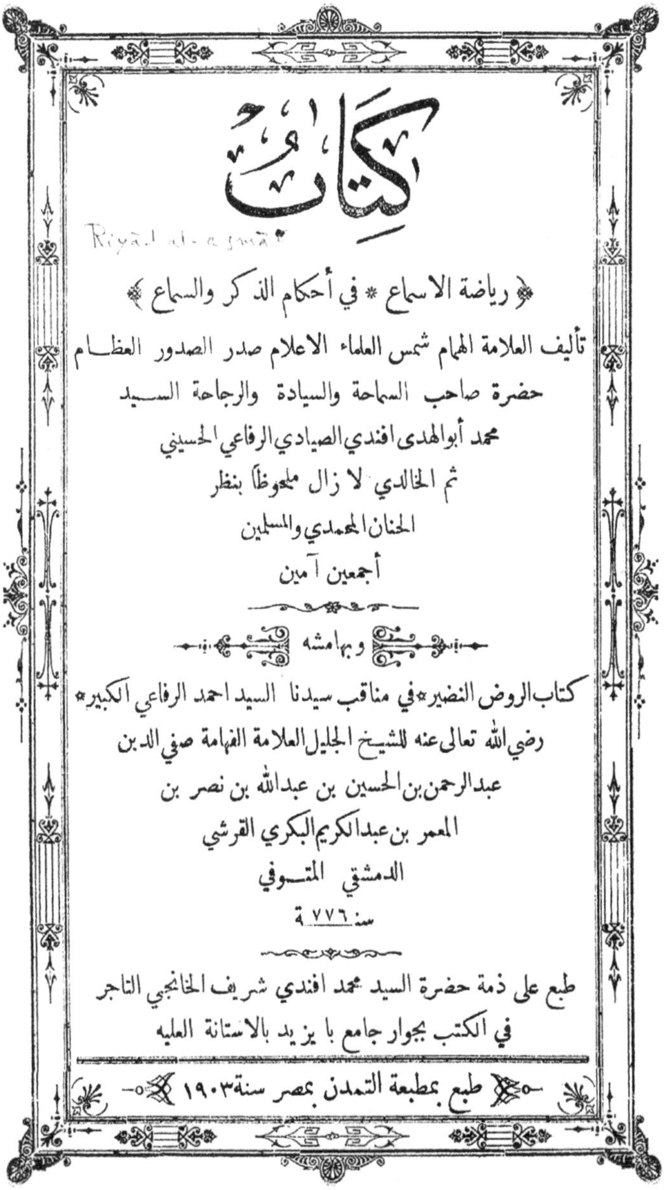
كتاب

رياضة الاسماع * في أحكام الذكر والسماع

تأليف العلامة الهمام شمس العلماء الاعلام صدر الصدور العظام
حضرة صاحب السماحة والسيادة والوجاهة السيد
محمد أبوالهدى افندي الصيادي الرفاعي الحسيني
ثم الخالدي لا زال ملحوظاً بنظر
الحنان المحمدي والمسلمين
أجمعين آمين

وبهامشه

كتاب الروض النضير * في مناقب سيدنا السيد احمد الرفاعي الكبير *
رضي الله تعالى عنه للشيخ الجليل العلامة الفهامة صفي الدين
عبدالرحمن بن الحسين بن عبدالله بن نصر بن
المعمر بن عبدالكريم البكري القرشي
الدمشقي المتوفي
سنة ٧٧٦

طبع على ذمة حضرة السيد محمد افندي شريف الخانجي التاجر
في الكتب بجوار جامع با يزيد بالاستانة العليه

طبع بمطبعة التمدن بمصر سنة ١٩٠٣

Abū al-Hudā al-Ṣayyādī, *Kitāb riyāḍat al-asmā'* (Cairo: maṭbaᶜat al-tamaddun, 1903), 91pp. A treatise by Ṣayyādī, with a thirteenth-century work on the miracles of the *Rifāᶜīyya* order founder printed on its margins. "Printed at the expense of (*ᶜalā dhimmat*) al-sayyid Muḥammad Effendi Sharīf al-Khānjī, bookdealer near the Istanbul Bāyezid mosque. Printed in maṭbaᶜat al-tamaddun in Cairo, 1903."

Copies of such works which had reached libraries in the region and beyond give us a fairly clear notion of their contents and style. But our knowledge of the scope and social span of this enterprise is lacking and partial. Often these works were printed for specific purposes, to serve a group's learning sessions and ceremonies, increase its adhesion, or strengthen it against rival groups. As such they were sometimes intended for internal use rather than for open circulation. Sometimes – there is no telling how frequently – local shaykhs ordered a work to be printed in a limited number of copies for their brethren only, and these may not have reached any library. An instance quoted by University of Bergen professor Sean O'Fahey from his own experience in Sudan, in the 1990s, might well be indicative of practices in earlier times as well. A pamphlet on ritual purification and prayer was printed in 1993 by the head of the Idrīsiyya order there, for inside use of its members. "Sayyid al-Idrīsī simply had a few hundred copies printed by an anonymous Printer in Omdurman – I suspect that I am the only person outside Sufi circles in that city to possess a copy! A friend was with the shaykh when they came from the Printer and passed a copy to me."[62] As we know nothing about the extent of occurrences such as this, we are left in the dark concerning an important segment of the region's pious printed output during the *nahḍa*. Even if we undertake the demanding task of screening all available lists of Arabic publications for their religious-oriented entries, we will still remain clueless about the pieces that had never reached any of these lists. Such pieces could be few or, just as likely, numerous. It thus seems that our knowledge about Arabic publications during the formative era is more limited with regard to religious products than to secular-oriented ones. This disparity compromises our ability to properly assess the broad sociocultural and political impact of either of these two categories. "The ephemeral nature of this kind of printing is obvious," O'Fahey observed with regard to the above pamphlet; "the need for scholars to be aware of it is, I hope, equally obvious."[63]

Before concluding the chapter, let us briefly consider the impact of this copious and variegated yield on the society's attitude to books. During the period explored here, the Arab printing industry turned out many thousands of books and booklets – between fifteen and twenty thousand entries should be a sensible assessment – hundreds of journal titles, newspapers, and pamphlets; and endless items of more transient nature. Did such varied multiplicity of publications change the way in which people regarded books and other written texts?

Printing became a fully acceptable method of book making, including the society's most sacred texts, and printed Arabic books came to be

[62] Ibid., 140–41.
[63] Ibid., 141.

treated with much respect. As we have seen, they were shelved side by side with hand-copied works and were viewed as perfectly valid complements to incomplete manuscript sets. Printed books, however, did not draw the same kind of reverence as manuscripts, especially older ones which projected an authority of old wisdom. Long cherished, old manuscripts were now considered even more valuable, more for being relics of a glorious past than for their contents, which could easily be duplicated. In that, they shared the same status as manuscripts in other societies. The mass production of books and the ease with which they could be reproduced by anyone perforce limited their individual attraction. We have no good way of measuring prestige, but there can be little doubt that a collection that contained manuscript items brought its individual or institutional possessors more repute than one with printed works only.

Other kinds of printed items were usually seen as a category apart from that of books. This was naturally so with the many types of printed ephemera, intended as they were for short-term uses, practical items that had little in common with books even though they were made by the same technology. It was also true of newspapers, despite the fact that, like books, they were carriers of knowledge. But newspaper knowledge was of a different kind, transient and superficial by definition. Designed to fulfill a short-term role, newspapers were not considered worthy of preserving or collecting like books and were usually disposed of after reading, like used train tickets, to the great loss of future researchers. The one kind of modern products that came to be treated with more regard, close to that accorded to books, were cultural, literary, and scientific journals (*majallāt*). The serious ones among them represented a middle case between books and newspapers. Though mass-produced and often dealing with down-to-earth matters, they had enough treasures in them to warrant respect and deserve to be kept: cultural observations by venerated scholars, historical knowledge, scientific intelligence, and serialized literary works. Publishers of early journals advised subscribers to collect the issues and bind them so as to turn them into books. "We are printing it as fascicules (*karārīs*) for the benefit of those who wish to assemble its issues into a book at the end of the year," the owner of one Beirut weekly announced in 1870, adding that the issues "well deserve to be collected in books, due to the valuable knowledge, historical lessons and beneficial crafts they contain." Other early periodicals likewise recommended this routine, and some of them offered their customers binding services to that end.[64] The more serious and enduring journals were indeed accumulated and kept in private and public libraries beside printed books.

[64] *Al-Naḥla*, 11 May 1870, 4. Similarly, *al-Zahra*, 1 January 1870, 3; *al-Jinān*, 1 November 1870, inside front cover; *al-Najāḥ*, 22 May 1871, 560; *al-Muqtaṭaf*, February 1876, 15.

In collections which the new technology enriched at modern-time speed, quality periodicals were deemed worthy entries.[65]

The technology for mass production of written works thus modified the standing of canonic Arabic texts and created new categories of lower-value writings. As in other societies which assimilated printing – and as always when a precious product becomes plentiful – the value of books was diminished by their mass multiplication. Not so the value of the works themselves, from sacred writings to popular epics, which were now more readily available to many more people, to access and venerate.

[65] Khalidi, 54–55 and note 62 on p. 227. Examining the al-Aqsa and Khālidiyya libraries in Jerusalem in the 1990s, Khalidi found scores of leading nineteenth-century periodical volumes, among them *al-Jawāʾib, al-Muqtaṭaf, al-Hilāl, al-Manār*, and *al-Mashriq*. They had originated in private collections of local educated families and were bequeathed to the libraries.

4 Diffusion Channels

In the previous two chapters, I examined Arab printers and publishers and their products. Later chapters will look into the consuming public of these works, the readership, which likewise grew dramatically within the same historic period. The proliferation of written works and the growth of their consumer market were two sides of a coin, that of enhanced Arab literary activity during the final Ottoman half-century. As with all coins, in between the two visible sides laid an interlocking layer that joined them together – a vital layer that permitted the flow of products from printers to readers. Its constituents were many: middlemen of all stripes, technological mechanisms, working procedures, and several functional institutions. This intermediary tier has been the focus of inquiry by students of book history in Europe and the West in recent years. But it has been largely overlooked in the Middle East, where it has received still less attention than either the publishers or the readers. An indispensable link with a significant imprint on the quality and rhythm of change, it warrants a closer consideration. In the present chapter and in the next, I will look at some of its main constituents.

A mediating layer of this kind has been part of every system in which written texts were meant to reach an audience. It had existed, on a small scale, during the manuscript era as well, comprising a range of book traders and sellers. But printing, with its massive scope and hurried tempo, vastly increased the need for it as well as its complexity. As Robert Darnton has shown in one of his most quoted studies in book-history,[1] the route from the author's desk to his readers was long and lined up with many stations. Darnton's famous "communication circuit," largely based on his research of eighteenth-century France, has proven most valuable as an organizing model for the study of diffusion in other times and places. Beyond the writer's door, Darnton has reminded us, were printers, proofreaders, binders, shippers, warehouse keepers, wholesale

[1] Darnton, "What Is the History of Books?" See also his "The Forgotten Middlemen" and "'What Is the History of Books?' Revisited."

book dealers and small bookshop owners, distribution agents, post-office personnel, mailmen and local deliverymen, street newspaper vendors, and more. A set of support mechanisms, such as advertisement; promotion techniques, such as subscription and readers' clubs; and institutions that permitted access to books, such as libraries and reading rooms, were all just as essential to the dissemination process. These middlemen and the various services they ran determined whether distribution was slow or dynamic; whether publications reached the periphery and countryside or remained confined to the major urban centers; whether access to them in a given neighborhood was smooth or problematic; whether authors and publishers got their due pay on time, or at all; and, in the case of periodicals, whether their flow was orderly or interrupted.

In the Middle East as elsewhere, modest mediating agencies linking writer and reader had existed before printing and had been adequately effective for serving the limited circles of customers that needed access to written texts. Here as elsewhere, these limited old services would become ineffectual when faced with the heightened flow of writings once printing had begun. To remain useful, the infrastructure linking publishers and customers had to expand as dynamically as both production and readership. In adjusting these services to the changing needs, new kinds of occupations related to book diffusion came into being, traditional ones were modified, and new methods and practices were devised. Arabic-speaking societies and their pool of reading elites were spread across vast territories from Morocco to the Persian border and beyond – unlike Europe, with its many realms of distinct languages – and this meant a consumer market that required stretched-out circulation services if they were to reach remote corners. In the developments discussed below, the entire Arabic-speaking area is considered as one distribution zone, one body with two beating hearts, one in Egypt and the other in Lebanon, from which arteries were extended to the various parts of the region.

Functional transport and communication systems were critical to delivery. They had long determined the pace and span of the flow of information in the region, the traffic of official letters, notices, and books and the written exchanges of views and polemics. The advent of printing coincided with rapid developments in these areas, and in other infrastructure systems, borne by the grand changes of the nineteenth century. "Of all economic activities in the Middle East," noted Charles Issawi, an astute observer of the region, "transport was the one most deeply revolutionized in the course of the 19th century"; Issawi also extended the assessment to communication means such as telegraph and telephone.[2] These shifts would facilitate

[2] Issawi, *An Economic History . . . North Africa*, 44.

more effective diffusion of publications from the early days of Arab printing. It would be worthwhile to look briefly at their general contours before examining specific developments in distribution.

Hardly a unique Middle Eastern occurrence, rapid changes in mobility was a global historic phenomenon in the nineteenth century. Technological advancement made movement by land and water ever faster in many parts of the world, first in Europe and North America and then elsewhere, and telegraph facilitated prompt communication across vast distances everywhere. Rendered easier and faster, human movement for many purposes increased in scale, amounting to what some scholars have described as a "culture of mobility." So did the scope of trade.[3] Ottoman territories were naturally affected by these developments. As early as the 1830s, British, French, and Austrian steam-powered ships were navigating the eastern Mediterranean, carrying men, goods, and mail from European to Ottoman harbors and among the region's seaports.[4] These services increased in volume and frequency after mid-century. The tonnage of ships calling at the Alexandria port, for example, witnessed a twenty-five-fold increase between 1830 and 1913; in Beirut it grew forty-two-fold during the same period.[5] Local seaport facilities were upgraded, and communities of foreign settlers formed around terminal towns of these routes. River navigation, primarily in the Nile, Euphrates, and Tigris, was being modernized during the second third of the century and likewise allowed faster and more reliable travel. These last goals were attained on a still grander scale by the digging of the Suez Canal, inaugurated in 1869. Concurrently, land transport was enhanced. Rail traffic, begun in Egypt in the 1850s, expanded there dynamically thereafter. In Syria, Lebanon, and Palestine, it began during the last two decades of the century, and between Syria/Palestine and the Hijaz after its end. Railways connected not only main cities – e.g., Alexandria–Cairo–Suez (1850s), Jaffa–Jerusalem (1892), Beirut–Damascus (1895), and Damascus-Maᶜan–Medina (1908) – but also suburbs, smaller towns, and countryside locations, often via narrow-gauge rails. Just as important, railways linked the region to Europe, with lines that, from the 1880s onward, connected Paris, Vienna, Munich, and other cities with the imperial center in Istanbul. Railroads were coupled with land roads, which facilitated the replacement of sluggish animal-back traffic with faster cart and carriage movement. The early initiatives appeared, again, in Mehmet ᶜAlī's Egypt,

[3] For an overview, see Huber, 9–20.
[4] Servantie, 507–12.
[5] Issawi, *An Economic History . . . North Africa*, table on p. 48. In Alexandria it increased from 140,000 to 3.5 million tons and in Beirut from 40,000 to 1.7 million tons.

most famously with the Cairo–Suez road (1830s), and continued under his heirs. In Syria, Lebanon, and Palestine, they began during the second half of the century, e.g., the Beirut–Damascus road (early 1860s) and Jaffa–Jerusalem road (late 1860s). By the close of the century, the region's sea and river traffic was dominated by steam navigation. Carriages and even some motorized cars were now traversing about 20,000 km of paved roads that crisscrossed the Ottoman territories, and trains connected towns along some 5,000 km of rails. Numerous small spots hitherto inaccessible came to be integrated into the burgeoning networks, and everything moved faster. The slow passage by sailboats and beasts was gradually relegated to the region's fringes and peripheral spots. In the busy centers, it was relegated to history.[6]

With better transport came better communications. The boosting of sea and land traffic facilitated the development of postal services in the region. A limited, horseback-operated Ottoman system had existed since the 1830s, serving the empire's key cities. After mid-century, several foreign postal systems were granted concessions to operate in its territories: French, Austrian, Russian, Italian, and German, competing with the Ottoman system and with each other in service speed and quality. An autonomous Egyptian service was also launched in the mid-1860s. Relying on the extending transportation networks, these services spread out grids with scores of stations throughout the region, in big and small, even isolated, towns – such as ᶜAslūj, Majdal, and Ṣamaḥ in Palestine[7] – which tied them to each other and to the world. Telegraph was introduced in the empire in the mid-1850s, and its entry was quickly followed by what one scholar has depicted as "an orgy of extended telegraph construction," comprising Ottoman and imperialist initiatives.[8] A cable network of 6,490 km in 1863 had by 1904 swelled to 36,640 km throughout the empire. Parts of this network were spread in the Arab provinces, linking the main cities in Syria, Lebanon, Palestine, Iraq, and the Hijaz to the imperial center in Istanbul. To these should be added another 14,700 km of cables in the province of Egypt (which was connected to Europe via Malta by submarine cables).[9] The entry of telegraph into the empire and its provinces was a development of major implications. Its main effect was enhancing state governability and control by rendering the center's links with the periphery speedier and more direct than before. Telegraph also served essential strategic and economic

[6] Issawi, *An Economic History . . . North Africa*, 44–61; Issawi, *The Economic History . . . 1914*, 248–57, 406–15; Barak, 26–32; Sehnaoui, 38–40; Hanssen, 92–96.
[7] Collins and Steichele, 41, 153, 184. Mail service expansion will be discussed further in Chapter 5.
[8] Davison, 136.
[9] Wishnitzer, 292; Barak, 40–44, 126–31, 136–37; and Davison.

interests of the European powers. For us, however, its important contribution was in enhancing public communications: Telegraph would allow reception of up-to-date news and their distribution in print, either through direct access to a terminal or by using the services of news agencies, which began to enter the region in the 1860s.[10] Telegraph was followed sometime later by telephone, which first appeared in the region in the early 1880s and became common in official and business use after the turn of the century.[11] The entry of steam navigation, railways, paved roads, telegraph, and telephone within a few short decades stimulated profound changes in all spheres of life. In the field of printed communication, their impact was nothing short of revolutionary.[12]

We may now return to the diffusion of printed texts and its agents. As we have seen in Chapter 2, before the advent of printing, people used to get their books from local booksellers or stationers or access them in public libraries. When books became mass products, the need for their enhanced diffusion was met by upgrading the old conduits and by devising new techniques. The rest of the present chapter will deal with mechanisms of the former, older kind. Newer methods will be examined in Chapter 5.

Booksellers and Bookshops

The selling of Arabic books has a history as long as that of authoring them. This history is yet to be systematically explored, a knotty task especially with regard to the preprinting era, given the paucity of evidence. But if fractional, available sources do reveal the general outlines of the old routine of book selling and buying. The key figure in the book trade was the *warrāq* (or *kutubī*), the retailer who would carry a stock of texts in his vending spot and handle specific orders by obtaining the requested items from afar or producing a copy. Special book markets, typically clusters of book-dealer booths, operated in big cities such as Cairo, Baghdad, Basra, Aleppo, and Damascus at least since the eleventh century and in Istanbul at least since the mid-sixteenth. The sources tell us of manuscript dealers traveling across the Islamic countries with their treasures; of special "book criers" announcing the sale of manuscripts in city streets and markets;

[10] Barak, 127–31. Reuters news agency opened its first office in Alexandria in 1865, also serving the French news agency Havas.

[11] Barak, 205–10.

[12] There was another side to the introduction of these swifter means: they allowed a tighter government control over the movement of people, which sometimes slowed it down rather than speeding it. See, e.g., Huber, chapter 6, regarding the employment of modern control means to hamper the mobility of pilgrims to Mecca.

and of precious, high-quality books being sold to the wealthy by auction (*nidāʾ*). Booksellers are reported to have been sometimes organized in guilds, headed by a shaykh, together with book copiers and binders. Handwritten, hand-illustrated, and hand-bound works varied in value and price according to their authors' prestige, their commonness or rareness, and their physical and esthetic quality.[13]

Like other businesses, the Arab book trade before printing had its ebbs and flows. The available evidence suggests that, by the time printing arrived in the Arab Middle East, books were a commodity in small demand on the whole, notwithstanding a certain rise in public interest in some places during the previous century or two.[14] Writing from Cairo in the 1830s, Edward W. Lane reported the presence of eight book dealers in that city, not a small number for a town of some 240,000 inhabitants at the time; but, he noted, "their shops are but ill-stocked." Lane's description of their trade leaves an impression of a humble business with a small, perhaps selective, clientele: "Whenever a valuable book comes into the possession of one of these persons, he goes around with it to his regular customers," looking for a buyer.[15] Around the same time in Syria, John Bowring was struck by the fact that he "could not find a bookseller in Damascus or Aleppo" and was told that "no scribe could now get his living in copying MSS for sale."[16] Similarly, a survey of Jerusalem shops in the late 1860s, before the mass arrival of printed products, found only two booksellers among 1,932 registered businesses, a Jew and an Armenian.[17] The situation in other cities in the region was apparently similar.

Arabic newspapers, first appearing in the late 1850s, are a major source for us on book diffusion, mostly through adverts for printed books and for their vendors, which they carried from the very start. The early papers mentioned several booksellers in the region: five or six in Beirut, one in Damascus, one in Aleppo, and one in Alexandria.[18] There could have been a few others here and there which did not advertise themselves, including the eight Cairo shops mentioned in Lane's account.[19] For most of these, we know nothing but their names; quite likely they were old-style

13 Ṭarrāzī, *Khazāʾin al-kutub*, Vol. 3, 909–17; Pedersen, 49–53; Hanna, *In Praise*, 93.

14 For the assumed surge in demand in sixteenth- to eighteenth-century Egypt and Syria, see Chapter 2.

15 Lane, 210. Cairo's population estimate on p. 33. Another (anonymous) European visitor to Cairo in the mid-1840s counted just five shops in the Cairo book bazaar; quoted in Schwartz, 216.

16 Bowring, 106 (writing in 1838).

17 Warren, 491–92. There were also seven bookbinders, six Jews and a Muslim.

18 Details in Ayalon, "Arab Booksellers," 77–78 and passim.

19 Lane, 210, and see also Nuṣayr, 465–71.

warrāqīn, who could now carry printed books as well. There were also a couple of businesses in Beirut, whose published notices at that point seemed to portend an upcoming change. A bookshop owned by one Fatḥāllāh Tājir, advertising itself in 1859, noted that it had been in operation there "for a long time." The shop offered locally printed books as well as items in Arabic and Turkish imported from Cairo and even from Paris. No fewer than forty-four books were listed in one of its announcements, many of them rather expensive (100 ghirsh apiece, or more), creating an impression of a somewhat exclusive business – a little like the Cairo manuscript dealers in Lane's account, several decades earlier.[20] Another dealership in that town, whose owner was khawājā Ilyās (or Lyās) Fawāz, publicized itself regularly in the early Lebanese press with lists of books for sale, all of them of local printing and more modest prices. Neither of the two shops provided its address or location, suggesting that they were both well known to the city's potential buyers.[21] Sometime later, in 1867, a Beirut bookshop owned by a Frenchman announced the sale of both local and imported books and journals.[22] These, and a handful of similar shops in the region's urban areas, were in place to handle the limited output of locally printed books and some foreign imports that first arrived in small quantities. It was a modest volume, quite unlike that which was soon to gush into the region.

When Arabic books and journals began to flow out of the presses in bigger quantities, the few existing dealerships could at first handle the flow. Announcements on the sale of books through a range of other outlets, however, were fast multiplying and suggesting that the old bookshops were too few for meeting the challenge. A common practice in these early years – we hear about it mostly in the Beirut press, the source of much of our evidence for that period – was a sale of books by merchants who normally traded in other kinds of goods. They now added books to the products they vended, apparently as a provisional practice. Such, for instance, seems to have been the case with one ʿAbd al-Qādir effendi al-Anjā, who happened to have "a quantity (*kamiyya*) of [copies of] *kitāb ṭabaqāt shuʿarāʾ al-ʿarab* by Iskandar Aghā Abkāryūs"; he put them "on sale for 25 *ghirsh* [apiece] in the shop (*dukkān*) of al-sayyid Muḥyyi al-Dīn al-Kubba in the butter (*sammāna*) market" in Beirut.[23] The butter market

[20] *Ḥadīqat al-Akhbār*, 8 September 1859, 4. Book prices in other adverts of the time were usually markedly lower, 20–30 ghirsh or less.

[21] E.g., *Ḥadīqat al-Akhbār*, 15 December 1859, 4; 15 March 1860, 3; 22 March 1860, 3–4; 19 January 1865, 4; 20 April 1865, 2–3; 13 November 1865, 4.

[22] *Ḥadīqat al-Akhbār*, 21 May 1867, 3 – *al-maktaba al-faransawiyya*, owned by Charles Béziès.

[23] *Ḥadīqat al-Akhbār*, 15 March 1860, 4.

dukkān of al-sayyid al-Kubba was, quite likely, not a bookshop, but it was a facility that could be used to that end for lack of a more suitable place. Al-Anjā, who had obtained a stock of copies of the book – how, he did not say[24] – offered them for sale in the place he found most expedient.

In like manner, notices in the Beirut press of the early years advised potential buyers to get their books in a *dukkān, maḥall,* or *makhzin* of this or that seller, all generic terms for "shop" or "depot" of any kind.[25] The institution of *maktaba,* or bookshop – as distinct from all other shops – was then still in the future, as was the term denoting it. Such other stores were often located in bazaars or business centers. Like al-sayyid Kubba's depot in the butter market, places where books were sold were "in the perfumers' market (*sūq al-ᶜaṭṭārīn*)"; "in [an unspecified] shop (*dukkān*) near the *khān* of al-khawājāt Bustrus"; or in another one, "near the palace (*sarāyā*) gate," a common business locale.[26] Sellers mentioned in book adverts were often identified by titles that could be their names or, just as well, indicate their trade. Books were sold by *al-saᶜātī* (literally watchmaker), *al-dukhānī, al-tunbākūjī* (both tobacconist), *al-ḥakkāk* (lapidary), *al-ṭarābīshī* (tarbush maker), *al-ḥallāq* (barber), *al-tājir* (merchant), and the like (sometimes the title appeared in addition to a three-barrel name, e.g., "Muḥammad effendi Khalīfa al-tarabīshī," which makes the last part more likely the men's vocation).[27] At other times, potential buyers were advised to get books "*ᶜinda* so and so," that is, "in [the place of] ...," without further elaboration, presumably because these men and their location were public knowledge.

Let us look more closely at one example. Ibrāhīm Bek al-Najjār, the *qā'imaqām* and chief physician of the Ottoman imperial troops in Beirut around mid-century, was also the author of several works. Having written a book on the history of the Ottoman state, entitled *Miṣbāḥ al-sārī wa-nuzhat al-qārī,* he had it printed in 1855 and wished to market it.

24 Two years earlier the same book was already on sale in the American Press in Beirut, for thirty ghirsh a copy; *Ḥadīqat al-Akhbār,* 14 August 1858, 4. Conceivably, al-Anjā acquired some unsold copies at a reduced price.

25 E.g., *Ḥadīqat al-Akhbār,* 8 September 1859, 4; 31 December 1859, 3; 15 March 1860, 3; 26 February 1868, 3; 13 November 1863, 4; 20 April 1865, 3; *al-Najāḥ,* 29 May 1871, 604.

26 E.g., *Ḥadīqat al-Akhbār,* 29 November 1859, 4; 15 March 1860, 3–4; 20 April 1865, 3; 10 January 1865, 3; 8 February 1866, 3. In Tunis a shop was called *ḥanūt* and customers were similarly referred, e.g., to "the *ḥanūt* of the bookseller *(kutubī)* sayyid Muḥammad al-Saʿīdī, adjacent to the door of the great Zaytūna mosque on the cemetery side"; *al-Rā'id al-Tūnisī,* 5 April 1865, 4, and similarly 22 June 1860, 1; 12 April 1872, 4. For similar developments in late nineteenth-century Tehran, where bookshops were likewise emerging out of other bazaar businesses, see Marashi, 92–93.

27 For these examples, see *Ḥadīqat al-Akhbār,* 13 November 1863, 4; *al-Jawā'ib,* 3 September 1868, 4; 8 March 1870, 4; *al-Waṭan,* 12 November 1881, 1; 21 April 1883, 4; *al-Janna,* 30 April 1884, 4; *Miṣr al-Fatāt,* 5 January 1909, 2.

In 1858, when the just-born paper *Ḥadīqat al-Akhbār* offered a new channel for mass publicizing among readers of Arabic, al-Najjār approached the paper to promote his book. The paper announced the availability of the work through its own Beirut office, as well as "*ᶜinda* ᶜAlwān effendi al-Ghurr in the perfumers' market, *ᶜinda* al-khawājāt ᶜArab and Malḥa near the palace gate, and *ᶜinda* al-khawājā Ilyās Fawāz" in Beirut. Only the last one is known to have been a book dealer. Buyers were also advised, just as laconically, to get it "*ᶜinda* al-khawājā Dīmitrī Ḥamawī in Damascus" and "*ᶜinda* al-khawājā Shukrāllāh Naṣrāllāh Khūrī in Aleppo."[28] Their locations in these cities were not indicated, presumably because their businesses (of unspecified nature) were known to the public or to potential book buyers. Five years later, the same book was still on sale, now "in the *dukkān* of the khawājā Ḥabīb al-Jalakh and Iskandar Khurshīd al-Sāᶜātī" in Beirut.[29]

Circulating books through nonbook businesses was a useful practice, given the scarcity of bookshops. We may imagine vendors of various other goods, aware of the new merchandise and perhaps of a nascent public demand for it, adding books to the choice of items they would try to sell. The practice continued for some time while new shops that traded mainly in books and journals were coming into being, which gradually sidelined and then eliminated the former provisional solutions. In smaller places, where demand for printed works remained low, such mixed businesses persisted longer; thus in Ṭanṭā (Egypt) in 1900, books were offered for sale "in the al-Ittiḥād pharmacy (*ijzākhāna*)."[30] There were also shops whose main business was with books, journals, and newspapers, and sometimes related items such as stationery and school needs, but which also carried other goods in order to supplement their income. In a way, this was a step forward in the evolvement of modern Arab bookshops. Now it was books and journals, not foods or perfumes, with which the shop mainly dealt, and other items were supplementary. Amīn Hindiyya's shop in Cairo is a good example of this. It would eventually grow into a thriving business, a bookshop-cum-publishing house which would put out several books, including at least one of Hindiyya's own writing

[28] *Ḥadīqat al-Akhbār*, 30 October 1858, 4; 15 December 1859, 4. Similarly, 29 December 1859, 4; 22 March 1860, 3; 19 January 1865, 4; 20 April 1865, 2; 29 February 1866, 4. In 1858 al-Najjār opened his own press, al-maṭbaᶜa al-sharqiyya, in which he continued to print the book. Details in Shaykhū, 104.

[29] *Ḥadīqat al-Akhbār*, 23 October 1863.

[30] *Al-Mu'ayyad*, 15 February 1900, 4. Similarly, *al-Muqaṭṭam*, 11 March 1889, 4 – potential customers referred to a pharmacy in Cairo. In Beirut, likewise, buyers were occasionally advised to obtain books from pharmacies; e.g., *Thamarāt al-Funūn*, 23 September 1895, 4. In remoter places the practice continued beyond the period examined here – see e.g., Ayalon, *Reading Palestine*, 83ff for twentieth-century Palestine.

(see Chapter 2). But back in the late 1880s, when Hindiyya opened it in the Muskī quarter, making a living from retailing books and newspapers was difficult, given the limited public demand. To make ends meet, the young Hindiyya also offered a range of other items: In addition to "Arabic, Turkish, Persian, French and English books, scientific, literary, legal, historical, entertaining, and more," from Istanbul, Syria, and Egypt, his shop also carried "writing tools, such as paper, ink, pencils, and school needs," as well as, more interestingly, "tarbushes, fitting silk buttons, light slacks (*dūblīn*), and double-sided bath robes (*ṭuqūmat ḥammām*)."[31] Tarbushes and bath robes in a bookshop – this was the typical mark of the trade then. Other businesses in those infancy days of book diffusion sold just about everything: cloths, foods, home utensils, and more. The Cairo "Egyptian Bookshop" carried oil paintings in addition to books, journals, and stationery; Mikhā'īl Raḥma, a bookseller in Beirut, also sold "exquisite pictures and other ornaments"; a bookshop in the tanners' market in Hamāh (Syria) offered "superb tea" for sale; and so did khawājā Ibrāhīm Ghandūr's shop (*maḥall*) in Jaffa, where buyers could find local newspapers along with "the best brands of English tea."[32] The phenomenon was a familiar feature of the nascent printed-book business, in the Middle East and elsewhere. Edmund Crull, an early eighteenth-century bookseller in England, also sold "pills and powders for physical purposes as well as food and medicine for mental"; and in mid-nineteenth-century Ontario, books were vended in a "general-purpose store" which also carried shoes, spades, sugar, and pork.[33] Written goods alone would be an inadequate source for sustaining a business then.

As shops engaging mostly in book and journal selling began to emerge in the region, a term was devised to denote this business in its new dress: *maktaba* (pl. *maktabāt* or *makātib*). The word was coined around mid-century, its literal sense being "a place of writings." It was first applied to libraries and book collections, and then was extended to shops selling books, journals, and other items related to reading and writing.[34] Singling

[31] Advert for Hindiyya's shop in Āsāf and Naṣr, *Dalīl*, 228. A slightly different version appeared in ʿAbd al-Masīḥ, inside back cover, and in *al-Ahrām*, 20 April 1889, 3. Several years later Hindiyya reported an expansion of his successful business and, again, advertised a set of books for sale along with a variety of other items, mostly apparel, in the same notice; *al-Hilāl*, 15 July 1895, advert appendix, 6.

[32] Al-Maktaba al-miṣriyya, 1–4; *Lisān al-Ḥāl*, 11 January 1899, 1; 16 December 1913, 4; *Filasṭīn*, 29 January 1913, 4.

[33] Shaylor, 136; Wiseman, 18–19.

[34] The term appears neither in Edward Lane's *Arabic-English Lexicon* (London: Williams & Norgate, 1863–1893) nor in A. Biberstein-Kazimirski's *Dictionnaire arabe-français* (Cairo: Impr. Egyptiènne, 1875). R. Dozy's *Supplément aux dictionnaires arabes* (Leiden: Brill, 1881), relying on mid-nineteenth-century dictionaries, defines *maktaba*

out written products from other goods sold in "shops," it lent bookselling the specificity it deserved under the changing circumstances. In the 1870s, *maktaba* began to be used with reference to bookshops along with the older, more generic terms; by the mid-1880s, it had effectively replaced all the others.[35]

As well as designating a bookshop, *maktaba* came to be applied to a set of other institutions and practices, some of them innovations in the region. A library or book collection, a stationer's business, a book-lending shop, a publishing house, a newspaper-vending place, all came to be identified as *maktaba*, with the inevitable uncertainty that such laxity entailed. While contributing to specificity, then, the new term also generated ambiguity, which would delude later-time observers of these institutions. The terminological fluidity reflected the looseness that marked some of the new practices related to the making and diffusion of Arab books and journals. As we shall see, businesses calling themselves *maktaba* often combined two or more functions, engaging in publishing (sometimes even possessing their own presses)[36] or running book-lending operations, in addition to retailing books and journals. Often they would carry writing tools, office implements, school needs, postage stamps, and the like, goods whose potential customers would usually be book and journal buyers, that is, educated people or those in the process of getting education. Stationery was a natural match for books and newspapers, in the Middle East as in other places. A *maktaba* could be a tiny newspaper-vending kiosk or a big store with a selection of printed items and an ambitious distribution project. The smaller ones apparently resembled modest *warrāq* shops of the old style, keeping to the previous plain setting while dealing with goods of a new kind. The most common *maktaba*s everywhere were of this kind, usually one-man ventures whose owners tried to make ends meet by relying on the expanding printing

as "cabinet d'étude, bibliothèque, librairie." In Buṭrus al-Bustānī's *Muḥīṭ al-muḥīṭ* (1871) the word denotes "a place for laying books" (*mawḍa*ᶜ *waḍ*ᶜ *al-kutub*).

35 For early appearances of *maktaba* as a name for bookshop, see: in Beirut – *al-Jinān*, 29 February 1876, inner and outer back cover; *Lisān al-Ḥāl*, 4 May 1878, 4; 15 October 1879, 4; *al-Muqtaṭaf*, March 1879, inner back cover; May 1880, inner front cover; August 1882, 87; May 1883, 280; *Thamarāt al-Funūn*, 5 July 1882, 4; 2 June 1884, 1. In Cairo – *al-Muqtaṭaf*, January 1886, 254; August 1886, 703; Āsāf and Naṣr, *Dalīl*, 189, 228.

36 Numerous books from the last third of the nineteenth century carried the name of a maktaba as publisher. For some early examples, see: Muḥammad Ḥaqī Nāzilī, *Khazīnat al-asrār jalīlat al-adhkār* (Cairo: al-maktaba al-tijāriyya al-kubrā, 1286 [1869]); Aḥmad Būnī, *Shams al-ma*ᶜ*ārif al-kubrā* (Cairo: maktabat ᶜAbd al-Raḥmān Muḥammad, 1291 [1874]); *al-Ṭarīqa al-waḥīda ilā al-bayyina al-rājiḥa* (Damascus: al-maktaba al-salafiyya, 1299 [1882]); Muḥammad Khalīl al-Murādī, *Silk al-durar fī a*ᶜ*yān al-qarn al-thānī* ᶜ*ashar* (Cairo: maktabat al-ᶜArabī, 1291–1301 [1874–1883]).

industry and growing public interest. Bigger places sometimes grew into grand enterprises that had their own order-catalogs, networks of agents, promotion apparatuses, and regional, even international, ties.

New bookshops were set up in different parts of towns throughout the region. They appeared in market alleys (*sūqs*) of old city quarters, around central mosques, in the city-gate vicinity, near the big commercial *khāns*, and, toward the end of the century, in the newer sections of fast-expanding towns, outside the walls. Here they were sometimes grouped in one area, reminiscent of the historic manuscript sellers of the old urban markets (and of similar clusters in European cities). Such, for example, were Cairo's Clot Bey street (north of Ezbekiyya gardens), where we hear of at least six bookshops in the 1880s and 1890s, and Fajjāla (Faggāla) street (north of Ramsīs square), which became a hub of book publishing and selling around the turn of the century. Such was also Beirut's *sūq al-ḥamīdiyya*, around the same time.[37]

Let us visit one small shop of this kind, whose opening seems to have made a difference in the cultural setting of its vicinity. The bookshop ᶜAbdāllāh al-Rifāᶜī launched in 1902 in Tripoli, Lebanon, was apparently the first of its kind in that city.[38] Tripoli, a seaport town 85 km north of Beirut, had a mostly Muslim population of ca. 25,000 at the time. With no good road or railroad connecting it to Beirut(there was a trade route leading east, to the country's interior), it was a peripheral place on the margins of Arab cultural developments. Still, the town was not cut off from the changes that affected the region's other parts. Missionaries, both Catholic and Protestant, who arrived there around the middle of the nineteenth century established several schools that exposed their pupils to new concepts. Printing was introduced in 1893 by Muḥammad Kāmil al-Buḥayrī, whose *maṭbaᶜat al-balāgha* remained Tripoli's main (though not only) press until the end of the Ottoman era.[39] Buḥayrī also started a weekly newspaper that year, *Ṭarābulus al-Shām*, which became the press's principal project and Tripoli's only periodical for the next fifteen

[37] Details in Ayalon, "Arab Booksellers," table on p. 85. For a discussion of bookshop clustering in specific sections of seventeenth- and eighteenth-century London, see Johns, *Nature*, 62–74.

[38] A cursory note in *Thamarāt al-Funūn*, 1 June 1896, 3, mentions one earlier *maktaba* in Tripoli, *al-maktaba al-qāwūqjiyya*. It could refer to a bookshop or, just as well, to the private book collection of the Qāwūqjīs, the famous family of Tripoli *ᶜulamāʾ* (see Mārūn ᶜIsā al-Khūrī, 49–50).

[39] Buḥayrī's press was also known as maṭbaᶜat ṭarābulus. More Tripoli presses – al-maṭbaᶜa al-ᶜilmiyya, maṭbaᶜat al-isᶜāf, and al-maṭbaᶜa al-waṭaniyya – are mentioned in books issued in 1312 (1894–1895), 1900, and 1912 respectively, found at the Princeton University library. More details in Mārūn ᶜIsā al-Khūrī, 31–36; Ṭarrāzī, *Ta'rīkh al-ṣiḥāfa*, Vol. 4, 24; Gulick, 22–23, 27.

years.[40] The town had its educated class, whose members became attentive to the sounds of the *nahḍa* resonating from the south. During the last quarter of the century, some of them attempted to form and run literary-scientific societies, with partial success. Quite a few of the city's learned subscribed to Arabic journals published elsewhere, whose agents operated in the town from as early as 1859. Many Tripoli names appeared among those who sent letters to the editors of such journals and exchanged views with readers in other places (over forty names of Tripoli residents appeared in the "readers' questions" sections of the two leading periodicals, *al-Muqtaṭaf* and *al-Hilāl*, from 1883 to 1907). Scores of others subscribed to Buṭrus al-Bustānī's encyclopedia, *Dā'irat al-maᶜārif*.[41] Members of the Tripoli educated class could access Arabic books and journals in different ways, but buying them in a local shop was not one of them, prior to ᶜAbdāllāh al-Rifāᶜī's initiative.

Rifāᶜī, of whose background we know little, must have assessed that there would be a favorable market in his city for printed goods, which were flowing in at an increasing pace from Beirut and other places. He began selling books from his home or from another shop he might have had sometime before opening his book business. In book adverts appearing in Beirut prior to the opening of his shop, potential buyers were advised to obtain them, among other places, "from Shaykh ᶜAbdāllāh effendi Rifāᶜī in Tripoli."[42] In April 1902, Rifāᶜī published the following announcement in the Beirut newspaper *Thamarāt al-Funūn*:

> By God's grace, I have managed to open a bookshop, which I have named *al-maktaba al-rifāᶜīyya*. It is located in one of the stores (*makhāzin*) on the government's palace avenue. I have brought to it loads of Arabic, Turkish and French books, printed in Istanbul, Egypt, Beirut, India, and other countries. They include every brand and kind of scientific Arabic books of interest to scholars, as well as elementary texts for schoolchildren, Arabic, Turkish and French dictionaries, copybooks, and all other school needs. If a certain book is missing in the shop, as might sometimes happen, I undertake to bring it in as quickly as possible. I also accept books and suchlike [items] to be sold on consignment, according to the usual custom or in a manner to be agreed upon between the agent and the seller. Come and enjoy our efficient and honest service and our low prices.[43]

Rifāᶜī was realistic. There were book and journal readers in his town, pupils who needed school texts and writing gear, and businesses with

[40] The press also printed a few books, apparently no more than a handful. Worldcat (accessed 1 September 2015) has only four books printed in maṭbaᶜat al-balāgha or maṭbaᶜat ṭarābulus in Tripoli.

[41] Details in Ayalon, "Syrian Educated Elite," tables on pp. 137–45; also Mārūn ᶜIsā al-Khūrī, 19–25, 37–66.

[42] E.g., *Lisān al-Ḥāl*, 15 April 1901, 1; *Thamarāt al-Funūn*, 18 November 1901, 8.

[43] *Thamarāt al-Funūn*, 28 April 1902, 8.

office needs. There was thus room for a bookshop combined with stationery depot that would address these needs and provide its owner with a livelihood. Books, periodicals, and writing tools could be imported from other cities in the region and beyond it mostly by sea, a fairly quick, one- or two-day trip from Beirut or Istanbul at the time. Rifāʿī knew that to survive, his business must sell as varied a line of products as possible, both to individuals and wholesale, and offer additional related services, such as retailing books and "suchlike" items (*al-kutub wamā māthalahā*) on consignment. More ambitiously, he endeavored to be his own publisher, issuing books and selling them. Several years later – the exact date is unclear – the shop published a work by Ḥikmat Sharīf, a contemporary Tripoli historian, "printed at the expense" of Rifāʿī. An advert added at the end of the twenty-four-page booklet listed five more works previously published by the shop (three of them apparently rather skinny, if their modest price of three qurush apiece is any indication). The shop's promotional notice elaborated the various goods it carried in great detail. For example, the books on sale comprised "every kind of scientific, literary, and history books in different languages, books on religion, exegesis, grammar and language, stories, plays, anecdotes and tales of the most recent printing, dictionaries in Turkish, Arabic, Persian, French, English…" and so on and so forth. Similarly, the shop offered a rich selection of writing tools, office needs, drawing equipment, and designing implements. The note encouraged clients to buy large quantities of books, offering a discount for mass acquisition.[44]

Al-maktaba al-rifāʿīyya operated at least until the outbreak of World War I; it may or may not have persisted thereafter. Adverts in Beirut newspapers regularly referred book buyers to Rifāʿī's shop at least until mid-1914, that is, twelve years after its opening.[45] Such longevity would in itself be a mark of relative success, though we do not know if Rifāʿī's business really prospered or just barely survived. With no direct evidence on the shop's routine functioning, we may imagine it as a small-size outlet for books and journals brought in by sea from Beirut, Istanbul, and perhaps other places, which also sold the locally published newspaper, *Ṭarābulus al-Shām*, and whatever books printed by the town's humble presses. The impression one gets from the shop's periodic notices and the press references to it is of a small-scale venture, whose owner had to show

[44] Ḥikmat Sharīf, *Saʿādat al-maʿād fī mukhtaṣar sharḥ bānat Suʿād* (Tripoli: al-maktaba al-*rifāʿīyya*, n.d.), 22–24. There are clear indications that the book appeared before World War I.

[45] E.g., *Lisān al-Ḥāl*, 16 December 1911, 4; 24 October 1913, 4; 16 December 1913, 4; 23 May 1914, 4. A promotional notice by the shop itself appeared *Lisān al-Ḥāl*, 25 November 1913, 4.

much creativity if he were to sustain it during the childhood days of the printed book market in a peripheral town like Tripoli. In that, Rifāʿī seems to have typified many of his colleagues who started similar businesses then. Sensing a rising public demand but also aware of its limitations, the more successful entrepreneurs displayed much resourcefulness. They would bring in books and periodicals from other parts of the region and from Europe, equip their shops with writing paraphernalia and various other goods, promote their business in the press and on book covers, issue sales catalogs or book lists to attract the public, and offer discounts for massive purchases. They would also serve as agents for journals and newspapers, local and other, and devise other services that would bring books closer to the public, such as in-house reading corners and book-lending arrangements.[46]

None of the works which *al-maktaba al-rifāʿiyya* announced as published or about to be published could be traced in available catalogs of research libraries. There is no telling if they were ever issued; conceivably, at least some of them were not.[47] If so, this would be one sign of the gulf between Rifāʿī's aspirations and his ability to carry them out. Difficulties of many kinds characterized the trade during that early stage of modern book retailing. Facing economic and other obstacles, most of the small businesses were short-lived, usually shorter than Rifāʿī's. Typical of these hardships was the phenomenon of people starting a bookshop on their own or with a partner and after a while moving on to another shop or partnership. For example, Nakhla Fawāz collaborated with Luṭfallāh al-Zahhār in *al-maktaba al-waṭaniyya*, in Beirut, in 1881; two years later, we find Fawāz in *al-maktaba al-sharqiyya* in the same city, in partnership with Khalīl Fawāz (his brother/son?).[48] Similarly, Nakhla Qalfāṭ, a renowned writer, opened a bookshop called *al-maktaba al-sūriyya* in Beirut, in 1880; by 1901, he had been a partner of Salīm Maydānī in *al-maktaba al-kulliyya* there.[49]

As is often the case in most trades, alongside the many transient shops were a few bigger and more successful ones that persisted for many years and made their impact on Arab book dissemination. Such a success

[46] E.g., *al-maktaba al-ʿaṣriyya* in Suez – *al-Hilāl*, 15 February 1900, 318; *al-maktaba al-kulliyya* in Beirut – *Lisān al-Ḥāl*, 3 May 1901, 3; an [unnamed] bookshop in Nablus around 1900 – Darwaza, 160.

[47] We only know of one other book by a local author which the *maktaba* published in 1909 or 1910: Muḥammad Amīn Ṣūfī al-Sukkarī, *Samīr al-layālī* (Tripoli: maktabat al-*rifāʿiyya* [sic.], 1327–1328 [1909–1910]).

[48] *Al-Janna*, 11 February 1881, 4; 22 June 1883, 4. In adverts from later years, al-Zahhār appears as the sole owner of *al-maktaba al-waṭaniyya*; e.g., *al-Janna*, 13 February 1884, 4.

[49] *Al-Muqtaṭaf*, May 1880, inside front cover; *Lisān al-Ḥāl*, 3 May 1901, 1.

sometimes suggested the unusual vision and unique business acumen of one individual; but more often, it resulted from the bookshop being a part of a bigger enterprise, usually a publishing house or a journal, on whose infrastructure it could lean. Thus Khalīl Sarkīs, our acquaintance from Chapter 2, who ran a big printing and publishing project and issued an important newspaper also had a bookshop attached to his business, *al-maktaba al-adabiyya*, where he sold the works his firm published and more. So did several of the other leading Arabic papers, e.g., *al-Jawā'ib, al-Muqtaṭaf, al-Mu'ayyad, al-Ẓāhir*, and *al-Hilāl*. The shop of this last journal illustrates the success that could stem from the backing of a prosperous journal with a gifted proprietor. Jurjī Zaydān, a self-made intellectual and owner of the literary monthly *al-Hilāl*, had started the journal in Cairo in 1892 and soon turned it into one of the most influential Arabic periodicals of its time. Its office in the Fajjāla quarter, Cairo's busy printing center at the time, at first served as a sales outlet for books, including some of Zaydān's own authorship. In 1896, he moved to add a bookshop to the business, "in response to the urging of friends and subscribers and out of a desire to contribute to the spread of knowledge." The note announcing the opening of *maktabat al-hilāl* projected a bold foresight: The place would be stuffed with books, journals, and newspapers from Egypt, Syria, Istanbul, Europe, and America, for customers to buy or to browse free of charge. The shop would also include a bookbinding section and a lending library.[50] Regular references to the *maktaba* in later months and years suggest that it grew into a busy enterprise. Its catalog was often reported to meet with a great demand and even run out of print, something that required repeated reprinting.[51]

Bookshops proliferated in the region during the last third of the nineteenth century and in the early twentieth, more often akin to Rifāʿī's business than to Zaydān's. No fewer than 123 such shops operated in urban centers of the Arab provinces from 1870 to 1914, two-thirds of them from 1890 onward, according to one study, whose findings are less than comprehensive.[52] The biggest concentrations were unsurprisingly in Cairo, Beirut, and Alexandria, but they also appeared in other cities, such as Damascus, Aleppo, and Baghdad, and in many smaller towns, among them Manṣūra, Ṭanṭā, Suez, al-Maḥalla al-Kubrā, Hamāh, Lādhiqiyya,

[50] *Al-Hilāl*, 1 October 1896, 119–20; 1 November 1896, 200; 1 January 1897, 400; 1 March 1897, 488; 1 April 1897, 595. The book-lending arrangements in this shop will be discussed below.

[51] *Al-Hilāl*, 1 November 1897, 186; 1 May 1898, 672; 15 January 1899, 248; 1 October 1901, 32; 15 February 1902, 324; 1 May 1906, 504.

[52] Ayalon, "Arab Booksellers." Since the publication of this study in 2010, I have located several additional bookshops from the period that had not been included in my lists.

Jerusalem, Jaffa, Haifa, Nablus, Tripoli, Sidon, Baalbek, Karbala, and Mecca. Other places will see their first modern bookshop only after World War I. Served by better sea and land transport and advanced postal services, the new network of outlets brought books and journals to audiences in the remotest ends of the region. The expansion of vending sites selling a multiple range of goods in small places away from the main urban centers indicated a major change in the access to books. The industry was now reaching out to the consumers closer to their homes, in town quarters and markets.

Bookshops were predominantly an urban phenomenon, for obvious reasons. To be sure, people in the rural areas did get access to written texts, both before and after the introduction of printing – typically to works of religious guidance and epic stories, which for the most part would be read there collectively.[53] But village people who could read and wished to obtain books and journals had to get them elsewhere, normally from sellers in a nearby town. In some places, however, another option began to pose itself toward the end of the nineteenth century: itinerant peddlers, who made periodic tours of villages, would bring in some printed merchandise from the city and sell or lend it there. We hear of this practice in the Egyptian countryside around the turn of the century from two witnesses who depicted the routine in some detail, Ṭaha Ḥusayn and Sayyid Quṭb. The former – later a celebrated writer and intellectual leader – grew up in an Upper Egypt village. He recorded his memories of "booksellers (*bāʿat al-kutub*) who used to journey through villages and towns with an assorted stock of books (*asfār*)" and sell them wherever there was demand.[54] His contemporary, Sayyid Quṭb, told of another rural part of the country in some more detail. Quṭb remembered visits by a peddler who would come in annually for a few days each time, "shouldering a sack full of books ... He would set himself in the village small marketplace, sit crossed-legged on the sack after having emptied it, and spread the books for sale, some twenty or thirty of them, in front of him in rows according to their value or subject." He would sell these books, usually for a trifling price, or lend them for local reading, for a pittance.[55] Both Ḥusayn and Quṭb elaborated on the kinds of books these sellers brought with them, which were of a traditional nature (tales of saints, stories from the Islamic legacy, popular epics) alongside more modern items (e.g., Sherlock Holmes). How widespread the phenomenon was in Egypt and other places is a matter for further exploration. During the

[53] See e.g., Tamīmī and Bahjat, Vol. 1, 98–100; Sāmī al-Ṣulḥ, Vol. 1, 13–14.
[54] Ḥusayn, 97–100.
[55] Quṭb, 118–22. There are more illuminating details on the culture of books and reading habits in the village in Quṭb's memoirs. See also Chapter 6.

period under discussion, demand for books in rural areas hardly justified more than the periodic visits of such roving vendors, who would bring in goods that fitted the modest number of customers and their limited buying power. The countryside remained for a long time on the margins of the cultural-literary shifts prompted by the entry of printing. But if marginal, at least some parts of it were well within the circle that was gradually opening to these developments.

Libraries and Reading Rooms

Members of the society's educated class, if affluent, could purchase books, subscribe to journals, and build copious collections without difficulty. But to read books or journals, one did not need to buy them. One could reach them where they were available without charge, in libraries. The practice had deep roots in the Middle East. The collections of the earliest libraries, from Umayyad times onward, were open to the learned who used them for reading and copying. Libraries were usually institutional, attached to mosques and *madrasa*s, with stocks that were gradually augmenting through bequests by private individuals. They permitted entry to whoever wished to consult or copy items from their collections, and many of them had facilities to assist readers and copiers, including writing tools and papers, as well as supportive staff. Books could be used in situ or be borrowed one or more at a time, with or without a deposit, to be read or copied at home. The overall scene emerging from recurrent references in the sources and from recent studies on the subject is of a well-organized system in many places and periods; it has even been suggested that "Muslim libraries were in every respect centuries in advance of those in the west."[56] We ought to bear in mind, however, that while our knowledge about the prescribed regulations of these services may support such an impression, we know much less about the scope and nature of their actual use by the public. We may also assume that the quality of library services fluctuated in different times and places, reflecting changes in general circumstances among different localities.

By the onset of Arab printing, the level of public library activity in the Arab provinces was apparently low. The reading habits of the young Nāṣīf al-Yāzijī (1800–1871) offer one indication of that. Yāzijī grew up in an educated Lebanese home (his father was a famed physician and poet) and as a child showed signs of remarkable intellectual curiosity. His compatriot Fīlīb dī Ṭarrāzī, who recorded his biography, depicted an inquisitive

[56] Heffening-Pearson, EI^2. See also Hirschler, 124–63; Eche, 368–80; Rosenthal, *Technique*, 6–12; Sibai, 100–15; Ibn Dohaish; Pinto; Giladi; Bilici; and Frenkel.

young man during the first quarter of the nineteenth century who was ever groping for books. However,

> only few books were around then, and the number of printed ones was small due to the scarcity of presses in Syria and Egypt, which turned out scholarly works only rarely. He would therefore rely on borrowing books from some monasteries and old libraries. He would read some of them once, memorizing their best parts, and hand-copy some of the others. Many of them are still kept with his family.[57]

Plausibly, this is a reliable illustration of the literary reality of the time, at least in Lebanon. A few decades later, Buṭrus al-Bustānī would lament that reality in gloomier terms: "Due to the stinginess of [book-collection] owners and superintendents, on one hand, and the unreliability of book borrowers, on the other, [books] remain locked behind iron doors, left at the mercy of moth and consumed by dust. What is the use of so many books if no one reads them?"[58]

If the scene of public reading facilities was indeed disheartening, it began to change after mid-century. With increased production at home and expanded imports from abroad, the shelves of public collections started filling faster. Old library stocks, having comprised mostly items of a traditional, largely religious nature, changed in size and makeup. Taking in mostly printed works, they were gradually becoming more relevant to readers with modern interests. The collection of al-Azhar library, for example, reportedly reached a total of 37,000 volumes by the eve of World War I; of these, some 26,000 volumes (more than two-thirds) were now printed works.[59] Meanwhile – and this is of greater importance to our discussion – new reading institutions were coming into being: more public libraries, libraries of literary societies, public reading rooms, and book-lending shops.

New public libraries, a modern version of the old, were somewhat atypical among the mediatory mechanisms that linked books and readers. Unlike with the other channels we are examining here, serving the educated public was only a secondary priority for these libraries. Their prime objective was different: preserving the depleting treasures of handwritten works and retaining the growing lots of printed ones. Providing access to the expanding readership, though a part of their purpose once they had opened, was not a sufficient cause for founding more of them. These priorities shaped the role they played in the process we are exploring here. The first of these new institutions and the biggest in any Arabic-speaking country was the Khedivial library (*al-kutubkhāna al-khidīwiyya*), founded

[57] Ṭarrāzī, *Ta'rīkh al-ṣiḥāfa*, Vol. 1, 82–84. The account is from 1913.
[58] Bustānī's 1859 *khiṭāb, al-Jamʿiyya al-sūriyya*, 115.
[59] Zaydān, *Ta'rīkh adāb*, Vol. 4, 463.

by Khedive Ismāʿīl in Cairo in 1870 (it would later become Egypt's National Library, *dār al-kutub al-miṣriyya*). Toward the end of that decade in Damascus, the Ẓāhiriyya library was opened at the initiative of education inspector Ṭāhir al-Jazā'irī, who assembled scattered literary treasures from various local collections and placed them under one roof. Al-Jazā'irī also played a role in setting up another prominent public library, the Khālidiyya in Jerusalem, around the end of the century.[60] These three libraries opened their doors to "anyone wishing to visit, read, write [i.e. copy], or consult" a text, free of charge.[61] The Khālidiyya catalog stated that the library, born out of a private collection, was reorganized as "a house of general knowledge" (*dār ʿulūm ʿumūmiyya*) for any individual wishing to read (*man yarghab al-muṭālaʿa min ayy fard kān*) on site, though not to borrow. It was to be open from dawn to dusk, and a set of written regulations, posted in the reading room, indicated the kind of working routine the owners had in mind: "Readers must not engage in excessive conversation, shouting, or argument so as not to distract those who are reading or copying." In the same vein, "smoking of cigarettes and water-pipes inside the reading room of the library [is] strictly forbidden, regardless of who is concerned."[62] The owners, then, did expect the public to visit the place.

Adhering to operational norms known in traditional libraries, the new institutions were reminiscent of the old in more ways than one. But there were also major differences, in both scope and contents. These facilities availed their readers with fast-expanding stocks of printed books and journals, classical as well as modern, in Arabic and foreign languages. They encompassed thousands of volumes (tens of thousands, in the case of the Khedivial library).[63] If still a far cry from the mythological stocks of the classical collections with their legendary hundreds of thousands of entries, the new libraries were bigger than known collections of more recent times and, moreover, carried a promise for rapid growth. As the seven-volume catalog of the Khedivial library from 1888 to 1892 reveals,[64] a reader frequenting the place at that time would have access – in addition to traditional-style manuscripts and copies of the books and

[60] For the Khedivial library, see Sayyid, 21–28, 233–54; for the Ẓāhiriyya, Commins, 41–42, 91; Muḥyī al-Dīn, 37–39; Buḥayrī, 59–61; *Sālnāme-i vilāyet sūriye* 1317, 333–34; for the Khālidiyya, see Chapter 3 above.

[61] "Al-kutubkhāna al-khidīwiyya al-ʿāma," in *Dalīl wādī al-nīl*, 36–37.

[62] Al-Maktaba al-khālidiyya, pp. b–g; Conrad, 201–02. For a description of reading rules in the Khedivial library, see *al-Hilāl*, 1 May 1900, 474.

[63] According to Zaydān, *Ta'rīkh adāb*, Vol. 4, 461–63, the Khedivial library had some 70,000 volumes on the eve of World War I.

[64] Dār al-kutub al-miṣriyya, *Fihris al-kutub*. The data below are from Vol. 5 (published 1890), which covers history and certain other fields.

journals produced in Egypt since the outset of printing – also to works written or printed in various languages in Istanbul, Beirut, Tunis, and Calcutta, as well as Paris, London, Leiden, and Gottingen. He would also find a range of current periodicals, local and foreign, that continued to accumulate rapidly. Over a quarter of the Khedivial library collection in 1887 were items in European idioms (most, if not all of them printed), a rate which by 1908 had increased to ca. 45 percent. In the Ẓāhiriyya in 1896, over a quarter of all books were printed, and over half of them have been identified as dealing with "nonreligious" subjects. And in the Khālidiyya, as we have already seen, more than half of the 2,100 holdings were printed items, many of them new works on modern topics.[65] The dynamic quality of these institutions was thus all too obvious. More public libraries, usually growing out of private collections, began to open in Egypt, Syria, and the Hijaz during this period.[66] Though smaller and less illustrious than the ones mentioned above, they reflected a similar desire to collect and preserve written and printed works and put them at the public's disposal.

On the whole, however, during the period explored here, such libraries played a limited role as places of public reading. Located in a few big cities, they were conveniently reachable only by those residing in their neighborhood, not in the remoter quarters or beyond. One Cairo scholar indeed complained, in 1900, that "the only library open to the people is *al-maktaba al-khidīwiyya*, but it is difficult for the large Cairo public to reach it."[67] People living in smaller towns, let alone the rural areas, were still less fortunate in that respect. "Nowadays it is imperative that public libraries exist in every town and even every village," Muḥammad Kāmil al-Buḥayrī, a journalist from Tripoli, suggested when visiting the Ẓāhiriyya in Damascus, in 1902; but his own peripheral town could boast no similar institution. "Would that our town had one like it, or even close to it," he lamented.[68] Even where the new public libraries were reachable, they made no special effort to attract readers, let alone newcomers to the world of reading. As already noted, serving the public was their secondary purpose, after book preservation. Especially proud of their manuscript holdings, the image they seem to have projected in the early years was one of old-style learning institutions, associated more with scholarship and erudition than with mass modern reading. The Qur'ānic phrase "*fīhā kutub qayyima*" ("sound/valuable books inside"), inscribed

[65] Rushdī, 10 of the Arabic text; *al-Hilāl*, 1 February 1910, 316–17; Commins, 16–17; al-Maktaba al-khālidiyya, passim.
[66] Zaydān, *Ta'rīkh adāb*, Vol. 4, 458–94; Batanūnī, 254–55; Ochsenwald, 83.
[67] Khalīl Thābit in *al-Muqtaṭaf*, April 1900, 314–15.
[68] Buḥayrī, 59–61.

above the Khālidiyya doors in 1900[69] and above those of many other libraries both before and after that, implied this preference: The place was first and foremost a repository of precious works, and it allowed members of the public to come and browse or read, as had been customary in mosque and *madrasa* libraries. In that sense, the new public libraries represented a kind of a passive link in the chain of intermediary mechanisms. They permitted, but did not actively encourage, readers to come and use their collections. This view of their purpose was largely shared by the readership itself, which customarily regarded libraries as places designed for scholarly pursuit rather than for public browsing and reading. Lūīs Shaykhū, the editor of an important Beirut monthly who in 1900 called for erecting a public library in that city, explained that such an institution was needed "for the intellectuals (*udabā'*) to turn to for their explorations, for school students [to help them in] their studies, and for newspaper and journal owners [to serve them in] their inquiries."[70] The last two groups, students and journalists, were new categories of potential library users now added to the more obvious intellectuals. But Shaykhū saw no need to include the wider circle of readers that was expanding through schooling. Members of this new circle were not thought of, nor did they regard themselves, as library customers. As we shall see in a later chapter, this common view was reflected in the small numbers of library users in the early years. It would change slowly and only partially at a later stage.

A different kind of libraries that appeared around mid-century, first in Lebanon and later elsewhere, were those of literary and scientific societies. These were usually exclusivist forums. The society named *majmaᶜal-tahdhīb* (Beirut, 1846), for instance, would accept as members only "those who can read and write, age sixteen and above, who do not quarrel and do not use foul language," as its regulations stipulated.[71] These societies were just as particular in making their book collections and reading rooms accessible to members only. The celebrated "Syrian Society" (Beirut, 1847) had upon its initiation a library with 756 books, mostly donated by its members, including 229 printed volumes in foreign languages. The library had a superintendent (*amīn*) whose duties included purchasing more books and journals, cataloging them, and overseeing the use of the collection for reading and borrowing by the

[69] Qur'ān, 98:3. The 1900 sign with this phrase at the Khālidiyya appears in many photographs from that time; e.g., Gidal, 88, picture 48.

[70] *Al-Mashriq*, 15 January 1900, 92–93. The term he used was "comprehensive (*shāmila*) library."

[71] *Al-Jamᶜiyya al-sūriyya*, 5. *Majmaᶜ al-tahdhīb* was the first known such society in the region.

eligible members.[72] More such societies were set up in Lebanon and Egypt, and later also in other parts of the Fertile Crescent, some of which had book collections and reading facilities.[73] They were usually similarly exclusivist and aristocratic. Thus, the "Syrian Scientific Society" (Beirut, 1868) – a resurrected forum of the defunct "Syrian Society" – launched a club with a library that was opened to those paying a "subscription" fee. Its rate was 150 qurush for Beirut residents and 50 qurush for nonresidents (who enjoyed fewer privileges), a substantial sum of money affordable only by the well-off. Such society collections offered important advantages to the social layer whose members were accustomed to consuming written enlightenment. To them, the gain of easy access to ever-increasing pools of books and journals was considerable.

Two additional conduits of bringing books closer to readers appeared in the region around the same time: public reading rooms and book-lending shops. In a way they represented an extension of libraries and offered services which had customarily been identified with them. Reading rooms and lending shops were set up as outlets of using books and journals for a fee. The novel thing about both was their being private ventures based on a business interest, whose owners sought to profit from the new kind of public demand. As many would-be customers had more curiosity than resources, paying a small sum for reading the text instead of purchasing the product itself made much sense to them and to the businesses as well. With no antecedent in the region's experience, they were typical *nahḍa* institutions that assumed some of the roles of traditional libraries in a new dress. The available information on them is scanty; concerning their actual functioning, it is almost nonexistent. But there are enough mentions of them in the sources, mostly notices on their opening, for us to treat them as links of some significance in the diffusion chain.

Reading rooms – *ghurfat* (pl. *ghuraf*) *al- qirā'a*, or *dār* (pl. *dūr*) *al-qirā'a* – began to appear in the region in the mid-1870s. The concept was simple: allowing reading without acquisition of a changing pool of printed texts for a modest fee. Typically they were used for reading newspapers and journals more often than books. This convenient arrangement had European (and American) precedents with deep historic roots. There, alongside the reading halls of literary-cultural clubs (*Lesegesellschaften, cabinets littéraire*), commercial reading rooms appeared (*Leihbibliotheken, chambres de lecture*), where people of wider classes could read books and

[72] *Al-Jamʿiyya al-sūriyya*, 12–14, 19–22, 120 (including many details on the library contents and operational rules); "Gesellschaft der Künste," 382–84; *Ḥadīqat al-Akhbār*, 14 August 1858, 4.

[73] *Al-Jamʿiyya al-sūriyya*, 123–29; Zaydān, *Ta'rīkh adāb*, Vol. 4, 428–54.

journals for a monthly payment and sometimes borrow them for reading at home. Institutions of both kinds existed in Europe and North America in the eighteenth century, here and there even earlier, and proliferated in the nineteenth. Commercial reading rooms played a role in drawing substantial groups in Western societies, those left out of the more refined reading clubs, into the circle of regular book and journal consumers.[74]

The Middle Eastern version duplicated the European practice with or without having been inspired by it. Here too, starting such places was motivated by a business-driven desire to profit from a growing popular demand. An 1876 initiative to open such a place by the diligent printer-publisher Khalīl Sarkīs casts light on this kind of institution. In an advert in *al-Jinān*, Sarkīs announced his plan to launch "a new project" (*mashrūᶜ*) in Beirut which he called *al-maktab al-sūrī*, "Syrian office." His motivation, he explained, derived from the belief that public reading facilities "are among the greatest means to the betterment of society," and from his sense that Beirut was in dire need for such a place. The design was ambitious. The "office" was to consist of a meeting hall for merchants and businessmen, a bookshop, a printing press, and "a well-organized hall, where Arabic and foreign books and newspapers will be available for browsing and enjoying." The place, to be centrally located in the city, would be open to subscribing members, but nonmembers would also be permitted to use its facilities for a fee per entry.[75] Sarkīs's announcement was also publicized in subsequent issues of the journal for a while, but later sources, including his own newspaper *Lisān al-Ḥāl*, made no mention of the opening or operation of the scheme. There is no evidence that he actually opened such a place. More likely, the launching of a newspaper in the following year consumed his energies and his financial resources and made him give up the bold idea.

Such projects, more modest than Sarkīs's visionary plan, were started around the same time in Beirut and elsewhere. A group of intellectuals, mostly teachers and graduates of the Syrian Protestant College, opened a reading room in Beirut and stuffed it with Arabic and other periodicals, as well as "the best books that elevate and enlighten the minds." It was reported to have become a meeting place for a "group of reading lovers of all factions."[76] A similar venture, designed to enlighten youth, was started in the city by American missionaries. They rented a big shop in a central

[74] Altick, 322–23, 328–29; King, 163–86; Wittmann, 303, 305, 308–11; Barbéris and Duchet, 440–45; Richter, 24–27, 83–85, 114, 213–15; Whitmore, 119–29; for America, see McHenry.

[75] *Al-Jinān*, 31 March 1876, inside and outside back cover.

[76] Zaydān, *Ta'rīkh adāb*, Vol. 4, 488–89.

location and supplied it with no fewer than 3,400 Arabic and European books and journals. Offering tea and coffee at low prices to make reading more pleasant, they were reported to have scored a considerable success.[77] Reading rooms were also opened in Egypt. In Alexandria, the launching of a "public office (*maktab ʿumūmī*) for the reading of cultural books (*kutub adabiyya*) of every kind, as well as Arabic, Turkish and European newspapers" was announced in 1876.[78] And a bookshop owner in Suez publicized his shop as, also, a place for reading (*muṭālaʿa*).[79] Unsurprisingly, the evidence on reading rooms, modest as it is, comes from the two centers of literary activity, Lebanon and Egypt, to the exclusion of other Arab provinces. The practice would later expand to more places including, reportedly, rural areas.[80]

Small-scale book-lending businesses began to pop up in towns of the region during the last decade of the nineteenth century, usually as sections of existing bookshops. The arrangement was simple and advantageous to all: For a small periodic fee the customer could access multiple printed treasures while the shop owner would profit from lending the same items time and again. This convenient deal, too, had been popular in Western Europe and North America during the eighteenth century and a part of the nineteenth, thriving mostly on lending novels and collected stories (there, along the selling-and-lending bookshops, were also private libraries that dealt only with lending). The subsequent upgrading of public library services and the proliferation of inexpensive books and journals forced most such ventures to close toward the end of the nineteenth century, when the Middle Eastern variation of it was just beginning.[81] We will recall that Jurjī Zaydān, who in 1896 opened his *maktabat al-hilāl* in Cairo and furnished it with local and international books and journals, also announced his intention to introduce book-lending arrangements. He proposed to make novels (*al-riwāyāt*) and *adab* books borrowable for a monthly fee of fifteen qurush (ten for *al-Hilāl* subscribers), one volume at a time. Clients would be permitted to "take [the books] to wherever they wished" and exchange books as frequently as

[77] Ṭarrāzī, *Khazāʾin al-kutub*, Vol. 2, 564. Similarly, *al-Muqtaṭaf*, April 1900, 313–14.

[78] *Al-Ahrām*, 19 August 1876, 4. Similarly, 19 August 1877, 1.

[79] *Al-Hilāl*, 15 February 1900, 318.

[80] Zaydān, *Taʾrīkh adāb*: "Reading rooms were opened in many villages [in Lebanon]. Villages with a population no bigger than several thousand set up reading rooms and appointed committees that supplied them with books and journals." For similar developments in early twentieth-century Iran, where reading rooms were called *qirāʾatkhāna*, see Marashi, 95–96.

[81] With some notable exceptions, e.g., "Mudie's Select Library," which operated until 1937, and "Boots Booklovers' Library," until 1966, both in England. Wittmann, 306–08; Allen, 44–45; Altick, 59–66; Wiseman, 23; and "British Circulating Libraries."

they desired, "even every day." The service was also offered to those residing out of Cairo, who could receive the books by mail provided they paid for postage.[82] Similar arrangements appeared in other places. We hear, for instance, of *al-maktaba al-kulliyya* in Beirut, which in 1901 invited "whoever wishes to subscribe for reading stories, novels and the like on a monthly basis to [come and] find in [our shop] new books to gratify him."[83] We may also assume that other sellers with a healthy business sense offered this kind of service in their shops without advertising it in the press. Such, for example, was shaykh Ṣāliḥ al-Khafash, owner of a small bookshop in Nablus, Palestine, around 1900, who had "books and story-booklets to be lent for a fee," as one of his young customers recalled, many years later.[84] At a time when there was no local press in the province, his business, like all others, must have been known mostly to people in the vicinity. Shops of this kind were likely more widespread than the few of which we know, basing their businesses mostly on lending novels and storybooks, as in Europe. They would become more common in the region in the twentieth century.

The impression emerging from extant evidence is that, in the overall endeavor of bringing publisher and reader closer together, libraries, reading rooms, and lending shops played a relatively small role. It also seems that the number of their users was limited in these early years, and began to grow slowly only toward the end of the period (I shall examine this last point in Chapter 6). Bookshops and journal-vending places seem to have been more numerous and widespread than libraries, reading rooms, and lending shops put together. It is impossible, however, to assess the relative roles played by these different institutions in mediating between text makers and their customers, and we must make do with the notion that all of the channels considered in this chapter contributed to this mediation to some, greater or smaller, extent. Other mediating mechanisms were no less important, and we will look at them in the chapter below.

[82] *Al-Hilāl*, 1 October 1896, 119–20.
[83] Notice in *Lisān al-Ḥāl*, 3 May 1901, 3. Its owners were Nakhla Qalfāṭ and Salīm Maydānī.
[84] Darwaza, 160.

5 Advancing Circulation

New Conduits: Mail Delivery and Distribution Agents

Bookshops and libraries multiplied in the region, but they were not opened everywhere. For many potential readers, the nearest such outlet was in another town, sometimes a remote one, and practically beyond reach. Despite their ongoing expansion, bookshops, libraries, and reading rooms were too few and far between to make printed publications accessible across the region. Looking for new channels to complement the old, publishers had two more options at their disposal, both facilitated by the changes in communications: sending the published items to clients' homes by mail and selling them through itinerant agents, who were positioned in or traveled around faraway places. Both books and journals were thus circulated.

From very early on, books advertised in newspapers were announced to be "available at the paper's office." The standard formula in book adverts was "*yubāʿ fī*..." (on sale at...) or "*yuṭlab min*..." (to be requested from...) followed by reference to the paper's bureau. Sometimes this was the only way to get the book; at other times, it was obtainable there in addition to some shops or sellers. Let us look at some examples. We will recall that Ibrāhīm al-Najjār's *Miṣbāḥ al-sārī*, which was sold by several merchants in Beirut, Damascus, and Aleppo, was also available at the office of *Ḥadīqat al-Akhbār*, the newspaper advertising it.[1] This routine became standard until the end of the century, and occasionally beyond.[2] Journal mediation in bookselling was sometimes expanded into a "sales section," whereby newspapers publicized lists of printed works, not just single items,

[1] "*yubāʿ fī bayrūt fī maktab ḥadīqat al-akhbār*" – *Ḥadīqat al-Akhbār*, 30 October 1858, 4. See previous chapter.

[2] E.g., *Ḥadīqat al-Akhbār*, 15 March 1860, 4; 31 May 1860, 3; *al-Jawāʾib*, 8 March 1870, 4; 14 January 1886, 4; *al-Najāḥ*, 29 May 1871, 604; *Lisān al-Ḥāl*, 18 May 1878, 4; 6 April 1897, 1; *Thamarāt al-Funūn*, 25 September 1881, 4; 19 December 1883, 4; 1 May 1893, 4; *al-Muqtaṭaf*, March 1883, 223; March 1885, 383; August 1886, 704; *al-Waṭan*, 21 April 1883, 4; *al-Janna*, 22 May 1883, 4; *al-Hilāl*, 15 October 1894, 158; *al-Bayān*, 16 December 1897, 544; *al-Muʾayyad*, 20 January 1900, 4; *al-Qibla*, 5 Rabīʿ al-Thānī 1335 [1917], 4.

available in their office.[3] More ambitious journals, like *al-Jinān, Lisān al-Ḥāl*, and *al-Hilāl*, opened what seem to have been full-fledged promotional wings in their offices.[4] Similarly, readers were advised to order books directly from the press that printed them,[5] or straight from the author, whose name was frequently noted without an address. Thus, a book on the history of Damascus, printed in that city in 1879, was available "from the author in Damascus" (*ᶜinda al-mu'allif fī al-shām*) with no further particulars; a book on religious faith, printed in 1897, "should be requested (*yuṭlab*) from its author in Manṣūra"; and a religious tract printed in 1899 was to be "ordered from its esteemed writer in Suez."[6]

How were customers to get the books they craved from the author, the journal office, or the printer? If they lived in the same city as the author or the press, that should not be too difficult. But for residents of remoter places, an additional connecting conduit was needed. Effective postal services, the obvious arrangement that comes to mind in this connection, were anything but obvious in the Ottoman provinces of the mid-nineteenth century. Old norms of communications, based as they were on an irregular movement of official and other messengers when necessary, began to be replaced by more organized practices in parts of the empire in the 1830s and 1840s, and evolved into a reliable and extensive system only toward the end of the century. Once in place, this system would become the backbone of regular book and journal distribution.

Enhanced sea and land transport permitted the emergence of a postal network with branches in small towns and rural places and with more frequent service. Smaller places could now be linked to the big cities, and hence to each other, by steamers and by a system of relay stations that

[3] See, e.g., the announcement of nine books and booklets sold in the office of *Ḥadīqat al-Akhbār*, 29 March 1860, 3. Similarly, *al-Jawā'ib*, 20 April 1869, 4; *Thamarāt al-Funūn*, 31 December 1883, 4.

[4] For the first two, see Chapter 2; for the third, see Chapter 4. *Al-Jinān* (1 May 1873, inside front cover, and 1 February 1874, inside front and back covers) publicized lists of over one hundred books on sale at the office of the Sarkīs-Bustānī *maṭbaᶜat al-maᶜārif*, which published the journal. Similarly, *al-Ẓāhir*, 14 June 1904, 4, advert of the paper's bookshop.

[5] E.g., *Thamarāt al-Funūn*, 20 June 1876, 4; *al-Muqtaṭaf*, December 1879, outside back cover; *Lisān al-Ḥāl*, 15 October 1879, 4; *al-Janna*, 11 February 1881, 4; *al-Ahrām*, 8 November 1892, 1; *al-Ẓāhir*, 21 September 1904, 3.

[6] For these examples, see: *al-Muqtaṭaf*, March 1879, 88; December 1879, outside back cover; *al-Rā'id al-Miṣrī*, 26 November 1897, 1071; *al-Hilāl*, 1 May 1899, 478–79. Similarly, *al-Muqtaṭaf*, June 1880, inside front cover; *al-Janna*, 15 May 1883, 4; 18 May 1883, 4; *al-Hilāl*, 1 December 1892, 189; 15 April 1899, 447; *Thamarāt al-Funūn*, 1 June 1896, 1; 18 November 1901, 8; *al-Rā'id al-Miṣrī*, 17 December 1897, 1120; *al-Nafā'is al-ᶜAṣriyya*, January 1911, 46–47. Sometimes references were more specific: a book on first aid, published in Cairo in 1908, was sold by "its author, in his pharmacy on *jāmiᶜ al-banāt* street, opposite the residence of the mufti al-ᶜAbbāsī in Cairo"; *Miṣr al-Fatāt*, 29 December 1908, 2.

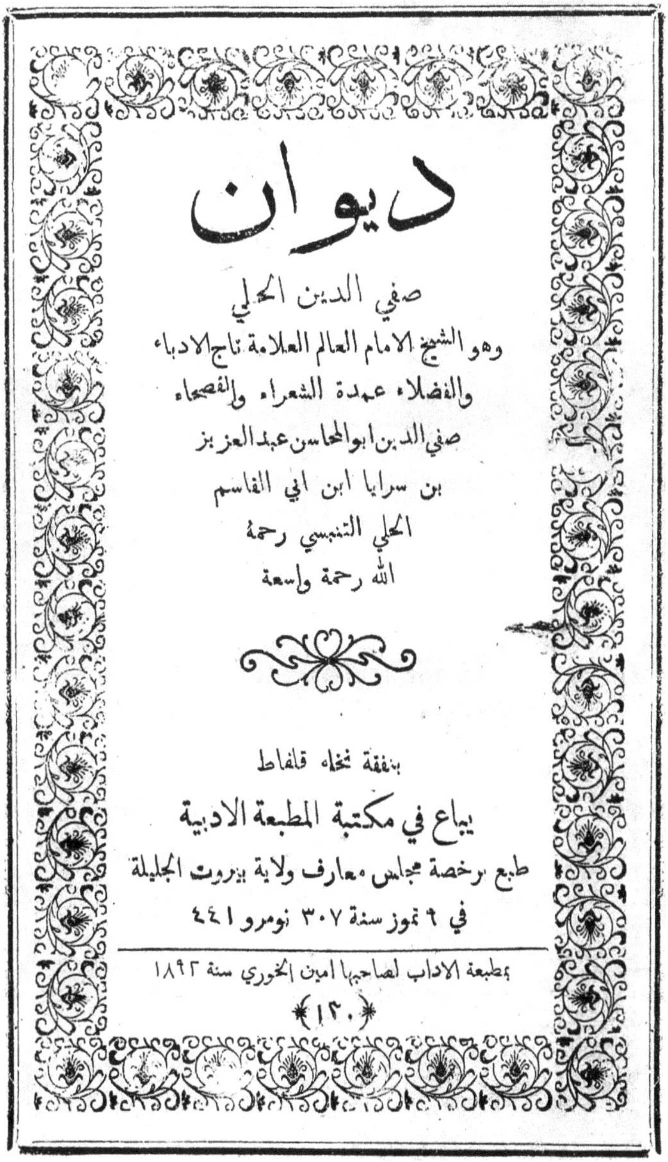

ديوان

صفي الدين الحلي

وهو الشيخ الامام العالم العلامة تاج الادباء

والفضلاء عمدة الشعراء والفصحاء

صفي الدين ابو المحاسن عبد العزيز

بن سرايا ابن ابي القاسم

الحلي السنبسي رحمة

الله رحمة واسعة

بنفقة نخله قلفاط

يباع في مكتبة المطبعة الادبية

طبع برخصة مجلس معارف ولاية بيروت الجليلة

في ٩ تموز سنة ٣٠٧ نومرو ٤٤١

بمطبعة الاداب لصاحبها امين الخوري سنة ١٨٩٢

﴿١٢٠﴾

Dīwān Ṣafī al-Dīn al-Ḥillī

(Beirut: maṭbaᶜat al-ādāb, 1892), 528pp. "Printed at the expense of (*bi-nafaqat*) Nakhla Qalfāṭ. On sale (*yubāᶜ*) in the bookshop of *al-maṭbaᶜa al-adabiyya*. Printed by permit of (*bi-rukhṣat*) the exalted education council of the province of Beirut, 9 Tammūz [1]307, number 441, in maṭbaᶜat al-ādāb owned by Amīn al-Khūrī, 1892."

operated carriages and horse-riders.[7] By the end of the century, post offices were densely spread out across much of the region. To illustrate, Palestine had nine Ottoman post offices in 1870: in Jerusalem, Jaffa, Haifa, Acre, Bethlehem, Gaza, Nablus, Hebron, and Tiberias. That in itself should be a fairly thick coverage of the small land, although, of course, it left much of the countryside unlinked. By 1914, the number had rocketed to sixty-six branches in both urban and rural places, among them villages such as Shafa ᶜAmr, Masmiyya, Salfīt, and Ṭanṭūra.[8] The Ottoman postal system in Palestine was supplemented by foreign networks – three by 1870, five by 1914 – with more efficient service on the whole and with branches in the country's large towns and beyond.[9] Service frequency was also upgraded, from once a week between main cities in the early part of the period to three times weekly, or even daily, toward its end (service to smaller and remoter places was sparser). In the 1870s, a book, a journal, or a letter sent from a Beirut post office to an address in Jaffa or Alexandria would take four to ten days to reach its destination and perhaps twice as long if sent to inland stations, e.g., from Jaffa to Jerusalem or Bethlehem, or from Alexandria to Manṣūra or Damyāṭ.[10] By the end of the century, delivery times had been reduced on many lines, especially to localities reachable by rail or a good carriage road. For residents of towns that were easily reachable, such as Tripoli (Lebanon), Jaffa, or Suez, to buy a book from a Beirut or a Cairo publisher would entail sending an order letter and then waiting for the dispatched book, which together could take perhaps two to three weeks at any time throughout the period. If someone from an outlying place such as Baṣra, Nablus, or Ḥamāh requested a book from, say, Ṭanṭā in the Egyptian Delta,[11] the procedure might well have taken a month, or two.

When Buṭrus al-Bustānī published his encyclopedia *Dā'irat al-maᶜārif* and sold it from Beirut (see the next section below), his journal *al-Jinān* regularly publicized customer names, sometimes also the dates on which they ordered their subscription. The gulf between these dates and the publication time of the issue mentioning them reflected the pace of postal

[7] Details in Okan, 66–77.
[8] See the elaborate study of the Ottoman post and telegraph in Palestine and Sinai, by Collins and Steichele.
[9] Okan, 79–94.
[10] According to an 1868 handbook for travelers in Syria and Palestine, a weekly mail service was operated between Beirut and Jerusalem, "performing the distance" in about four days. There was also a biweekly service between Damascus and Beirut, cutting the distance in "22 hours in fine weather, but occasionally a fortnight in winter." A once-weekly service from Damascus to Istanbul via Homs, Ḥamāh, and Aleppo took twelve days. See Porter, xlvi.
[11] Such as the one advertised in *al-Hilāl*, 15 April 1899, 447.

movement at the time. The notion it gives us is rough, since other factors were involved in this process, but it is nonetheless indicative. In the mid-1870s, subscribers in Beirut and nearby places would usually see their names in the journal seven to ten days after registering.[12] Buyers from more distant locations, such as Cairo, Alexandria, Damyāṭ, Aleppo, Baghdad, and Baṣra, would have them recorded after some two to three weeks, sometimes later.[13] On occasion, the process was quicker: It happened that customers from Baghdad, Aleppo, Asyūṭ, and Nazareth were notified of their registration within ten days,[14] and the subscription of a man from al-Ṣalṭ was noted within a week.[15] Between a few days and a couple of weeks, this was the pace then. By that time, printed products were obtainable via this channel in urban and large rural centers most everywhere in the region.

A functional means for remote access, postal services in the region at first encountered impediments that hindered their efficacy. This was naturally truer in the earlier part of the period than later on and more typical of the Ottoman system than of the foreign ones. The service relied on the existing infrastructure and on old norms of human performance, whose adaptation to the new needs was often slower than the erection of post offices. The distribution of mail to customers' homes, for example, required a serviceable address system, especially in the urban areas, with street names and house numbers, but this was absent most everywhere in the region until after the end of the Ottoman era. The locations of presses, publishers, and bookshops, and of course the customers, were indicated in formulas such as "near the mortgage bank," "close to the school," "in [such and such] a market," and the like,[16] which must have encumbered the flow of mail when it began to arrive in bigger quantities. There was also the challenge of educating the public on the proper use of this new system, especially the need to pay for postage in advance. This turned out to be a slow process, as can be seen, for instance, from repeated reminders to journal readers, that all correspondence be prepaid (*khāliṣ al-ujra*), "or they would remain in the post office (*tabqā fī*

[12] E.g., *al-Jinān*, 15 January 1875, inside back cover; 31 August 1876, inside front cover. Bustānī first named the project *al-Kawthar*, after one of the rivers in paradise (also meaning "the plentiful"), but altered the title before starting publication.

[13] E.g., *al-Jinān*, 15 January 1875, inside back cover; 1 March 1875, inside front cover; 1 June 1875, inside front cover; 1 July 1875, inside front cover.

[14] *Al-Jinān*, 1 June 1875, inside front cover; 30 November 1876, inside front cover; 15 December 1876, inside front cover.

[15] *Al-Jinān*, 1 February 1876, inside front cover.

[16] E.g., *al-Ahrām*, 5 August 1876, 1; *Lisān al-Ḥāl*, 4 January 1997, 8; *Filasṭīn*, 5 July 1913, 3–4. For a discussion of the phenomenon, focusing on the example of Ottoman Jerusalem, see Wallach, 134–42.

al-būsṭa)."[17] Just as problematic was instilling dynamic working habits in the system's employees. An "important message to subscribers" in Bustānī's *al-Jinān* portrayed in gloomy colors what it meant to dispatch a journal (and obviously also a book) by post in the early 1870s, in this case from Beirut:

We have received numerous complaints from our agents and subscribers in the province of Syria, in Aleppo, Adana, Baghdad, Baṣra, and Jeddah, claiming that the journal reaches them irregularly, or not at all ... Having explored the matter here and in the provinces, we have learned that the reason for this is the negligence (*ᶜadam ḍabṭ*) of post officials, who often deliver the journal to the wrong people, sell them (*yabīᶜūnahā*), or relay them to the wrong place. We have even discovered, on more occasions than one, that the journals reached a certain provincial department, where they were opened and read while their real buyers were awaiting their arrival ... Similarly frequent remonstrations have reached us from Egypt, where ... the distributors (*muwazziᶜīn*), who take the papers from the post office in order to deliver them [to customer homes], have been selling them instead to school students, for a pittance.[18]

Many items had been misdirected, the message went on. Papers addressed to Java (*jāfā*) landed instead in Jaffa (*yāfā*). And a set of copies dispatched by sea from Beirut to Tripoli disappeared, so the journal owners had to send a replacement set and pay for it again, but then the first set was discovered on a ship that had traveled to Istanbul and back. "They went on a trip to Europe," the paper suggested acerbically, "we were fortunate that they did not stay there to wait for the opening of the Vienna world fair [scheduled for some ten months later]." Another issue of *al-Jinān* reported that subscribers had been told they could come in person to the post office and collect their copies, so as to preempt being mishandled by the local clerks. This solution, however, required precise timing, namely, arriving in the office shortly after the ship with the papers had docked in the city port, and it elicited another wave of remonstrations, with customers insisting that the paper be delivered to their homes.[19] The owners of *al-Jinān* then tried to shift from the Ottoman postal service to the Austrian, French, and Russian ones, which were supposed to be more competent, but that did not prove to be of much help either. "We do not like to hear from the Europeans that people of the

[17] *Al-Rā'id al-Tūnisī*, 29 Ramaḍān 1280 [1863], 1. Similarly, e.g., *al-Jawā'ib*, 14 September 1861, 1; *al-Jinān*, 1 November 1870, inside front cover; *al-Najāḥ*, 22 May 1871, 560; *al-Ahrām*, 5 August 1876, 1; *al-Muqtaṭaf*, June 1877, outside back cover; *Lisān al-Ḥāl*, 22 October 1877, 1; *al-Zamān*, 25 September 1882, 1; *al-Muqaṭṭam*, 14 February 1889, 1; *al-Rā'id al-Miṣrī*, January 1897, 325; *al-ᶜAlam*, 7 March 1910, 1.

[18] *Al-Jinān*, 1 July 1872, 433–34.

[19] *Al-Jinān*, 1 December 1872, 793; 15 December 1872, 829.

East (*al-sharqiyyīn*) are unable to run their affairs properly,"[20] Bustānī remarked in dismay.

Such malfunctions were frequent during the early decades of postal services, and in that the Arab provinces were not different from other parts of the empire. As well as hampering the orderly circulation of periodicals, these snags must have hindered the ordering and supplying of books between the publishing centers and their remote customers. Complaints about such problems would become fewer in later years, but would not entirely disappear.[21] Whether or not the "people of the East" were slow in adapting to modern communications, as Bustānī implied, it is clear that diffusion by mail in the region during the early decades was marred by difficulties. It mirrored the problematic physical and operational conditions that burdened the entire cultural shift.

Seeking to bypass the obstacles and expedite circulation, Bustānī and other publishers resorted to an old-new functional idea: appointing agents to act on their behalf in faraway places. Not long after the inception of mass Arab printing, a network of agents was spread across the region and it grew ever denser with time. The arrangement proved indispensable for the distribution of journals and newspapers, given their periodic recurrence and the complexity of handling the payments. It was less vital, but still highly convenient, in distributing books. Employing agents had been an old practice in the region's history, especially in commerce. A "merchants' agent" (*wakīl al-tujjār*) who represented his employer in remote transactions was a well-known figure. A *wakīl* (pl. *wukalā'*) could act for several businesses concurrently, just as a single business could employ several agents.[22] The Western press offered an example of how the practice could be applied in distributing mass-printed publications. The Paris-based *Journal des Debats*, for instance, had agents in Rome, Naples, Cologne,

[20] *Al-Jinān*, 1 July 1872, 433–34. Reports on customer grievances appeared in *al-Jinān* regularly, from mid-1872 onward. In addition to the references in this and the previous note, see also *al-Jinān*, 1 January 1873, 1; 15 March 1873, 181; 1 November 1873, 721. See similar complaints in *al-Muqtaṭaf*, January 1879, inside front cover; *al-Janna*, 18 December 1883, 4. Abū al-Saʿd, 56, quotes sources from Baghdad in the 1870s, describing similar problems. Just as often, journals reported difficulties in transferring money through the banks from the provinces to the journal's Beirut office, another facet of the operational snags in the communicational underpinnings at the time.

[21] For example, American consuls in Jerusalem repeatedly complained about the unreliability and carelessness of the Ottoman postal services there in the 1880s and 1890s. There were also reports of disorder in the Jaffa post office on the eve of World War I. Kark, *American Consuls*, 148–50; Kark, *Yaffo*, 193 (quoting US consular correspondence and the Jaffa newspaper *Filasṭīn* from 1911 to 1912).

[22] Mawil Y. Izzi Dien, "Wakāla," in *Encyclopaedia of Islam*, 2nd edn.

and London already in 1860, and the *New York Tribune* had them in London, Vienna, and Berlin in 1870.[23]

Appointing agents to similar ends thus seemed a natural move in the Middle East. The practice was born together with the Arabic press. The first private paper, Khalīl al-Khūrī's *Ḥadīqat al-Akhbār*, publicized a list of its agents from the very outset in 1858; six of them represented the paper, in Istanbul, Damascus, Aleppo, Baghdad, Alexandria, and Cairo.[24] The next important journal, Fāris al-Shidyāq's *al-Jawā'ib* (Istanbul, 1861), likewise had six agents upon its inauguration, in Tunis, Beirut, London, Malta, Cairo, and Tripoli.[25] Ambitious publishers like Khūrī and Shidyāq saw the entire Arabic-speaking region as one potential market for the journals and books they wished to disseminate. Shidyāq, who started off with half a dozen agents in 1861, had them in no fewer than twenty-four locations by 1870, including places in Egypt and the Fertile Crescent, the Hijaz, North Africa, India, Malta, France, and England. In the following year the number climbed to twenty-eight.[26] The semi-weekly journal *al-Najāḥ* (Beirut, 1870) published in its second year a list of twenty-eight agents across the region from Tunis to Baghdad, as well as in India, Marseille, and Manchester; the news weekly *Thamarāt al-Funūn* (Beirut, 1875) employed thirteen agents in Syria, Palestine, Anatolia, and Cyprus from the start; *al-Ahrām* (Alexandria, 1876) appointed twenty-two agents upon its launching, in locations in Egypt, Istanbul, Damascus, Aleppo, Beirut, Acre, Jaffa, and Baghdad; the monthly *al-Muqtaṭaf* (Beirut, 1876) started off with twelve, but within a year, their number rose to forty-five; and the biweekly/monthly *al-Hilāl* (Cairo, 1892) began with fifteen, employed thirty-two a year later, and had as many as sixty-one agents in its third year – in Egypt and the other Arab provinces, India, England, and the United States.[27]

Each of these agents represented a spot on the distribution map of books and journals. Predictably, there were large concentrations of them close to the hubs of cultural activity in Egypt and Lebanon: Out of forty-five

[23] *Journal des Debats*, 1 January 1860, 1; *New York Tribune*, 2 July 1870, 4. Both papers replaced their agents from time to time, as can be seen from earlier and later issues. Other papers of the time provided no data on their agents; e.g., *Les Temps, L'Opinion, Le Moniteur Universel.*

[24] *Ḥadīqat al-Akhbār*, 22 May 1858, 1. At that early stage they were not yet referred to as *wukalā'* but as "those who take care of subscribers," *alladhina tuktab ʿindahum al-asmā'* (literally: "those with whom names are registered"), reflecting the newness of the practice.

[25] *Al-Jawā'ib*, 14 September 1861, 1.

[26] *Al-Jawā'ib*, 5 April 1870, 8; 12 February 1871, 4.

[27] *Al-Najāḥ*, 22 May 1871, 593; *Thamarāt al-Funūn*, 20 April 1875, 4; *al-Ahrām*, 5 August 1876, 4; *al-Muqtaṭaf*, July 1876, inside front cover; December 1877, outside back cover; *al-Hilāl*, October 1892, November 1893, February 1895 – lists on outside back covers.

al-Muqtaṭaf agents in 1877 (still issued from Beirut then), nineteen were employed in Mount Lebanon and around it, from Zaḥla to Marj ᶜUyūn; and of the sixty-one agents employed by *al-Hilāl* in 1895, forty-two were located in the Nile Valley and the Delta. More important, however, was the placing of agents in locations where few if any publishing activities took place prior to the twentieth century. There, the role of agents as links to the centers of production was truly crucial. As early as 1871, eighteen of these were already in place in the cities of Syria (excluding Lebanon), Palestine, and Iraq. A medium-size town like Jaffa had at least eight different agents during the decade starting in that year, and Lādhiqiyya had seven.[28] By the end of the century, hundreds of such intermediaries had been employed throughout the region. There were also traveling agents (*mutajawwilūn*) who, like the itinerant booksellers we have met earlier, went on periodic tours of small towns and villages where retaining permanent representatives would have made little business sense.[29] Obviously, not all places were served by agents all the time, and towns were occasionally left without them for a while. On the whole, it was a dynamic scene of an expanding system that was stretching its nerves to ever-farther places.

Of the personal identity of these agents, their sociocultural background, and their other occupations, we know little. For the great majority of them, all we have is their names. The evidence at hand does not tell us why they were picked for the post, what their relationship to cultural activity was, and how successful they were in fulfilling their duties. But a scrutiny of the extant data reveals some valuable details about their collective profile. A great many of them had Christian names, such as Jirjis, Yūḥannā, Niqūlā, Buṭrus, Mikhā'īl, and the like, reflecting the broad involvement of that community not only in making but also in disseminating printed products. Their family names, too, often indicated belonging to the urban educated class, many of whose members are known to us from their role in the region's intellectual discourse, e.g., Qasāṭlī (Damascus), Maᶜlūf (Zaḥla), Dabbās (Beirut), Zurayq (Jerusalem), and Ṣayqalī (Haifa). Yet another clue to their social background is provided by titles regularly attached to their names. Most common of these was *effendi*, a standard designation for an educated urbanite, but there were also other honorifics, such as the Ottoman *rifᶜatlū*, *faḍilatlū*, and

[28] In 1871, agents represented newspapers in Damascus, Aleppo, Lādhiqiyya, Iskandarūn, Jerusalem, Jaffa, Acre, Haifa, Baghdad, and Mosul. Jaffa during the 1870s had agents for *al-Jawā'ib*, *al-Najāḥ*, *Thamarāt al-Funūn*, *al-Muqtaṭaf*, *al-Jinān*, *al-Janna*, *al-Iskandariyya*, and *al-Ahrām*. Lādhiqiyya had agents representing all of these but the last.

[29] E.g., *al-Hilāl*, July 1893, 528.

ᶜizzatlū, all subtle variations of "his highness."[30] One agent of *al-Muqta ṭaf*, appointed in Jerusalem in 1878, was referred to as "*janāb al-fāḍil al-ad īb al-arīb al-shaykh Yūsuf effendi Fashfash al-akram*" – a string of lavish honorifics that would make little sense to translate, which puts the man squarely within the intellectual elite.[31] Sometimes agents were identified by their other occupation: consul, vice-consul, or consulate translator; department of customs secretary; telegraph inspector; physician; lawyer; merchant; and teacher.[32] Such trades had little relationship to publishing or journalism, and the publishers may have enlisted the services of these men due to their education or social standing. The appointment could also be incidental: "Our agent in Jizzīn, Milḥim effendi Nāṣif, has been appointed chief secretary in the criminal department of central Lebanon," *al-Muqtaṭaf* informed its readers in February 1880. His new responsibility did not permit him to serve the paper any longer, hence "we have passed the agency on to his brother Salīm effendi Nāṣif, a police officer in Jizzīn."[33]

An official in the customs department, or a physician, who accepted to act as an agent for a publisher apparently did so as a side responsibility unrelated to his main business. But there were also those for whom representing a publisher was consistent with their own trade, most typically bookshop owners. An Aleppo bookseller was hired as a newspaper agent already in 1858,[34] and many others followed. Such was Ḥabīb Gharzūzī, a big trader in books and journals in Alexandria, whose name appeared as agent in numerous papers published in Egypt, Beirut, and Istanbul, from the late 1860s onward.[35] Such was likewise a Tunis bookshop, which in 1872 acted as an agency for various Lebanese and Egyptian journals; and a Cairo bookshop in 1880, which upon its launching undertook to represent several journals from Cairo, Alexandria, and Beirut.[36]

30 Of twenty-eight agents of the Beirut semi-weekly *al-Najāḥ* in 1871, nineteen are mentioned as effendis; *al-Najāḥ*, 22 May 1871, 593. Similarly, *al-Muqtaṭaf*, November 1881, inside back cover.

31 *Al-Muqtaṭaf*, March 1878, outside back cover.

32 For these examples, see: *al-Jawā'ib*, 5 April 1870, 4; 9 November 1870, 4; *al-Muqtaṭaf*, June 1877, outside back cover; September 1878, inside front cover; January 1881, outside back cover; March 1881, inside front cover; *al-Janna*, 13 July 1879, 1; *al-Hilāl*, December 1892, outside back cover.

33 *Al-Muqtaṭaf*, February 1880, outside back cover.

34 *Ḥadīqat al-Akhbār*, 22 May 1858, 1. In the 29 December 1859 issue, the agent (Shukrāllāh Naṣrāllāh Khūrī) is referred to as a trader in books.

35 *Al-Jawā'ib*, 21 April 1868, 1; *al-Najāḥ*, 22 May 1871, 593; *Rawḍat al-Akhbār*, 13 December 1874, 1; *Thamarāt al-Funūn*, 20 April 1875, 1; *al-Ahrām*, 5 August 1876, 4; *al-Iskandariyya*, 13 March 1879, 1.

36 *Al-Rā'id al-Tūnisī*, 12 April 1872, 4; *al-Muqtaṭaf*, February 1880, outside back cover; *Thamarāt al-Funūn*, 14 November 1881, 1.

Agents were hired mostly by journal owners, and their primary responsibility was seeing to the smooth flow of newspapers, collecting the fees for them, and delivering the payments to the journal owners on time. Sometimes they were involved in promoting sales and procuring adverts for the papers they represented; and, especially early on, their employers also relied on them to report on events in their neighborhood: "We beg our esteemed agents . . . not to be lax in keeping us informed on important events in their area" was a common appeal.[37] Equipped with the paper's letterhead, seal, and receipt book, the agent was a subsidiary link in the diffusion chain of periodical publications. The availability of such remote offshoots was regularly utilized by the publishers who employed them, and by others, to help in book dissemination as well. Many newspaper adverts for books on sale referred potential buyers to journal agents in the provinces.[38] Similarly, these agents were often charged with handling payments for future books whose publication would be financed through a presubscription deal (see the next section of this chapter).[39]

With a working infrastructure, efficient services, cooperative customers, and well-trained agents, the system would permit an uninterrupted flow of books and journals to near and far places. But, as should be clear by now, conditions in the region during the early decades of the *nahḍa* were different. Numerous obstacles hampered the work of agents. One of them was the lack of client cooperation, especially on matters of payment for journal subscription. Agents everywhere complained about customers who were slow to pay their dues or avoided it altogether, a widespread occurrence (this, if we will, was the mirror image of buyers not receiving their journals on time).[40] More to the point here, the agents themselves were often a source of continuous difficulties. Recurrent references to agents' incapacity (*taqṣīrāt*) and negligence (*ihmāl*) reflected what seems to have been a serious problem in appointing fit agents during the early years. While some of them (notably owners of big bookshops) proved

[37] *Al-Ahrām*, 5 August 1876, 4. Similarly, 4 November 1876, 1; 20 January 1881, 3.

[38] For a few examples, see: *al-Rā'id al-Tūnisī*, 12 April 1872, 4; *al-Ahrām*, 4 November 1876, 4; *al-Muqtaṭaf*, December 1879, outside back cover; *Lisān al-Ḥāl*, 9 June 1880, 4; *Thamarāt al-Funūn*, 14 November 1881, 1; 19 December 1883, 4; *al-Janna*, 3 September 1881, 1; *al-Waṭan*, 21 April 1883, 4; *al-Hilāl*, 15 October 1994, 158.

[39] E.g., *al-Jinān*, 1 January 1870, inside back cover; 1 May 1873, inside back cover; 1 April 1878, inside front and back cover; *Lisān al-Ḥāl*, 16 October 1878, 1; 15 October 1879, 4; 7 October 1901, 4; *Thamarāt al-Funūn*, 20 April 1875, 4; 1 November 1881, 1; *al-Ahrām*, 7 April 1877, 4; 11 May 1877, 4; *al-Muqtaṭaf*, October 1878, inside back cover; March 1879, 88; May 1883, 280. A prominent example of this routine was the circulation of Buṭrus al-Bustānī's multivolume *Dā'irat al-maᶜārif*, which was sold to subscribers throughout the region and whose circulation was administered for some ten years by agents of Bustānī's own biweekly *al-Jinān*. See further below.

[40] Ayalon, *The Press*, 208–10, quoting many examples.

trustworthy and efficient, others were patently inept. There is no way of telling how extensive the problem was, although one manifest indication – the high frequency of agent rotation in many places – would suggest that it was widespread. For example, the agent for *al-Muqtaṭaf* in Jerusalem, in December 1877, was Khalīl al-Jamal; in March 1878, it was Yūsuf Fashfash; in May, Yūsuf Asᶜad and Yūsuf al-Jamal; and in October, Yūḥannā Qusṭa Gharghūr – five agents in less than a year.[41] Whether choosing to resign or being replaced by the publisher, an agent employed for such a fleeting moment could barely be useful as a link in the diffusion chain.

Publishers often complained about their agents' sloppy performance, most commonly with regard to collecting subscription fees and forwarding them to the journal. We shall recall Fāris al-Shidyāq's complaint, in the mid-1860s, about his newspaper agents in Lebanon, Tunis, and Algiers who refused to pay, paid only partially, or delayed payment (see Preface) – a state of affairs that undermined the paper's viability.[42] In Alexandria in 1894, the agents of one paper had hired distributors, who "had been found to be greedy":

> They are selling the paper for five millieme, claiming that it is sold to them for three millieme and that the extra two millieme are their profit. The truth is that we sell it to them for two millieme, and their profit should be one millieme. We beg the readers not to pay more than three millieme. We are not publicizing their names, so as not to stain their repute.[43]

Other agents acted in a contrary way, but their performance reflected similar problems. "It has been brought to our attention," *al-Muqtaṭaf* editors wrote in 1881,

> that the journal's agents in Alexandretta, Damyāṭ and Marj ᶜUyūn have been paying out of their own pockets for a few subscribers during a period of three years, in order that the subscription fees reach us on time. We are grateful to them for their initiative. Would that they had stopped delivering the papers to those who obstruct [their work] like that and [thus] display such contempt for knowledge.[44]

Complaints about the poor performance of agents usually related to hitches in the circulation of periodicals and the payment system associated with it. They hardly ever appear with regard to book dissemination

[41] *Al-Muqtaṭaf*, December 1877, outside back cover; March, May, October 1878, all on outside back covers. Another example may be quoted from Aleppo: June 1878 – Ḥabīb Yūsuf Kūsā and Rizqāllāh Rūfā'īl Ṣabbāgh; March 1880 – Mikhā'īl Anṭūn Saqqāl; November 1881 – Aḥmad effendi Wahbī. See *al-Muqtaṭaf*, June 1878, outside back cover; March 1880, outside back cover; November 1881; inside back cover.

[42] Shidyāq's letter, quoted in ᶜImād al-Ṣulḥ, 99.

[43] *Lisān al-ᶜArab*, 2 August 1894, 1.

[44] *Al-Muqtaṭaf*, January 1881, inside front cover; March 1882, inside front cover.

by the agents. Still, we might assume that, wherever the agent system malfunctioned, it must have encumbered the flow of books as well. Such shortcomings, like those of the other links in the diffusion chain, reflected the system's novelty. They represented the infancy diseases of the new practices, which would gradually be gone later on.

Advertising

Until they were relegated to irrelevance by modern changes, *nassāḥ* and *warrāq* were highly regarded callings in Arab societies. It is an "age-old, honorable trade" (*ḥirfa qadīma sharīfa*), noted the author of a "Lexicon of Occupations in Syria," composed around 1900, who also suggested that these vocations generated "abundant income."[45] We need not doubt the public esteem for the trade of making, copying, and selling books, but its lucrativeness is somewhat questionable. More likely, there was a wide range of profitability in that, as in any profession, with the diligent and resourceful prospering more than others. Those who were fortunate enough to be in the business in times of rising public demand – of the kind detected by Nelly Hanna in sixteenth- to eighteenth-century Cairo (see Chapter 2) – were likewise better off than their occupational peers in other times and places. On the whole, however, the book trade had a modest commercial promise, given the limited pool of potential customers. The rules of economic logic usually maintained equilibrium between the limited demand and the pace of production.

This equilibrium was upset by the opening of presses in the region. The productive power of the new machinery was greater than the public ability to absorb its products, even with the growing thirst for intelligence. The book and newspaper market was flooded with goods, and, as ever in a buyers' market, the makers of the new products had to labor to promote their merchandise and allure consumers. The present section looks at some of the promotional techniques that typified the formative phase of Middle Eastern book diffusion.

Before electronics, mass written notices were the foremost way to advance the sales of any merchandise. Written and graphic advertising relied on the printed press and, to a lesser extent, on written announcements of different formats in public places. Reading ability was of the essence, of course; where it was limited, so was the promoter's path to potential clients. Such was the situation in the Middle East at the time when printing, newspapers, and advertising entered the region all around

[45] Qāsimī, Vol. 2, 269–70, 383–84. Qāsimī uses the Syrian term *ṣaḥḥāf* for the *warrāq's* trade.

the same time. Advertising books and journals was particularly challenging. Trumpeting new goods or services is ever more demanding than marketing familiar ones, as it entails persuading people to acquire new habits. The task is all the more tricky when cultural considerations are involved.

Commercial adverts in the Arabic press first appeared in the Egyptian official *al-Waqā'iʿ al-Miṣriyya* and, after the mid-nineteenth century, also in private journals. With the flourishing of commercial activity, the expansion of the press, and the rise in literacy, they gradually proliferated as well. By the end of the century, Arabic papers, especially in Egypt, were already devoting a sizeable part of their volume (sometimes around 25 percent of their space, or even more) to private and public advertisement, both local and foreign. This activity would intensify after World War I, there and elsewhere in the region.[46] Books were not a new commodity in the Middle East, of course, but there was novelty in their printed format, which made them distinct from their handwritten antecedents both as objects and as symbols of cultural values. The disparity was still greater with books of hitherto unfamiliar nature, such as works translated from European languages, or Bustānī's modern encyclopedia, let alone periodical publications which represented an utter innovation. Not everyone who was accustomed to buying or collecting manuscript books would necessarily be as attracted to printed ones; the shift required enticement.

Periodical publications were the main vehicle in inducing the public into buying books and subscribing for journals. They targeted their own readers, who were obvious prospective customers, seeking to convince them to consume more. Arabic journals advertised themselves, and sometimes each other. But far more regularly they carried adverts for books. *Ḥadīqat al-Akhbār* in the 1850s, *al-Jawā'ib* in the 1860s, *al-Jinān* and other papers in the 1870s, all featured books as prominent items in their commercial notices. So did the official Egyptian press in the 1860s and 1870s.[47] Advertisements were placed by everyone in the industry with interest in promoting sales: authors, printers, publishers, and booksellers. Most typical were notices by presses which published both the promoted books and the journals announcing them. The simplest format was listings of books for sale, with details on prices and the way to obtain them and with no promotional remarks. Just as common were notices that sought to lure readers into purchasing the book on offer, often by using arguments that relied on traditional norms of book quality and prestige.

[46] Shechter, 180–82; Russell, 49–61; Ayalon, *The Press*, 202–05.
[47] Nuṣayr, 471–77.

Like early European printers, who during the industry's infancy had to grapple with a demand for books "as esthetic as manuscripts,"[48] early Arab publishers had to mind the expectations of their would-be customers, whose taste for books had been shaped before printing. Books were meant to be made with deference to proper rules of scribing, reverence for the Arabic language and style, and regard for beauty. Promoters, therefore, often tried to convince potential buyers that the new products were as good as the old, or better. One recurrent point was emphasis on the rigorous care with which the book had been executed, so as to meet the standard criteria: the publisher's utmost efforts to "correct its wording and upgrade its style (*iṣlāḥ ᶜibārātahā lughawiyy*^{an} *wa-taḥsīn uslūbahā*)"[49]; to carefully produce it "with high-quality letters, printing, and paper"[50]; and to arrange it so as to be "consonant with good taste (*al-adhwāq al-salīma*)."[51] A printed edition of a *dīwān* by a ninth-century poet, produced from an eleventh-century manuscript, indicated on its title page that it had been made "with highest precision and perfection (*fī ghāyat al-ḍabṭ wa'l--itqān*)." Another edition of the same book, reprinted later by another publisher, repeated the assertion and added that "a highly learned scholar" had supervised its "printing, meticulous editing, and critical revision."[52] To pick yet another example, a lengthy advert for a book noted its having been "printed in a clear manner, as if it were drawn by pen, or even prettier and more perfect than handwriting in its arrangement (*abhā naskh*^{an} *min al-khaṭṭ wa-atamm*)."[53] Close attention to accuracy and regard for esthetics, essential in setting a book's value in the manuscript era, thus continued to affect the attitude to books after the entry of printing. Later, with the mounting influx of machine-made books, such adherence to old standards would give way to other kinds of priorities.

Another common promotional device was extolling the book's author for his scholarly stature, his repute, and his skills. Such acclamations were not necessary for reproduced works of classic scholars, but they were required for books by less famous contemporary authors, whose precipitous multiplying generated the new need. For example, Buṭrus al-Bustānī's learner's guidebook for the English language (1866) was promoted on the basis of its author's eminence and "proficiency (*barāᶜa*) in the two languages, Arabic and English [which] is sufficient guarantee for the book

48 Febvre and Martin, chapter 3; Eisenstein, *Printing Revolution*, 23ff.
49 *Al-Jawā'ib*, 21 April 1868, 1. Similarly, *al-Jawā'ib*, 3 September 1868, 4.
50 *Lisān al-Ḥāl*, 5 December 1889, 1.
51 *Al-Waṭan*, 21 April 1883, 4.
52 Al-Walīd al-Buḥturī, *Dīwān*, first part (Istanbul: maṭbaᶜat al-jawā'ib, 1300/1882, and Cairo: maṭbaᶜat hindiyya, 1911).
53 *Al-Jawā'ib*, 7 July 1868, 4.

being the best possible bridge" across the two idioms.[54] In works rendered from alien languages, in particular, the translator's philological credentials were often accentuated. An Egyptian translator of La Fontaine's fables was hailed as "one of Egypt's more skillful men-of-letters (*udabā'*)."[55] and Salīm Nawfal, who translated Roger de Beauvoir's *Marquise de Fontanges*, was acclaimed as "by all accounts one of the most prominent among those who have elevated the Arabic languages to the summit of all current idioms."[56] A different kind of reasoning used in promotional notices was presenting a work as a key to the civilized nations. "The Arabs need books in their language, but the old books do not include all the scientific innovations, revelations and inventions of our time," one writer observed; "the Arabs ought to obtain all of that, so as to equalize their standing [with that of other nations] and to nurture the essentials of progress, civilization, affluence, comfort, learning and knowledge ... and join their contemporaries ... the civilized countries."[57] This argument appeared repeatedly in notices for books dealing with modern matters. The Tunisian statesman Khayr al-Dīn al-Tūnisī's tract, *Aqwam al-masālik* (1867), was thus publicized as a book that "elucidates, in the most eloquent terms and clearest explanation" the "particulars of politics and the elements of civilization."[58]

The shifting emphases in the wording of adverts over time reflected a gradual change in the general public attitude to books. Printed books, especially works translated from, adopted from, or manifestly inspired by foreign examples, were often different from classical works in theme, style, and vocabulary. Insisting on linguistic propriety or grammatical accuracy would make little sense in books packed with foreign terminology, such as travel accounts to Europe or an adaptation of a Jules Verne story. More generally, the growing flow of printed works, both old and modern, seemed to render customary standards of correct style and "good taste" somehow less important. These habitual standards, which had figured in early promotional notices, gradually disappeared from them during the closing years of the nineteenth century. As in Europe several centuries earlier, people in the Arab provinces now seemed to pay

[54] *Ḥadīqat al-Akhbār*, 8 February 1866, 3. The book was al-Hadiyya al-saniyya li-ṭalabat al-lugha al-inklīzīyya.

[55] *Ḥadīqat al-Akhbār*, 30 August 1859, 4.

[56] *Ḥadīqat al-Akhbār*, 28 April 1859, 3. The description of Nawfal's linguistic qualifications was more flowery and spread over twelve lines. His translation, *riwāyat al-marqīz fūntānj*, was serialized in *Ḥadīqat al-Akhbār* in 1859.

[57] Bustānī in *al-Jinān*, 15 May 1874, note between pages 328 and 329; Bustānī et al., *Dā'irat al-maʿārif*, Vol. 1, 2.

[58] *Al-Jawā'ib*, 20 October 1868, 4. Likewise, an ornate advert in rhymed prose elaborated the many benefits of a book on Napoleon I; *al-Jawā'ib*, 21 April 1868, 1.

less heed to old norms of format, layout, and fonts. Most people would happily possess printed copies, even if less esthetic, of works that would be beyond their reach in their handmade version. The style of the adverts brightly mirrored this change of attitude.

Obviously, it was mostly the literate who were potential book and journal buyers, and promoters commonly addressed them politely as *adīb* ("man-of-letters"; pl. *udabā'*), or its various derivatives: *muḥibbū al-ādāb* ("literature/culture lovers"), *banī al-adāb* ("children of culture"), *al-jumhūr al-adabī* ("cultured public"), and the like.[59] That this was at first a small, somewhat exclusive circle seemed clear to book makers. Beyond politeness, such an approach placed the *adīb* in a select class and lent him prestige. It also implied a duty to the community; for who, if not the *udabā'*, would elevate the society to a loftier level of culture? "All men of perception and knowledge," Buṭrus al-Bustānī suggested in a promotional note for *Dā'irat al-maᶜārif*, "and those interested in disseminating [these values] among speakers of the Arabic idiom East, West, North and South, and in spreading knowledge and civilization among the many millions who speak that idiom, should subscribe to this important project and act for circulating it among our compatriots."[60] If you are educated, Bustānī urged his readers, you have a responsibility to pioneer culture by supporting the industry. This argument was frequently voiced in the early years of printing but disappeared toward the close of the century. It gave way to adverts promoting printed works for their specific worth, no longer justifying it by cultural or communal reasoning.

Books and journals were also promoted in other ways. Jurjī Zaydān's monthly *al-Hilāl* had a regular section since the early 1890s in which new publications that appeared in the region were surveyed. Under the title *al-taqrīẓ wa'l-intiqād* ("praise and criticism"), Zaydān listed or reviewed recent publications. *Al-Hilāl, al-Muqtaṭaf,* and a few other journals regularly referred readers to books while addressing their queries. Printers and publishers often used the books themselves – title page, back cover, or the book's last page – as a platform for further exposure. To pick an example, Salīm Ibrāhīm Ṣādir, publisher and bookseller in Beirut of the 1880s, advertised nineteen works printed in his shop on the back cover of *Kitāb al-falsafa li'l-qiss butīyīr* which he issued. In another book, *al-Tuḥfa*

[59] E.g., *Ḥadīqat al-Akhbār*, 9 April 1859, 3; 16 April 1859, 4; *al-Jawā'ib*, 28 April 1868, 4; 20 October 1868, 4. Sometimes the address was more elaborate: "We urge all Arabic-speaking *udabā'*, whether men of religion, philosophers, historians, poets, or those eloquent in the language, to move ahead and buy this book"; *al-Najāḥ*, 29 May 1871, 603.

[60] *Al-Jinān*, 1 March 1875, outside back cover.

al-saniyya fī ta'rīkh al-qusṭanṭiniyya, he entered a note on the last page, commending the book itself, promoting his shop, and encouraging readers to request the shop's catalog.[61] The printing industry, which served as a key instrument for advertising every other commodity, promoted itself with comparable zeal.

Regarding the entire Arabic-speaking region as one pool of potential consumers, advertisers targeted literate people throughout it. Perpetuating the old tradition of circulating written texts across the region, they promoted books and journals far away from their places of vending. A Beirut paper would announce a book sold in an Istanbul shop, a book available in Beirut would be advertised in Tunis, and an Istanbul paper would promote a volume vended in Alexandria.[62] One Beirut daily advertised a work by a Damascus author, printed in Beirut, available in bookshops in Istanbul, Damascus, Tripoli, and Lādhiqiyya, and composed in polemical response to a work published earlier in Cairo.[63] Assuming potential readers shared basically the same interests and taste everywhere, book promoters employed similar arguments to persuade them. Thus, an elegant notice on the front page of *al-Jawā'ib* (Istanbul) publicized a work printed in Beirut and offered for sale in Alexandria, using rhyme to render the message attractive: The book, it noted, was "a model of grace and excellence / and far from corruption and insolence ... it would coach rulers in caution / and instill in their subjects devotion ..." and so on, for another dozen lines, before concluding in a more business-like tone: "The book is sold in the *maktaba* of al-khawāja Ḥabīb Gharzūzī in Alexandria for 15 francs."[64] Advertising books and journals in faraway provinces embodied the transregional exchanges in print during the *nahḍa*. It narrowed the gulf between the centers of publishing and the parts where such activity was yet to begin.

61 *Kitāb al-falsafa li'l-qiss butīyīr* (Beirut: al-maktaba al-ᶜumūmiyya, 1883); *al-Tuḥfa al-saniyya fī ta'rīkh al-qusṭanṭiniyya* (Beirut: al-maktaba al-ᶜumūmiyya, 1887). For more examples in a similar manner, see: *Dīwān al-shāb al-ẓarīf* (Beirut: al-maktaba al-ahliyya, 1900), outside back cover; *Saᶜādat al-maᶜād fī mukhtaṣar sharḥ bānat suᶜād* (Tripoli: al-maktaba al-*rifāᶜīyya*, n.d.), last two pages; *Riwāyat ūtillū aw ḥayl al-rijāl* (Cairo: maṭbaᶜat al-tawfīq, 1899), last page.

62 *Ḥadīqat al-Akhbār*, 8 May 1859, 4; *al-Rā'id al-Tūnisī*, 29 Ramaḍān 1280 [1863], 3; *al-Jawā'ib*, 20 October 1868, 4; 7 March 1877, 4.

63 *Faṣl al-khiṭāb aw taflīs iblīs* (a response to Qāsim Amīn's *Taḥrīr al-mar'a*) – *Lisān al-Ḥāl*, 15 April 1901, 1.

64 "*Qad jamaᶜa amārāt al-faḍl wa'l-nabāha / wa-khalā min kull khalāᶜa wa-safāha. Wa-huwwa mā yuksib ... wulāt al-umūr taḥdhīr*^{an} */ wa-raᶜāyāhum haybat*^{an} *wa-ṭāᶜat*^{an}"; *al-Jawā'ib*, 21 April 1868, 1.

Creative Endeavors: Yūsuf al-Shalfūn and His "Book of the Month" Club

Yūsuf al-Shalfūn is almost unknown in the literature, despite his being a pillar of the *nahḍa* structure, somewhat like Khalīl Sarkīs whom we met in Chapter 2. Like him, Shalfūn was less of a celebrity than certain other men we have already encountered. But he was one of those nameless individuals without whose zeal and labor there would have been no literary awakening. Here we are interested in one of his several cultural projects, a pioneering scheme to boost book distribution. On the whole, it was not an important enterprise in the history of Arab publishing, and there is little surprise that it left such a trifling trace in the annals. Still, it is worth our attention as an instance of the trial and error which was

Yūsuf al-Shalfūn
Fīlīb dī Ṭarrāzī, *Ta'rīkh al-ṣiḥāfa al-ᶜarabiyya*, Vol. 1 (Beirut: al-maṭbaᶜa al-adabiyya, 1913), p. 120.

experienced by many who sought to implant literary works in the uninviting environment of Middle Eastern reading during the early phase.

Before examining this project, it would be useful to look at his overall role in the scene of cultural action during the early decades of the awakening. Yūsuf bin Fāris al-Shalfūn (1839–1895) came from an old Maronite family in Beirut, the grandson of a governor in the service of Bashīr Shihāb the Third. We first hear of him in the late 1850s, a young man of around twenty years, when he worked as a typesetter in Khalīl al-Khūrī's Syrian Press, the home of *Ḥadīqat al-Akhbār* since 1858. This was the start of a career that evolved along familiar *nahḍa* lines and bore many of the markings that typified its builders. Shalfūn stayed with Khūrī for a couple of years, refining his technical skills, and then moved on to work as a printer and editor for the Grand Vizier, Fu'ād Pāshā, during the latter's 1860–1861 mission to Beirut. Once the mission ended, Shalfūn applied for and received a license to open his own press, *al-maṭbaᶜa al-ᶜumūmiyya* ("public/general press"), in 1861 – the third private printing shop in Lebanon after that of Khūrī and another press.[65] Shalfūn ran his shop for several years, not only printing state and commercial documents but also producing more significant items. Under his ownership, *al-maṭbaᶜa al-ᶜumūmiyya* turned out some fifty books on religious (Christian) and historical subjects, local and translated literature, poetry, and *adab*. Most of these were small booklets, but a few were bigger volumes comprising hundreds of pages.[66] Shalfūn also used the press to publish two literary-informative journals consecutively, *al-Zahra* in 1870 and *al-Najāḥ* (in collaboration with Lūīs Ṣābūnjī) in 1871. Meanwhile, the government enlisted his skills once again. In 1867, Da'ūd Pāshā, the *mutaṣarrif* of Mount Lebanon, took him to set up a press for his Bayt al-Dīn headquarters and to manage it for a while, something Shalfūn did while overseeing his own Beirut shop. In 1873, he sold *al-maṭbaᶜa al-ᶜumūmiyya*, but in the following year he returned to the calling he knew best and opened another press, al-*maṭbaᶜa al-kulliyya*. He ran it until the early 1880s and printed in it at least a dozen books and a newspaper, *al-Taqaddum*, which appeared irregularly for some fifteen years.[67]

[65] The other private press was Ibrāhīm al-Najjār's *al-maṭbaᶜa al-sharqiyya*, which opened in 1858 and worked on a modest scale; Shaykhū, 104–05.

[66] Shaykhū, 97–101, listing forty-nine books printed in Shalfūn's press from its foundation in 1861 until (and including) 1873, apparently the year in which he sold his press (see below). The press continued to operate under a new owner, changing its name to *al-maṭbaᶜa al-ᶜumūmiyya al-kāthūlikiyya*. Shaykhū (101–03) lists over thirty titles printed in it during that later stage.

[67] Shaykhū, 95–104; Ṭarrāzī, *Ta'rīkh al-ṣiḥāfa*, Vol. 1, 120–21; Vol. 2, 8–9, 22–23, 51–52. There are some discrepancies in detail between these two sources, and it seems that the latter – which was written at a later time and is somewhat more credible – rectifies errors of the former.

In addition to being a pioneer printer and publisher, Shalfūn was also a writer. He authored substantial parts of his journals, including quite a few *qaṣīda*s, and wrote at least one novel and one poetry book.[68] Somewhat more prominently, he composed a manual of popular letter-writing, *Turjumān al-mukātaba*, which first appeared in the 1860s and then was repeatedly reprinted by presses in Beirut and in Cairo into the early twentieth century. Designed as a guidebook for scribes and inexperienced writers – a bridge to a modern cultural practice – its circle of users expanded with the spread of literacy.[69] Like others in his cultural milieu, he was able to use foreign languages: Some of his activities involved the use of French, several of his published literary works were adopted from French literature, and his press accepted jobs "in all European languages."[70] Finally, what could be more symbolic of a *nahḍa* maker than being a founding member of the Syrian Scientific Society in its second round (1868)? Shalfūn even read a *qaṣīda* of his in the Society's opening session, and was appointed the Society's librarian.[71]

In 1866, a time of publishing momentum in Shalfūn's *al-maṭbaᶜa al-ᶜumūmiyya*, he launched a project of a new type, a kind of "book club" which he named *al-Shirāka al-Shahriyya* or "monthly participation/partnership." By then his press had already printed over a dozen books, a few each year, but Shalfūn wanted more. He offered his readers a deal: For an annual fee, to be paid in advance, he would send them a new book every month. This was a forerunner of the subscription system, a procedure well familiar in Europe (and already known locally in a different mode in journal distribution), which would soon become routine, as we shall see below. Shalfūn singled out only the educated as his potential audience; the general public was beyond his business horizon, which is not surprising for that early stage. He set the annual price at fifty qurush for Beirut and Mount Lebanon, and sixty for other places, plus postage (literally, "the cost of delivering [the book] to [the customer's] place (*ujrat tawṣīlihi li-maḥallihi*)."[72] This was a reasonable rate, roughly in the range of

[68] *Ru'yat ḥifẓ al-widād* (al-maṭbaᶜa al-ᶜumūmiyya, 1866); *Anīs al-jalīs* (al-maṭbaᶜa al-kulliyya, 1874).

[69] Ben-Bassat and Zachs discuss the book and its influence in detail. They have traced its first appearance in 1869 (2, note 1). Shaykhū (99) mentions two earlier editions, in 1863 and 1865. The book was apparently printed in both of Shalfūn's presses, and the 1887 edition, produced in his *al-maṭbaᶜa al-kulliyya*, is presented as the seventh printing.

[70] Shalfūn's work with Fu'ād Pāshā in 1860–1861 involved editing and printing letters in French; Ṭarrāzī, *Tā'rīkh al-ṣiḥāfa*, Vol. 1, 120. For his press advertisement, see *al-Najjāḥ*, 22 May 1871, 593. European works he adopted and published were, e.g., Dumas's *Comte de Monte-Cristo*, Lamartine's *Genevieve*, and Bernardin de Saint-Pierre's *Paul et Virginie*, all rendered in Arabic and printed in *al-maṭbaᶜa al-ᶜumūmiyya*.

[71] Ṭarrāzī, *Ta'rīkh al-ṣiḥāfa*, Vol. 1, 120–21; Ben-Bassat–Zachs, 14.

[72] *Ḥadīqat al-Akhbār*, 22 March 1866, 3, and title pages of the series' first two books.

a year's subscription to some of the region's monthly journals in the following decade, which left people with limited means out of the consumer circle. Shalfūn evidently saw the educated Lebanese elite as an adequate reservoir of customers, whose tapping would allow him to maximize the advantages of owning a printing press and generate some profit. The evidence at hand makes it quite clear that the endeavor was motivated more by commercial considerations than by an urge to edify the public.

The oft-quoted historian of the Arabic press, Fīlīb dī Ṭarrāzī, erroneously counted Shalfūn's series of books as a monthly journal (*majalla shahriyya*), apparently because they came out in monthly regularity. The error was adopted by subsequent writers and scholars, who have considered *al-Shirāka al-Shahriyya* as one of Shalfūn's journals.[73] But the items in this series, which is extant in its entirety at the British Library, do not look anything like a journal; rather, they are a set of booklets. There are eight of them, printed in Shalfūn's press from January to August 1866, small opuses of 12 × 18 cm that comprise between thirty-four and ninety pages each. They make a rather disjointed mix of historical pieces, original and translated literature and poetry, including one novel by Shalfūn himself.[74] Difficulties in production, which would eventually cause Shalfūn to abandon the series after eight months, became visible when he was halfway through it. In a notice to his readers in book 5, Shalfūn begs them to "forgive our being so slow" in delivering books, "for reasons beyond our control." He also apologizes for having to discontinue the translation of *Count of Monte Cristo*, started in the previous installment, as the book was "too big" and would take a long time to render in Arabic. Instead, he sent his customers a novel of his own pen. From now on, Shalfūn promised, he would try harder. But after three more booklets – the shortest three in the series – he abandoned the project altogether. Shortly thereafter he was called upon to set up the government press at Bayt al-Dīn.

The book club was Shalfūn's idea of inducing his potential audience to consume more, so he could gain more from the new technology he owned. The plan itself was not quite original and seems to have been inspired by similar arrangements, based on subscription, that were

[73] Ṭarrāzī, *Ta'rīkh al-ṣiḥāfa*, Vol. 1, 68. Ṭarrāzī mistakenly referred to it as *al-Shirka al-Shahriyya*. For recent adoptions of this error, see e.g., Patel, 212; Zentrum Moderner Orient, *Chronology*.

[74] Books 1–3 are a summary of the Book of Josippon, by Josephus ben Gorion; 4 – a section from *The Count of Monte Cristo*; 5 – Shalfūn's novel *ḥifẓ al-widād*; 6 – *adab*, edited by Shalfūn; 7 – a *dīwān* of poetry by the fifteenth-century Sultan Khalīl al-Ashraf; 8 – an annotated *qaṣīda* by the eleventh-century al-Ṭughrā'ī.

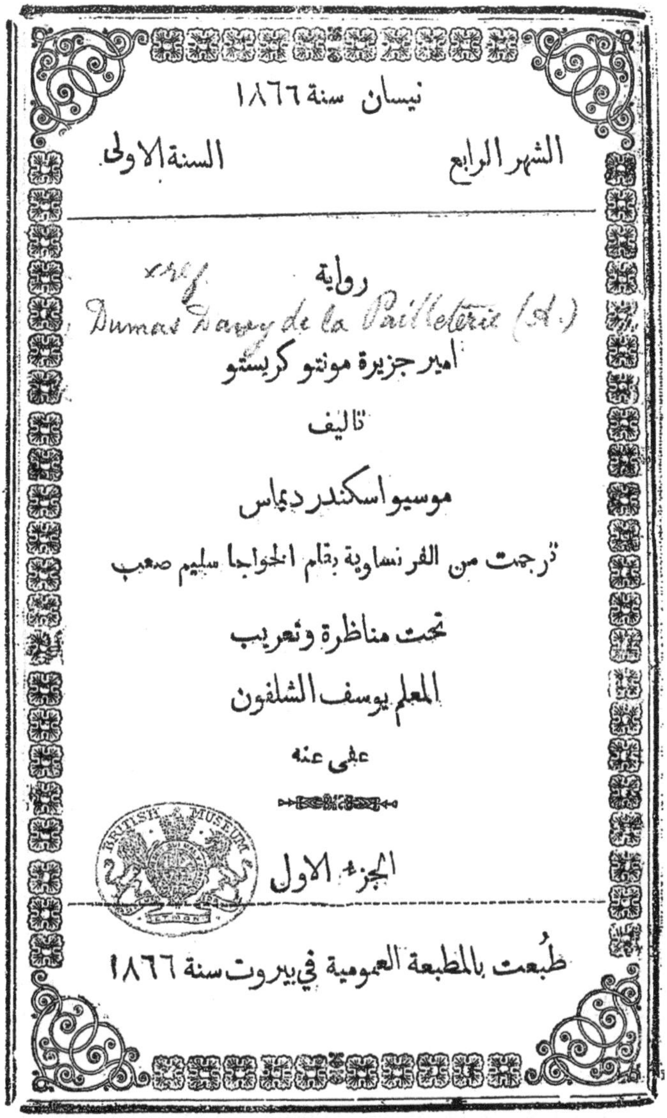
نيسان سنة ١٨٦٦

الشهر الرابع السنة الاولى

رواية

Dumas Davy de la Pailleterie (A.)

امير جزيرة مونتو كريستو

تاليف

موسيو اسكندر ديماس

ترجمت من الفرنساوية بقلم الخواجا سليم صعب

تحت مناظرة وتعريب

المعلم يوسف الشلفون

عفي عنه

الجزء الاول

طبعت بالمطبعة العمومية في بيروت سنة ١٨٦٦

Shalfūn's *al-Shirāka al-Shahriyya*, 4th issue (Beirut, April 1866), 51pp. Part 1 of Dumas's "Count of Monte Cristo," translated from the French by Salīm Ṣaᶜb under Shalfūn's linguistic supervision *(munāẓara wa-taᶜrīb)*. This was the first and last installment of that translation. © The British Library Board, 14599.d.1 (4), frontispiece.

widespread in Europe. The deal he proposed was meant to be beneficial at once to him and to his customers. Of the reasons for its termination after only eight months, we can only speculate; a record of the number of readers, their reception of the books sent to them, and their payments is unlikely to come to light, if it ever existed. "The series folded due to the slight value of its contents (*li-qillat mabāḥithihā*) and because the people did not care to read it," the knowledgeable Ṭarrāzī suggested – a sensible explanation that was applicable to so many other publishing initiatives.[75] Financial difficulties (Shalfūn's or his customers'); problems in managing book production or delivery, or in handling the payments; readers' disapproval of the contents – all of these are possible reasons, of the kinds that weighed down on attempts to craft a market of readers at that early stage.

Yūsuf al-Shalfūn's forgotten initiative was a failed attempt to extend the arrangement of prior payment from newspapers to books. Before too long, a variation of this practice would become common throughout the region.

Subscription

The deal through which Shalfūn sought to boost his sales was based on the same principle that underlay journal distribution: For a fixed prepayment, the publisher sends printed products to the customer's home at constant regularity. The arrangement came to be known as *ishtirāk*, literally "participation"; and subscribers were called *mushtarikūn*. In principle, the deal was better suited to periodicals than to books. Since journals and newspapers appeared at perpetual periodicity, paying for a whole set of issues would be more convenient to both publishers and customers than for the latter to buy them one issue at a time. The arrangement had its shortcomings: It required payment of a large sum up-front (and was thus affordable mostly to the well-off), and its success, which largely depended on the publisher's ability to deliver regularly, was subject to forces beyond his control, such as logistic problems, financial hardship, and government interference. In the late-Ottoman Middle East, the practice met with frequent difficulties owing to such constraints, as well as due to the very novelty of the concept and the lack of popular faith in it.[76] As we have seen, Shalfūn too faced difficulties when he tried to apply the method to book distribution.

[75] Ṭarrāzī, *Ta'rīkh al-ṣiḥāfa*, Vol. 1, 68.

[76] The difficulties in applying subscription in journal and newspaper distribution are discussed in Ayalon, *The Press*, 191–93, 206–11.

Deals like Shalfūn's book club appeared only rarely after that. But a similar procedure that entered the region around the same time struck roots and became common. That procedure was also termed *ishtirāk*, but in a slightly different sense: Rather than *participation* in a readers' "club" like Shalfūn's, it was used to denote the *sharing* of production costs. The practical meaning of such a sharing is that publisher and client agree to shoulder the expenses – the latter by paying an advance – and the project is executed if the publisher manages to gather enough sharers to cover the expected costs.

Ishtirāk, in the sense of sharing the costs, allowed publishers to plan production according to anticipated sales. The publisher would announce his contemplated project before starting production, or during its early stage, and offer beneficial terms (discounts or a convenient installment deal) to buyers who committed themselves beforehand. Often, actual printing would start only after a sufficient number of subscribers had been assembled to cover expenses and ensure profit. This arrangement facilitated the publishing of books that otherwise may not have been printed, putting them at the public's disposal and boosting sales. The concept was born in seventeenth-century England (it has been suggested that "this was a practice peculiarly suited to the English trade"),[77] from where it spread to continental Europe and North America. It became clear that this was "the most effective – and often the only – way to finance the printing of a truly substantial publication," based as it was on sharing expenses in the present with those who would be getting their return in the future.[78] The routine became standard in effectuating not only big projects such as multivolume encyclopedias (including the *Britannica* and *Grande encyclopédie*), dictionaries, and large sets of literature and poetry, but also more modest works.[79] The method encouraged publishing initiative and contributed to the development of the industry wherever applied.

The first to adopt the practice in the Middle East was apparently Buṭrus al-Bustānī. In the early 1860s, in notices in *Ḥadīqat al-Akhbār*, he appealed to the educated public and offered his upcoming two-volume modern dictionary, *Muḥīṭ al-muḥīṭ*, for sale. At that time he had already begun printing fascicules of it in *maṭbaᶜat al-maᶜārif*, the press he owned jointly with Khalīl Sarkīs. In the deal he proposed, customers would pay 200 qurush as an advance (*salafiyya*), and after receiving the first volume would be asked to pay another installment so as to enable production of

[77] Johns, *Nature*, 450.
[78] Ibid.
[79] Alston and others; Brewer, 139–40; Johns, *Nature*, 450–54; Curwen, 16ff; Tebbel, 158–60; Darnton, *Business of Enlightenment*, chapter 6 and passim.

the next. "Needless to say, our desire and interest in bringing the project to completion is incomparably bigger than yours," Bustānī reassured his customers in February 1866, when he had already printed some 600 pages, indicating that further progress in printing depended on additional payments.[80] Forging ahead with production, Bustānī periodically offered improved financial conditions to attract more buyers. He also set a deadline for joining the deal, after which, he noted, prices would rise markedly. "Whoever joins between now and the end of February will pay 4 Majīdī liras, provided the money had reached us by then," he announced in early January 1870; after that, the "gates of subscription will be locked" and the price will rise to five Majīdī liras "at least."[81] (The dictionary's price indeed exceeded 5 liras after its completion; in 1873, *maṭbaᶜat al-maᶜārif* put it on sale for 5.75 liras.[82]) Bustānī employed the same routine to produce and market the abridged version of this dictionary, *Quṭr al-muḥīṭ*.

While we have few details on the business facet of Bustānī's dictionary project, his tactic seems to have been a success, if one is to judge by the very completion of this ambitious project, as well as by the subsequent use of the method by many others. We have more data on another enterprise Bustānī launched sometime later, making use of the same procedure: his famous universal encyclopedia *Dāʾirat al-maᶜārif*. This was an innovative publication, grand in scope, structure, and contents, covering many matters that were discussed in Arabic writing for the first time ever (see Chapter 3). We know quite a bit about its business side, because Bustānī ran the exchanges with his subscribers publicly, through his biweekly *al-Jinān*. In it, he elaborated not only the financial and practical rules of subscription and supply but also the names of his many customers, their locations, and the changing state of their accounts. This pool of information, spread over a decade of the journal, is a treasure trove of evidence on an important section of the region's cultural life and its consumers, an unusually detailed and colorful document. Elsewhere, I have tried to show how these lists of names and places can contribute to a reconstruction of the educated classes in Palestine and Syria.[83] Here we are more interested in the technical details of the arrangement itself as a way to expedite production and circulation. "Printing large books of this type is impossible in any country except through subscription," Bustānī enlightened his clients in an early notice in *al-Jinān* and in a separate flyer

[80] *Ḥadīqat al-Akhbār*, 29 February 1866, 4.
[81] *Ḥadīqat al-Akhbār*, 7 August 1866: 3; *al-Jinān*, January 1870, inner back cover. See also June 1870, announcement facing page 352, and 1 March 1871, inner back cover.
[82] E.g., *al-Jinān*, 1 May 1873, inside front cover; 1 February 1874, inside front cover.
[83] Ayalon, "Modern Texts"; Ayalon, "Syrian Educated Elite."

he distributed, which laid out the rules.[84] To make registration easy, he even provided a form with a ready text of subscription acceptance, which customers just needed to sign and send back to him. In the first stage, potential customers were requested to notify Bustānī of their intention to buy, as "the number of copies in a publication like this would depend on the number of subscribers." Then, those who would choose to become subscribers would pay an advance of one Majīdī lira for the first volume, and once they had received it, they would keep paying one lira at a time for each upcoming volume. For his part, Bustānī undertook to try to produce a volume every year. He sought the largest possible audience, "not just a specific sector of the people but everybody: Statesmen, merchants, artisans, peasants, doctors, pharmacists, religious functionaries, scholars of every field, sailors, and so on." Bustānī promised to publish subscribers' names and the state of their accounts, "for their peace of mind" (and, perhaps, as an additional inducement to join the prestigious deal).[85] He also explained at length the great cultural value of this kind of project, and, to further promote it, he printed a sample (*mithāl*) comprising several exemplary encyclopedic entries and circulated it for free among prospective buyers.[86] On the whole, it looked like a fairly safe deal, and Bustānī's own repute as an intellectual and a teacher undoubtedly lent it additional credibility.

Bustānī lived for another eight years after the beginning of production, during which he fulfilled his part in the deal. Seven volumes came out in these eight years, so the promised annual rhythm was kept nearly to the full; four more volumes would appear thereafter at increasing intervals before the project would be discontinued. Fortunately for historians, Bustānī also kept his promise to publicize client names, long lists of which appeared in almost every issue of the journal for the first two years, and at decreasing regularity for several years thereafter. The great majority of them joined during the first two years, after which a trickle of new subscribers continued. The lists that came down to us in *al-Jinān*, a near-complete set,[87] include a total of 1,022 names of subscription applicants. Many of them changed their minds once it was time to begin paying, so the lists of

[84] *Al-Jinān*, 15 May 1874, note opposite page 329; Bustānī, *Iʿlān al-Kawthar*. I am grateful to Dagmar Glass for bringing this source to my attention.

[85] *Al-Jinān*, 15 May 1874; Bustānī, *Iʿlān al-Kawthar*, 12–14.

[86] *Al-Jinān*, 1 March 1875, inside back cover.

[87] Copies of *al-Jinān* in the collections of Princeton University library and the British Library have been examined. Both are nearly complete and largely complement each other in some cases of missing issues. Together they cover 90–95 percent of all issues. The subscribers' lists usually appeared on the inside part of the journal's cover. In some other academic libraries which possess a copy of *al-Jinān*, these covers were removed before binding.

اسماء مشتركي الكوثر تابع الاجزاء السابقة

اننا قد نشرناها بحسب تواريخ تعهدات الاشتراك واما الذين لتعهداتهم تاريخ واحد فبحسب ترتيب حروف اسمائهم الاولية

تنبيه ☆ ذكر سهوًا ان الخواجا عيسى فروجي من مشتركي بيروت وصوابهُ انهُ من مشتركي يافا

جناب الخواجه الياس هيكل	معلقة الدامور لبنان في ٣٠ ايار
جناب السيد الحاج محمد عمر فتح الله	بيروت في ٣٠ ايار
جناب الخواجه ملحم مطر صاحب اجزائية النحلة	بيروت في ٣٠ ايار
جناب الخواجه نخله كميد	بيروت في ٣٠ ايار
جناب الخواجه سليم خاشو	مرسين في ٣١ ايار
جناب الخواجه نقولا البرباري	مرسين في ٣١ ايار
جناب الخواجات قدسي اخوان	مصر القاهرة في ١ حزيران
جناب موسيو اكلير زغبي	بيروت في ١ حزيران
جناب امين افندي شقير كاتب في مجلس المحاكمة في لبنان	ارصون لبنان في ١ حزيران
جناب الخواجه انطون بشاره تيان	يافا في ١ حزيران
جناب الخواجا بشاره عرب ترجمان قنصلاتو جنرالية دولة المانيا	بيروت في ١ حزيران
جناب الخواجا جرجس افتيموس	دير القمر لبنان في ١ حزيران
جناب الخواجا جرجس نخله	بيروت في ١ حزيران
جناب خطار افندي ثابت كاتب مصارفات جبل لبنان	بيت الدين لبنان في ١ حزيران
جناب الشيخ خطار الدحداح من ماموري القلم الاجنبي في متصرفية لبنان	بيت الدين لبنان في ١ حزيران
جناب الخواجه ديمتري كحيل	مصر القاهرة في ١ حزيران
جناب روفائيل افندي اسطمبولي	بيروت في ١ حزيران
جناب الخواجه سليمان يعقوب الجاهل	دير القمر لبنان في ١ حزيران
جناب الخواجات نادر اخوان	مرسين في ١ حزيران
جناب نقولا افندي شبار	مرسين في ١ حزيران
جناب ابرهيم افندي سلوم مامور في الخزينة العامرة	بيروت في ٢ حزيران
جناب انطون افندي قصيري	بيروت في ٢ حزيران
جناب ثيودوروس افندي الياس مامور في عموم ليمانات وفنارات مصرية	الاسكندرية في ٢ حزيران
جناب الخواجا جبرائيل عبد الله خوري	اطنه في ٢ حزيران
جناب جبرائيل افندي نجار	مرسين في ٢ حزيران
جناب الخواجا حبيب صوايا	الاسكندرية في ٢ حزيران

List of subscribers for *Dā'irat al-maᶜārif* (here still called *al-kawthar*), three months after the project's announcement. *Al-Jinān*, 1 August 1874, inside front cover. Showing names from places in Lebanon, Egypt, Palestine, and southern Anatolia and the dates on which their applications were received.

actual payers are shorter than those of the original applicants, but they still comprise many hundreds of names. Unsurprisingly, the great majority of them, about two-thirds, were from places in Lebanon and Egypt, but there were also customers from Syria, Palestine, Iraq, and the Maghreb, and a handful from Europe and North America. Unsurprisingly, again, there was a dominant presence of Christians among them, a meaningful fact to which we shall return in the next chapter.

On the whole, the *Dāʾirat al-maᶜārif* project was a success story, at least during Bustānī's lifetime, as its orderly execution indicates. Bustānī managed to rally hundreds of *mushtarikūn*, sharers who funded a part of the series' production volume after volume. While the available sources do not reveal the project's financial balance sheet, the impression is that Bustānī's marketing strategy proved effective.[88] The success could be ascribed in part to his personal fame and intellectual leadership, perhaps also to a need that might have been felt by the educated for such a general encyclopedia in Arabic in a time of cultural ferment. But it was no doubt also due to Bustānī's smart management of the project. He gave it ample publicity, with persuasive elucidations of its value accompanied by attractive samples; followed production with regular reports in *al-Jinān*; publicly identified his customers (and thus formed a kind of prestigious club that people would wish to join); and put the efficient journal administration and agent system at the project's service. In principle, it was an elitist enterprise in both nature and price (and in that sense it resembled Yūsuf al-Shalfūn's "book club"). Tidily executed, it proved the usefulness of the method.

By the time *maṭbaᶜat al-maᶜārif* began to turn out volumes of *Dāʾirat al-maᶜārif*, the practice of attracting subscribers to finance book production was becoming standard. Bustānī himself used it in making other publications, not merely of his own writing. Thus, in 1873–1874, the press he owned jointly with Sarkīs announced its plan to publish al-Ḥarīrī's *Maqāmāt* by a subscription arrangement that people could "join only up to the termination of printing."[89] Other entrepreneurs likewise announced their intention to publish books and invited people to become *mushtarikūn* and to share expenses in return for alluring acquisition deals. The practice was employed in big, multivolume projects or those expensive to produce – e.g., Nakhla Qalfāṭ's six-part *Miʾa ḥikāya wa-ḥikāya*, ᶜAlī Pāshā Mubārak's four-volume *ᶜAlam al-dīn*, Zaynab Fawwāz's 552-page

[88] Bustānī also sought, and was granted, financial assistance from Khedive Ismāᶜīl and possibly also Ottoman Sultans. See Hourani, 114–15; Booth, *Classes*, 155 and note 4 on pp. 400–01.

[89] *Al-Jinān*, 1 May 1873, outside back cover; 15 January 1874, inside front cover.

large-format compendium of women's biographies, and a technically demanding Coptic–Arabic, Arabic–Coptic dictionary.[90] But it was also adopted as a way of funding more modest works. Here is an example of a notice on such a venture, published in a popular Cairo newspaper by the Egyptian writer Ḥasan Ḥusnī (al-Ṭuwayrānī):

My poetry collection (*dīwān*), entitled "the Fruits of Life" (*Thamarāt al-ḥayāt*) is now being printed in two large volumes, in the noble press of [the paper] *al-Waṭan*. It is arranged by subjects and alphabetically, so as to satisfy those with good taste. I have set a very small price for it, in order to make [its acquisition] easy for the public. I wish to notify the honorable and distinguished [customers] that three paying deadlines have been set: From the outset of rabīᶜ al-awwal to 17 jumād al-awwal, the price will be 10 francs; until 17 jumād al-thānī, 13 francs; and until 17 rajab 16 francs. After that it will be sold for 25 francs . . . We ask that the pay be [submitted] in advance.

The notice also presented a list of agents in Egypt through whom people could subscribe, and offered a discount to those purchasing a bulk of twenty copies.[91] Unable or unwilling to cover the costs of publishing his poetry, Ṭuwayrānī thought it more expedient to have prospective patrons pay for it in advance, in exchange for a reduction in its price.

Others likewise embraced the method, including those seeking to publish a single tome: A study on the history of Syria, a work on land engineering, a guidebook to daily medicine, a book on the language of plants, and so on, were offered to the public "by subscription."[92] Among them were small books, whose advance-sharing fee was as low as two francs (ca. eight qurush) per copy, or even less, by authors who had a text at hand, or just an idea for one, but no funds to publish it. The language of ads for such books often betrayed the author's absolute dependence on subscribers' support: "We trust people to help us with it" was a common formula. For instance, the author of a work on Islamic law, who offered a subscription for as little as three qurush per copy, indicated in his

90 *Al-Jinān*, 1 February 1878, inside back cover; *al-Muqtaṭaf*, August 1881, 79, and June 1882, 31; Booth, *Classes*, 31–33; *al-Hilāl*, 1 October 1894, inside front cover. For more big projects whose publishers sought to fund them by subscription, see e.g., *al-Jinān*, 1 April 1878, inside front and back covers; *Lisān al-Ḥāl*, 16 October 1878, 1; 5 December 1889, 1; *Ḥadīqat al-Akhbār*, 1 October 1885, 2; *al-Mu'ayyad*, 20 January 1900, 4; *Thamarāt al-Funūn*, 15 September 1902, 8.

91 *Al-Waṭan*, 21 April 1883, 4. The book was eventually published by the press of the same paper (1883).

92 For these examples see: *al-Ahrām*, 7 April 1877, 4; 31 December 1895, 4; *al-Bayān*, 16 December 1897, 544; *Lisān al-Ḥāl*, 26 June 1897, 4. For more examples, see: *Thamarāt al-Funūn*, 20 April 1875, 4; *al-Muqtaṭaf*, October 1878, inside back cover; August 1879, 88; February 1885, 320; October 1885, 64; *al-Ahrām*, 11 March 1880, 4; *al-Janna*, 11 February 1881, 4; 12 December 1882, 4; *al-Ṭabīb*, 31 December 1884, 400; *al-Hilāl*, 15 January 1897, 399; 1 August 1897, 920; *Lisān al-Ḥāl*, 7 October 1901, 4.

announcement that he had "full faith that my brethren, the believers, would assist me in this endeavor."[93] In such cases, printing depended on customers' sponsorship, without which the book might have remained a manuscript, or a mere idea.

The recurrence of such initiatives – many scores of them have been traced – showed subscription to have been a popular method for turning written texts into published ones. As it appeared to be a risk-free path to publication, many tried to pursue it, for the modest investment of advertising their call for subscribers in the press. Among them were obscure authors with their once-in-a-lifetime composing endeavor. It is important to bear in mind that our knowledge on this routine comes mostly from publishers' declarations of intent, which are often rich in details on the proposed deals but only rarely tell us about their actual implementation. It would therefore be foolhardy to try to assess the contribution of this procedure to Arab book publishing during the period explored here. In a cursory check, not necessarily representative, of fifty titles offered for subscription in late-nineteenth century newspaper announcements in Egypt and Lebanon, I have found that a little more than half were actually published, and copies of them have survived in libraries worldwide; for the rest, no trace has been found. This, again, is hardly indicative of any trend, certainly not in a quantitative sense. But it does seem to suggest that the method, employed as it was by so many, was a useful way to enhance publishing while also forming a consuming public that would be linked to the products during the early years of this industry, at least in a part of the cases in which it was attempted.

93 *Thamarāt al-Funūn*, 1 June 1896, 1. Similarly *al-Ahrām*, 29 January 1880, 2.

6 Reading and Readers

Imagine the Egyptian Shaykh Rifāʿa Rāfiʿ al-Ṭahṭāwī, who died in 1873, resurrected two or three decades later in his home city of Cairo. Ṭahṭāwī, a highly perceptive observer of human behavior who had spent years in other countries, was certainly a man of the world for his time and place. Still, had he been brought back to life in Cairo in, say, 1900, he would have been mystified by myriad sights and sounds unfamiliar and unimaginable in his own time. Among other phenomena, he would have been baffled by the multiplicity of bookshops, newspaper stands, and street vendors; the city streets being densely inscribed with shop signs, commercial posters, and personal notices; the ubiquity of people reading papers in cafés and elsewhere, silently and vocally; and the sight of money bills, *cartes de visite*, and tickets of various uses changing hands routinely. Since Ṭahṭāwī's passing away, written items of every form had become standard means for running public systems and for interpersonal interaction. Written messages, of course, can be useful when a significant segment of the people can make them out. And when an area that had been devoid of such signs, like Ṭahṭāwī's Cairo, becomes replete with them in a short time, we may assume a substantial shift in the reading habits of its inhabitants.

The decades around Ṭahṭāwī's passing indeed witnessed the dawn of a major change in Middle East reading, which in time would have far-reaching ramifications. The practice may have been on the rise among certain groups in Egypt, Syria, and Lebanon already prior to the nineteenth century (see Chapter 2), but now the change was markedly enhanced. An analogous transformation in reading habits had occurred during the eighteenth and early nineteenth century in parts of Western Europe and the United States, following a series of social and cultural developments: the accelerated spread of education, the expansion of publishing, and the burgeoning of various access channels. They entailed not only a swelling of the readership but also changes in reading patterns and in the read materials themselves. A reflective focusing on a limited selection of texts, often of religious-spiritual or literary nature, gave way to a lighter, more cursory browsing of writings of many types, including works of ephemeral substance that were becoming more affordable. To some historians, such wide-ranging adjustments over a few decades merited the title "revolutionary."[1]

Whether or not this last adjective is applicable to the changes of similar nature that occurred later on in the Ottoman provinces is a valid question, whose discussion, however, is best left for the book's conclusion. As we shall see, within several decades, the consumption of written Arabic texts saw a sharp upturn in scale and pace, substantial diversification in contents, and profound changes in reading modes. Many in the region were leaving behind the old notion of reading being the domain of specific groups – a convention that may have begun to crack already before the nineteenth century and was now openly replaced by a readiness to use written texts to many ends. More parts of society were coming to acknowledge the multiple benefits of exposure to writings of the new kinds. Reading would offer them a channel for getting updated on events, exchanging views with others across the community, and negotiating with the authorities. These social segments will be the focus of our discussion below. The big shift in the attitude to writing would underlie the emergence of a reading public in the Arab provinces, small at first but growing with considerable momentum after World War I.

Exploring Reading in the Middle East

If the study of book publishing and diffusion is trickier in the Middle East than it is in Europe, exploring reading – an intricate task in any society – is doubly thorny in our region, with its perennial dearth of evidence. As a human activity that is haphazardly recorded, reading is a notoriously knotty subject for historical research anywhere. Until several decades ago, the practice had not been considered to be worthy of scholarly attention. Reading had been regarded as, basically, a kind of unchanging human activity, governed by the human mind and physiology in all times and societies, a fixed variable that does not invite any special scrutiny. But once it was claimed and established that "reading has a history"[2] – that it may have been practiced in different ways in different times and places and plausibly with different effects – reading began to attract interest and grew into a distinct subfield of cultural history. Its accent, unsurprisingly, was on Western societies, for which we have by now a considerable corpus of research. Scholars have posed intriguing questions in this subfield and

[1] E.g., Eisenstein, *Printing Revolution*; Wittmann; Kaestle, "History," 52–64.
[2] Darnton, "First Steps," 155.

have devised creative methods to address them. Among other issues, they have examined the relationship between literacy, education, and reading; the size of reading publics and their sociocultural makeup; the materials read by different social sections; routines and modes of the practice; readers' reception of and reaction to what they had read; and, in turn, the impact of their reception on the authors. In grappling with these questions, historians have borrowed methods from sociologists, anthropologists, ethnographers, psychologists, and even neurologists, which have inspired them to examine evidence of kinds hitherto little known to historians. These have partly compensated for the paucity of more conventional evidence and helped reconstruct important parts of the reading experience in certain societies. Recalling Robert Darnton's "First Steps toward a History of Reading," first published in 1986, which was a call for diving into these unknown waters, one cannot fail to be impressed by the historiographical and methodological progress made in this field since then.[3]

Questions explored in works on Western reading are also relevant to the study of reading in other societies. In the Middle East, research in this field is still in its infancy, especially with regard to reading in the age of printing. We have works on private and institutional book collecting in the region – a few of them were mentioned in previous chapters – but little about their actual reading. There are also several specific studies on reading in the medieval Islamic world,[4] a few recent works on reading in the Ottoman period and the early Turkish republic[5] and another few on modern Arab societies.[6] All of these together are only beginning to scratch the surface. The main questions relating to reading in the Middle East in modern times are still awaiting a serious examination.

Only some of the many aspects of reading may be considered here, primarily those that are essential to the broad historic process probed in this book. The present chapter examines the emergence of reading publics in the Arab Middle East after the mid-nineteenth century, their size, spatial distribution, and sociocultural makeup. It also looks, more closely, at the personal experience of people who acquired the skills for independent use of written texts and set out to use them. The next chapter will look into the related phenomenon of collective vocal reading, a mode

[3] Among the most influential works in this field have been Darnton, "First Steps" (and some of his other studies); Ginzburg; Chartier, *Histoire*; Cavallo-Chartier, *History of Reading*; Saenger, *Space*; Brooks; Johns, *Nature* (esp. chapter 6: "the Physiology of Reading"). For a concise overview of the field, see Finkelstein and McCleery, *Introduction*, 101–18.

[4] Notably Berkey, *Transmission*; Hirschler; Leder; and Touati.

[5] Notably Fortna, *Learning*; a set of studies in issue 87–88 (September 1999) of *Revue des Mondes Musulmans et de la Méditerranée*; Georgeon, "Lire et écrire"; and Strauss.

[6] Holt; Baron, *Women's Awakening*; Yousef; Ayalon, *Reading Palestine* and "Modern Texts."

typical of the transition phase leading to mass reading, which markedly increased the circle of those exposed to texts. As we shall see, there was no dichotomy between the two manners of activity, but rather a continuum of situations. Other questions – for example, the contents of materials read by different groups (some aspects of which are examined in Chapter 3) and the ways in which each group was influenced by what its members read – must be left for another search.

In studies of reading in any society, the notion of literacy is usually at the hub of the discussion. This often lends ambiguity to the search, because "literacy" itself is a murky notion, a complex and multilayer concept rather than a precise one. So is its relation to reading, as well as the relation of both of them to education. Despite the extensive scholarly endeavor devoted to discussing these matters in recent years, much remains to be explained, certainly in the context of Arabic-speaking societies. Much of the vast literature on the subject deals with aspects beyond our concern here – especially when considering literacy in the broader sense of diverse competencies, way beyond reading – and there is no need for us to address it. But since literacy in its relation to reading is central to our concern, it is important that we define the intent of both as they are used here.[7]

"Literacy" implies a wide range of situations. Its loose semantic range is reflected in its lexical definition: The *OED* defines a "literate" person as one "acquainted with letters or literature; educated; instructed; learned." The semantic gamut is evidently wide. "Acquaintance with letters" indicates a variety of possible conditions, from an ability to identify letters, through reading them syllable by syllable, to composing meaningful words and sentences from them in both reading and writing. "Acquaintance with literature" and being "learned" are likewise as broad as an ocean. In addition to this elasticity, "literacy" is also a relative concept. One may be considered literate in one's own community but less so if moving to another social or intellectual environment. As recent studies have shown, the notion is also text-dependent. A person may be able to read texts of a certain type for which he or she had been trained, such as works of religious ritual, while being unable to decipher other writings– a journalistic report, for example. Or, one may be literate enough to read a press report but not quite so to approach sophisticated works of literature or scholarship, even when written in the same language. Finally, literacy could be temporary. A person who had acquired

[7] For some of the works that have informed the discussion below, see: Street (esp. chapters 4 and 5); Chartier, "Labourers"; Chartier, "Practical Impact"; Hall; Henkin; Griffiths (esp. chapter 2); Kaestle, "History"; Kaestle, "Studying"; Saenger, "Book of Hours"; Hanna, "Literacy"; Hirschler; and Yousef.

reading skills, especially in an imperfect way, and had not used them for a long time might relapse into functional illiteracy (a phenomenon familiar mainly in rural places). Literacy is thus an umbrella notion, which more often than not requires specifying adjectives to render it meaningful in a given discussion. People may be fully literate and able to read and grasp the meaning of every text, they may be fully illiterate and completely unfamiliar with any writing, or they may be at any point along the "sliding scale" (to borrow Jonathan Berkey's term)[8] between these two conditions, fixed at one point or moving along the scale.

In this study, we are interested in literacy not only as an individual capacity but also in its uses in the society at large, primarily as applied in group formats. This is a crucial point in the study of societies undergoing a transition in reading. Literacy works differently when applied in a collective mode: Groups possess mechanisms that allow them to amplify the potential of literacy held by some of their members, by making the latter share the fruits of their reading skills with others, vocally. The typical formats in which this practice takes place are sessions of collective reading, where the odd learned individual around makes the contents at hand accessible to the group by reading out the text aloud. The acquired competence of one person is thereby combined with the old routine of oral transmission to the benefit of all.[9] As in the hydraulic principle in physics, the strength of one element is multiplied to invigorate the entire system. The group's illiterate persons remain illiterate; but the community as a whole attains the desired objective of circulating the message. As a group phenomenon, then, the weight of literacy is unlike that in which it serves the individual. The value of this communal mechanism becomes especially evident in transition situations, when a largely illiterate society in a process of becoming literate is eager to get informed and employs the enhanced tool to that end. It will be examined at some length in the next chapter.

These intricacies of literacy limit the utility of relying on it in any study of reading. As a "sliding scale," the notion does not lend itself to quantitative assessments. Moreover, given the highly common routine of group reading, the rate of individual literacy loses much of its significance. Similarly, data on educational systems, especially premodern ones, are highly problematic because the competences their graduates take with them are ever varied.

Another term that requires a functional definition for our purposes is "readership." In the pages below, "readership" will be used as a two-tier notion, referring to two concentric circles of readers: an inner circle, of

[8] Berkey, *Popular Preaching*, 10.
[9] See Hirschler, 12–17.

people who were, or became, able to read independently; and an outer one, of people without such proficiency, whose access to texts was mediated by members of the former category, normally in vocal group reading. People who made up the outer circle should be regarded as a part of the consumer public, the "readership," especially of publications carrying news and their commentary. Independent readers and listening readers were thus two constituents of the readership, the former always and the latter in specific circumstances. Such a flexible, context-dependent definition best fits the Arab readership in the early decades of printing – although, admittedly, it leaves the question of size infinitely vague.

The Emergence of Arab Readership: The "Inner Circle"

In the Arab-Ottoman provinces of the early nineteenth century, people who were able to read made up a small fraction of society. Such a loose assessment is probably as specific as one can credibly offer at present for that era. Any attempt to be more precise would be speculative and impossible to verify, at least until more research had been conducted and more evidence had come to light. Historians who have propounded quantitative appraisals on that score have usually pointed to a single-digit literacy rate in the Ottoman Empire around the middle of the nineteenth century.[10] Reading and writing were traditionally practiced mostly by officials, men of religion, and a small number of intellectuals and curious people, who together formed a minor section of the society. Even if we take into account the presumed rise in book consumption before the nineteenth century suggested by historians such as Hirschler and Hanna (see Chapter 2), we may still assume that, for the vast majority of all Arabs prior to the middle of that century, reading was beyond the range of their skills, interests, and usual pursuit.

The entry of printing made a difference, first, in the reading habits of those already accustomed to it, the learned sector. Members of this group were the core of the publishers' targeted market, whose business success depended on their consumption. The market's increasing intake of printed works indeed reflected much interest on the part of old-time readers. This was especially visible with regard to journals, whose growing popularity and the lively exchanges among their subscribers mirrored the increasing role of reading in the routine of the educated. The advent of

[10] Fortna, *Learning*, 10, 20–21. Fortna quotes assessments of the empire's literate sector ranging from 2 to 10 percent, and notes the inutility of attempts to reach a more detailed evaluation.

cultural-literary societies – the Middle Eastern variant of eighteenth-century European "reading clubs" (see Chapter 4) – was another indication of this interest in the products of the printing press.

Of greater significance was the emergence of a massive Arab readership which comprised people who had not been used to reading before, namely, the popularization of the practice. The most important drive behind this historic change was the rising public need for information. The increasing demand for intelligence was a natural reaction to the rapid changes in the region's realities, which rendered the hitherto well-known environment less and less so. In many parts, mostly in the bigger cities and primarily those close to the Mediterranean, the physical surroundings were metamorphosing. State-initiated modernization projects, the construction of new urban neighborhoods and public buildings, the scheduled movement of trains and ships, the influx of foreigners, all altered the once-familiar surroundings. Take a resident of Cairo in, say, 1875: During the previous few years, he would have witnessed new urban quarters being erected, with new architecture and street lighting in the city center and suburbs; expanding roads, railroads, and telegraph lines in and around Cairo; new public institutions such as banks, a parliament house, an opera house, theaters, and a Khedivial library popping up; a long string of strangers flowing into the city, following the recent launching of the Suez Canal, and setting up businesses of every purpose; and fast increasing local colonies of foreigners that had multiplied eight-fold over the previous decade. All of these amounted to a makeover of the visible landscape.

The dazzling pace of these changes rendered the old ways of conveying news and elucidating them inadequate. As ever in times of rapid changes, these developments evoked an urgent demand for information. Beyond basic news on daily occurrences, explanations that would make sense of the broader trends were required. This necessity could now be met by the new means that came in with the many other novelties, presses and publications, especially periodical. The thirst for news and orientation, and quenching it through newspapers and journals, would play an important role in instilling the habit of obtaining knowledge from printed texts that would also be extended to books. This, in turn, would generate a motivation for receiving training in reading, something that would quickly prove to be an asset of multiple benefits.

Two other factors encouraged the emergence of Arab readership. One was the increasing presence of inexpensive printed works and of diffusion channels. These developments, examined in earlier chapters, and the expansion of reading fed each other in a circle: Low-cost books and journals attracted buyers, whose continuous multiplying in turn encouraged more publishing. Printed works were popularly adopted in response to a need; but the new kinds of knowledge they imparted and the new horizons they opened generated more appeal that further boosted reading and turned it into a habit. Once again, this was particularly so with periodicals, which, in addition to news and their elucidation also featured cultural-scientific essays and literary pieces that aroused curiosity and instilled new literary tastes. Sometimes, they appeared in serialized form, designed to elicit suspense and increase their lure. The option of active participation through exchanges with the editors and with each other was another attraction of the journals, which may well have increased their popularity.

The other factor was the expansion of education, organized and otherwise. In the nineteenth-century Ottoman Empire, as in much of contemporary Europe, public education was becoming a state concern. Where instruction, with its mainly spiritual objectives, had traditionally been the realm of religious guides, the state now marched in for the first time to assume a growing share in the responsibility for it. Both in Mehmet ᶜAlī's Egypt (and subsequently in Ismāᶜīl's) and, a little later, in the Ottoman capital and provinces, the government launched modern schooling projects as a part of its wider reforms strategy. By the time the state started building its new systems, missionary educational endeavor in Ottoman territories was already under way, competing with the government and offering attractive alternatives. So did private schools, founded by local religious communities and by several enterprising individuals. Together, these nonstate institutions outnumbered the government schools by a considerable margin.[11] State, missionary, communal, and private schools were now turning out literate graduates, at first hundreds and before too long thousands of them annually throughout the region. It is impossible to tell how many of these were fully competent potential "readers," but it is obvious that the schooling enterprises constantly and rapidly increased their numbers.

A growing urge for information, its plentiful availability in print, and the spreading of education combined to produce an increasing public of readers. Obviously, only a segment of those with a thirst for news and knowledge were at first trained to reach them independently. During this formative stage, the great majority had to obtain them through the mediation of the skillful few. The available figures regarding that smaller segment – the "inner circle" of proficient readers – are inadequate for drawing a reliable quantitative picture. But some of these data are worth quoting,

[11] Fortna, *Imperial*, chapter 2; Evered, 105–15. According to Fortna's evidence, in the province of Beirut – a locus of intensive nonstate educational activity – foreign and local communal schools around the end of the nineteenth century outnumbered state schools by a 3:1 ratio; Fortna, *Imperial*, 53.

because they give us at least a crude notion of scale. Egypt of the mid-1870s is said to have had some 140,000 students in the different schooling institutions. The great majority of these, ca. 80 percent, were rudimentary *kuttāb* pupils, who received limited training in reading, sometimes only a trifling taste of it; the rest attended the better organized government, foreign, and local private schools and apparently did take with them functional reading tools. By 1914, the overall number had risen to around 500,000 students (ca. 70 percent of them in *kuttāb*s).[12] The country's first official population census in 1897 found a total of ca. 400,000 people able to read (ca. 5.8 percent of all Egyptians), increasing to ca. 600,000 by the 1907 census and to ca. 850,000 by that of 1917.[13] These surveys were notoriously fraught with flaws of many kinds, and the data they quoted on this score most likely represented a mélange of fully literate, semi-literate, and slightly literate Egyptians in terms of their reading ability. What may responsibly be said on the basis of such loose figures is that in the early part of the period Egypt had several thousand – probably no more than 20,000 – people with good reading capability, and by its end several hundred-thousands of them. This reflects the rapid emergence of a large pool of potential book and journal consumers, regardless of their small share in the overall population. As for the other Arab provinces, available assessments are similarly tenuous. One appraisal, as sound as one can expect, notes that around 1914, about a quarter of the population of Syria (including Lebanon and Palestine) was able to read, as was some 5 percent of Iraq's, following several decades of educational activity.[14] Again, if these crude evaluations are anywhere near the mark, we may assume that several hundred thousands of all Fertile Crescent residents were functionally literate by the end of the period. By the eve of World War I, the overall reservoir of readers in the Ottoman Arab provinces (including Egypt), having multiplied several-fold since the onset of the *nahḍa*, comprised many hundreds of thousands of people with more or less functional reading skills. If a daring attempt at an appraisal is permitted, that pool could have reached close to a million, maybe even somewhat more, but apparently not as many as two million. This educated group, constantly increasing as it was, made up a promising market for the products of Arab print shops.

[12] Heyworth-Dunne, *Introduction*, 383–90, 440–41; Sāmī, 113, 118. Data quoted by Hoda Yousef (chapter 1) – ca. 161,000 students in total, in state, private communal, and missionary schools in 1913 – are in tune with the other assessments.

[13] Gouvernement Egyptien, Vol. 1, xx; Egyptian Government, *Census 1907*, 97; Egyptian Government, *Census 1917*, Vol. 2, 12–13.

[14] Issawi, *Fertile Crescent*, 30–32.

As significant as the increase in the reading public's size were changes in its spatial distribution and social makeup. For the most part, they marked a break with the past, in similarity to other places where the readership was transformed. In studying these changes, we may rely on findings that, while not very helpful in assessing readership size, are valuable in reconstructing its geographical spread and social profile. Such, for example, are readers' letters to journal editors, which often contain important clues to their locations and the social standing of their senders. Such are also extant lists of subscribers to periodicals and other publications, as well as data on newspaper agents, which are useful in putting together an approximate readers' distribution map. Looking at the scene one quickly reveals its unevenness: As one should perhaps expect in a formative phase, reading was asymmetrically distributed and limited to specific sectors of society, while other parts, the great majority, entered the circle only at a later time. Throughout much of the historic shift from pervasive illiteracy to extensive literacy, the scene was lopsided in every way.

Geographically, the largest concentrations of readers were in Lebanon and Egypt, with a thin spreading of more readers in the other provinces. The main centers everywhere were in urban locations; cities, more than the countryside, offered their residents material resources, access to education and to written and printed texts, and more free time. This was also truer of bigger towns than of smaller ones. Rural areas had far fewer readers, and they were especially rare in distant villages. These general contours of the scene, from the mid-nineteenth century onward, were reflected in newspaper-agent lists, most of whom were densely centered in Lebanese and Egyptian towns, while in other parts of the region, their presence was markedly sparser; in rural parts, it was rare.[15] This center/periphery pattern was also reflected in the distribution of readers' letters to journals, many hundreds of which were sent annually throughout the period, whose authors were predominantly residents of Lebanese and Egyptian urban locations.[16] The spatial compass of subscribers to Buṭrus Bustānī's *Dā'irat al-maᶜārif* closely tallies with the same pattern, as we have noted in the previous chapter.

Another factor affecting the Arab readership makeup was communal affiliation. In general, Middle Eastern Christians enjoyed better schooling

[15] See Chapter 5. *Al-Muqtaṭaf* and *al-Hilāl* seem to have been exceptional in that they maintained agents in small towns and even villages in Egypt.

[16] For a survey of readers' letters to journal editors, see Ayalon, "Modern Texts," 29–31. *Al-Muqtaṭaf* and *al-Hilāl* featured regular sections of readers' correspondence, indicating the readers' names and places of residence (several other journals carried similar sections more irregularly). This kind of source has obvious shortcomings, mainly the perennial uncertainty about the letters' authenticity. On the whole, however, they seem to offer at least a general notion of the readership distribution.

than Muslims and with better results. Arab Christians had high regard for education which emanated, among other things, from a faith in it as a vehicle to reducing their inferior minority status in society and from a religious belief that reading was related to self-salvation. Christians were also more receptive to missionary educational endeavors than their Muslim neighbors, who tended to view such foreigners with suspicion. Consequently, the Christian presence in Arab reading public was markedly weightier than their share in the population, just as they were prominent among writers and publishers. As has been shown in one study, reading became popular among Christians in Lebanon and Syria already in the seventeenth and eighteenth centuries, at first for religious reasons and then out of curiosity.[17] The situation was similar in other parts of the region. In turn-of-the-century Egypt, the literacy rate among Copts was more than double the rate among Muslims, according to the 1897 census.[18] The *Dā'irat al-ma*ᶜ*ārif* subscribers' lists are, again, another indicator: The great majority of the names publicized by Bustānī were unmistakably Christian – Mikhā'īl, Jirjis, Niqūlā, and the like. (One could suspect that Christians flocked to join the project because it was initiated and promoted by a coreligionist. But *Dā'irat al-ma*ᶜ*ārif*, far from being a communal publication, was a mine of universal knowledge which should have appealed to all intellectually curious people.) Christian names likewise dominated the lists of letter senders to journals, while Muslims were few. This Christian/Muslim gulf in literacy rates was of small significance in areas with communal homogeneity, e.g., Christian north Lebanon or the Muslim Egyptian Delta. It was of greater import in places with a mixed population, especially in big cities, where being educated meant clear socioeconomic and sometimes political advantages.

Two other distinctive attributes of the emerging Arab reading publics were the entry of women and the constantly increasing presence of youths. Few women and youngsters had been readers in the past. Their joining now, beyond being a typical mark of the literary transformation (a phenomenon familiar from other places as well[19]), was a development that bore some of the most far-reaching social implications of the entire process.

In Middle Eastern tradition, education and literacy had been characteristically a man's domain. Girls in learned families did get training in

[17] Heyberger.

[18] It was 15.3 percent among Copts, as against an overall 6.8 percent in the general population. Among Syrian immigrants in Egypt then the rate was 50.5 percent. See Reid, 45. Once again, such data should be regarded as indicating a general trend rather than as precise counting.

[19] For changes in this regard in nineteenth-century Europe, see Lyons.

reading, usually at home and mostly for pious purposes; we will look at some examples later on. But they were the exception to the rule, and not quite a sizeable one at that. That women had no need for such skills or for education in general was a popular conviction. If curious about written texts and eager to read them, a woman would have to face, besides the difficulties of obtaining the needed training, also her family's objection and people's frowning upon her engagement in this practice, which was typically regarded as an "ailment ... [that] brings devious ideas" to women's heads.[20] These old conventions, as well as their exceptions, were in force as the era of modern schooling was dawning. Both the authorities who built the new institutions and the parents who sent their children to be educated in them showed a preference for boys over girls as recipients of schooling. "A school for girls? What good will it do to teach the woman?" a group of young men reacted, "half amazed, half disgusted," when told of an American missionary intention to build one in Tripoli; "You had better establish a school for young men," they suggested.[21] Throughout the period examined here and long beyond it, both girls' education and female literacy, though slowly expanding, lagged behind those of boys and men, and women's share in the reading publics across the region remained small.

As reading was becoming more popular among men and modern education for (mostly urban) girls was advancing, women in modest numbers began to join the circle. This, and a set of other developments, portended a historic shift in the overall standing of Middle Eastern women, whose course and effects are beyond our concern here. The important thing for us is that, in departure from past practice, women now came to represent a distinct hue in the society's readership rainbow. Their voice, too, began to be heard through their participation in the printed public discourse across the region and in their own published books, starting in the late-1870s. Evidence of women reading and writing during the formative phase of the *nahḍa* is everywhere: in journals carrying their letters to the editors, in book and journal subscriber lists, in their own personal memoirs relating their experiences, in stories and novels some of them published, and in a host of periodical publications specifically written by and for women, from 1892 onward. Women in educated families, typically daughters of liberal-minded Arab intellectuals, led the way in this. Buṭrus al-Bustānī's daughter Alīs (Alice) and Salīm Salām's daughter ᶜAnbara, both from Beirut (a Christian and

[20] Baron, *Women's Awakening*, 80–81. The common attitude to women writing was even more unfavorable – see Yousef, chapter 3.
[21] Farah, 45, quoting a missionary archival document.

a Muslim, respectively), may be mentioned as two well-known examples of this trend. Both of them received broad education at home and in schools, and both tell us of their passion for reading (the former also published a novel, in 1891).[22] Women from the same sociocultural milieu opened literary salons in their homes that hosted prominent men of letters in learned gatherings – in Cairo, Alexandria, Damascus, and Aleppo.[23] Girls from other urban, not necessarily elite, families, whose parents sent them to get education in the emerging new schools, began to join the more refined daughters of the aristocracy in the new pursuit, in small numbers.

In her path-breaking study on the Egyptian women's press, Beth Baron documented these developments there in the late nineteenth and early twentieth century. Probing the emergence of journals by and for women as fora of printed exchanges, she portrayed women reading, writing, and calling upon members of their gender to do the same. Barred from public libraries until after World War I, Egyptian women had to make do with reading books and journals they could find in their homes. Oftentimes, they had to do so clandestinely because of relatives' unsupportive attitude. Over time, Baron showed, some of them formed a small "community of readers" around these journals, whose members corresponded with each other on matters of common concern.[24] Marilyn Booth, further exploring these changes in Egypt about the same time, similarly depicted a small but expanding circle of educated women accessing books and journals, writing for women's papers, sometimes also authoring novels or other works.[25] In Lebanon, the other *nahḍa* hub, such activities were reported earlier, starting from the mid-nineteenth century: As a study by Fruma Zachs and Sharon Halevi has shown, upon the 1858 inauguration of *Ḥadīqat al-Akhbār* in Beirut, there were already several local women among its readers.[26] There, from the very outset of the Arabic press, the female readership was deemed substantial enough to be taken into consideration by journal owners: "If we were not sure that these novels were read by a lot (*kathīrāt*) of women, we would not place them into the many issues that concern them," the editor of *al-Jinān* noted in 1873, referring

[22] For Alīs al-Bustānī, see Zachs, "Subversive Voices" (also surveying the writing activity of other women). For ʿAnbara Salām al-Khālidī's experience, see Baron, *Women's Awakening*, 85–86, and al-Jāmiʿa al-amīrikiyya fī bayrūt, *Muqābala*. Nāṣīf al-Yāzijī's daughter Warda was similarly instructed; Ziyāda, 16–17.

[23] Details in Tzoreff, 22–39; Zeidan, 41–73.

[24] Baron, *Women's Awakening*, 80–100. Also Booth, *Classes*, 136.

[25] Booth, *May Her Likes*, esp. chapter 4.

[26] Zachs and Halevi, "From *Difāʿ al-Nisā*," 617–18. Some of these women even wrote a letter to protest the paper's misogynous style, which it published in August 1858.

to original and translated literary pieces intended for a female audience and serialized in his paper.[27]

Their commercial value as customers notwithstanding, women remained a small minority among consumers, let alone makers, of the Arabic printed output up to World War I. There were apparently no more than a few hundred, at most a couple of thousand, of Arabic-reading women throughout the region at the beginning of the period and probably several thousand at its end.[28] Entering the field from a rather low point – lower literacy rates, restricted learning opportunities, and an unaccommodating social environment – women proceeded more tardily in setting a presence in the reading public. Like men, their exposure to printed materials through listening was greater than through direct access. But even with this broader circle of exposure, their share in the growth of readership remained on the whole meager at that stage. Its true significance, however, was not in its size but in being a portent of a historic change in the social status of women, which would gather momentum only at a later stage.

The other new color added to the fabric of readers was consumers of a younger age. In many ways, this was a weightier development in the expansion of reading publics than the entry of women. Targeting the society's young stratum, the new schooling projects in the region caused its reading class to expand at the bottom of the age pyramid. Consequently, youth and adolescents who were trained in schools – the likes of which had not been available to their parents – and who acquired the key to a knowledge that was in high demand came to form an increasing segment of the reading public, constantly bringing down its average age. The story of the Egyptian countryside teenager who, around 1914, became the local bookseller's "preferred client" (*zabūn mumtāz*) with special reading privileges, in contrast to the unlearned older villagers,[29] is one typical illustration of these circumstances. Obviously, not all boys and girls who attended schools came out with a passion for reading, but many of them did. While still students or as graduates of the system, youngsters displayed a zeal for books, an inclination that, perhaps unsurprisingly, was not always appreciated by the older generation.[30]

[27] Salīm al-Bustānī in *al-Jinān*, 1873, 826–27, quoted by Zachs and Halevi, "From *Difāʿ al-Nisā*," 620, and see also 618–19.

[28] Baron, *Women's Awakening*, 90–93, offers some partial assessments of readers of Egyptian women's journals during this period: between a few hundred and a couple of thousand in the first decade of the twentieth century – an assessment consonant with the above appraisal.

[29] Quṭb, 110–14. The periphery, in this case the rural area, often projects grand social changes at their sharpest. See more of Quṭb's account in the next section below.

[30] See e.g., Jurjī Zaydān's encounter with his father over the issue of buying books, in the next section of this chapter.

The reading habits of Arab boys and girls during this period are still awaiting a systematic research. Benjamin Fortna's instructive study, of Turkish youth entering the world of reading in late Ottoman and early Republican times,[31] is yet to be coupled by a similar exploration of young Arab readers. Meanwhile, what we have at hand is a set of testimonies by individual writers recalling their reading as young people, and some other contemporary references. They tell us that, beyond school texts which opened new horizons, Arab schoolchildren and graduates read stories, novels, and news reports in books and journals written for adults. We hear of youngsters (*shubbān*) in Iraq who read and even subscribed collectively for *al-Muqtaṭaf* in its early years, in the 1870s[32]; of a Damascus boy who, in the late 1880s, "started reading Arabic newspapers when [he] was 13 years old, during [his] last years in elementary school" and even subscribed to a couple of local and imported journals[33]; of a Beirut teenager around the same time who used to read books and journals in his room, as well as at work while helping his father in his restaurant kitchen[34]; and of an Egyptian youth who, as a first-year high school student in the early 1900s, used to "buy old and even new [journal] issues, despite their high price, and devour them from cover to cover."[35] We also hear of children reading their parents' books and journals at home, and of a critical observer complaining about the dearth of Arabic books fit for children, who must therefore resort to books written for adults whose "harm is greater than their gain."[36] The scope and trends of these practices are as yet too uncertain for a credible appraisal. But the rapid proliferation of reading youth is beyond question.

During the long interim between the outset of the process and the point, many decades later, when Arab literacy had become universal, school graduates also fulfilled the important role of mediating the printed knowledge to their elders and other unlearned people. We shall look at some instances of that later on. This side of the process was of great social significance. The possession of such a potent tool by a hitherto subsidiary section of the community, and the palpable edge it gave young people over their unschooled seniors, would shake old social norms and intrafamily relations.

Mostly Egyptian or Lebanese, predominantly urban, overwhelmingly masculine, typically Christian, and constantly declining in its average age – these were the main characteristics of the Arabic reading public on

[31] Fortna, *Learning*.
[32] *Al-Kitāb al-dhahabī*, 132–33.
[33] Kurd ᶜAlī, 50–55.
[34] Zaydān, *Mudhakkirāt*, 33–36. See a more detailed description below.
[35] Mūsā, *Tarbiyya*, 41.
[36] *Al-Muqtaṭaf*, 1 February 1890, 345–46. See also June 1889, 627–28; October 1893, 40–41.

the eve of World War I. Its expansion to embrace women, youth, and people from the periphery added more shades to the scene, not yet prominent at that stage but clearly identifiable. Members of these groups were becoming accustomed to ingesting daily news and insights from printed sources and to extending their intellectual and literary horizons by accessing them.

The "inner circle" of readers referred to in the title of this section seems to imply an identifiable segment of the public, whose members were connected by a shared pursuit. Did this segment make up a "community of readers"? The answer to this is equivocal. On one hand, there was an obvious unifying side to the practice of reading. Readers of Arabic everywhere were using the same devices to access knowledge of a similar kind that addressed issues of common interest. Many of them also participated actively in exchanges on such issues across the region through the new platform of periodicals. This was especially important during the early phase of the *nahḍa*, when the grand changes in the region were becoming visible and evoked similar dilemmas everywhere. Alongside the unifying side, there was also a comfortable equalizing facet to this discourse: Readers listened and responded to each other on equal footings, with no prescribed hierarchy among them.[37] This was the soil on which the local variant of the Andersonian "imagined communities" grew. On the other hand, however, members of the reading public also had their respective local, religious, sectorial, or gendered concerns, which led them to move, in addition or instead, in separate discourse circles, distinct from each other in size and focus: A Catholic Lebanese subscribing to the Jesuit *al-Bashīr* and absorbed in its missionary call was worlds apart from a Cairo woman who only read Rūza Anṭūn's *al-Sayyidāt wa'l-Banāt* with its accent on women's affairs, even though both were using the same modern device and both belonged to the same small segment, the educated part, of society. Many readers linked to local or sectorial reference groups that fit their priorities rather than to the big "community of Arab readers" with its region-wide dilemmas.

Entering a World of Reading

As already noted, the advent of Arab printing marked a major change even for those who had long been accustomed to reading: The bulky influx of writings, new contents, new styles, and new formats altered their reading habits and the role of texts in their life routine. But the truly big difference affected those who had not read in the past and

[37] Cf. Klancher, 22–26, discussing eighteenth-century England.

were now entering the circle. To them, the main novelty was in the praxis of extracting wisdom from written texts on their own through the newly acquired tools. As can be seen from the many journalistic essays of counseling for the novice and from the latter's numerous "how to" inquiries, adopting the habit was anything but smooth. Reading in its modern form necessitated acquaintance with some practical rules that had to be learned and applied. They were broadly discussed, mostly in the periodical press, both by seasoned readers and by those who recently joined them in this pursuit.

Betraying his tenderfoot state, one Muḥammad effendi Tawfīq from Bākūs (Egypt) wrote to the editors of *al-Muqtaṭaf*, in 1890, asking them to recommend "the most valuable book" for "someone who wishes to elevate his mind and extend his imagination." Another reader, Muḥammad effendi Aḥmad ᶜĀrif from Giza, was concerned with a different facet of the new practice: "Is much reading during the day harmful to the body, and how many hours at most should a person read?" Niqulā effendi al-Khūrī from Homs likewise asked whether it was "true that extensive reading in the dark could harm one's eyesight." And Shafīq effendi Saᶜdāllāh Ḥalāba from Cairo posed a slightly different version of the query: "If I read for a long time while lying down, I feel dizzy once I get up and start walking. This does not happen when I read sitting. What is the reason for that, and what is the best posture one should read in?"[38] These examples represented a widespread phenomenon. Journal editors and other writers, assuming a position of coaches for the new practitioners, addressed the queries with a distinct air of authority. The reader who asked about the "most valuable book" received a brief answer which might not have satisfied him: No single book can be labeled most valuable, and many of them fit the description. But as he was asking for a shortcut to "elevate his mind," he was offered one: encyclopedias, provided he was proficient in English or French. The editors also confirmed that reading in the dark or in dim light could harm the eyes. And the reader who had asked about dizziness after reading in bed received this learned explanation: "Obviously, much of your blood flows into your head when you read lying. Then, when you stand up the blood suddenly runs down and dizziness occurs, as in brain anemia. The best posture for reading is

[38] For these queries, see: *al-Muqtaṭaf*, 1 April 1890, 492; 1 May 1904, 452; 1 December 1904, 1097–98; 1 May 1916, 509. Similarly *al-Muqtaṭaf*, 1 August 1918, 194; 1 June 1924, 107; 1 December 1924, 577–78; *al-Hilāl*, 1 December 1896, 261. Such inquiries continued to arrive from different parts after World War I, as the dates of some of the cited references indicate, reflecting the ongoing flow of newcomers into the circle. Two terms were used interchangeably for "reading": *qirā'a* and *muṭālᶜa*; for their (often hazy) sense, see Hirschler, 13–15.

sitting upright with the head leaning a little forward and with the book in front [of you] parallel to [your] face."[39]

Such counseling to the neophyte marked the dawn of a new practice for many. But writers did not necessarily wait for queries from beginners before offering them guidance. Many took the initiative and wrote instructive pieces on aspects of reading which, they knew, would be attentively received. The monthly *al-Muqtaṭaf* carried some useful advice in its very first volume, early on in 1876, to "those with little experience in reading, in particular craftsmen." The editors proposed that they read deliberately and profoundly, so as to make sure they comprehended every detail, "even at the cost of great fatigue," since "obtaining knowledge is more tiring than obtaining money." They also extended a practical tip against forgetting the wisdom one had gotten from reading: taking written notes and retaining them, an idea many authors would later echo.[40] Subsequent issues of the journal carried scores of essays on the subject, under titles such as "beneficial reading," "a view on reading," "the proper way to read," and the like. Newcomers were congratulated on having assimilated reading, which was likened (with something of a juvenile enthusiasm) to "an adventure journey, allowing a man to see the country from one end to the other while still sitting under the roof of his own home."[41] Other journals followed suit. One did not have to "waste [one's] time in sailing across oceans and traveling to the end of the earth for months in search of news and reports [that were] obtainable in one hour of reading."[42] Newcomers were advised to use caution in selecting reading materials, so as not to waste their time on useless matters or expose themselves to harmful ideas, "like those who read just for entertainment and pastime." They should choose only serious works that would uplift their minds. How were "serious works" to be identified? One author offered a method: "If you wish to know whether the book you are holding deserves to be read, listen to your heart, your mind, and your feelings after having read a part of it. If you realize that it evokes in you noble principles and lofty emotions, then this is the book you should read."[43] Newspapers and journals, not just books, required some expertise in order to be properly absorbed. They should be read in their entirety, on a regular basis, with a critical approach, and without too much attention to the excessive praise they impart on people.[44]

[39] *Al-Muqtaṭaf*, 1 May 1904, 452; 1 December 1904, 1098; 1 June 1924, 107; *al-Hilāl*, 1 December 1896, 262.
[40] *Al-Muqtaṭaf*, 1 September 1876, 205–07.
[41] *Al-Muqtaṭaf*, 1 June 1906, 496.
[42] *Filasṭīn*, 30 September 1911, 3–4.
[43] *Al-Mawrid al-Ṣāfī*, Vol. 1, 2 (1910), 8–11.
[44] *Al-Muqtaṭaf*, 1 March 1903, 256–58.

Other practical aspects were also discussed. Veteran readers recommended taking breaks during reading sessions, in order to ponder about the read matters; to reread the same text two, three, or even four times and thus discover new facets in it each time; and to prepare written accounts of the read items so the reader could return to them and recover the impressions they had on him.[45] One writer reckoned that "working people can only rarely find free time for reading," but insisted that "it should not be too difficult to find some extra time for that, nonetheless." He proposed the following routine:

> If a person is used to getting up at six o'clock in the morning, it would do him no harm to wake up a quarter-of-an-hour earlier and engage in reading. When waiting for his food for ten minutes, he should use that time for reading. He who [really] wants it can find a whole hour for reading every day without difficulty, no matter how busy he is. Days of rest should be spent partly in reading and the other part outing. And whenever traveling or moving from one place to another, a man should have a useful book in his pocket, which he should read in the appropriate time ... However, the reader should be careful not to exhaust himself by reading or engage in it to the point of fatigue or beyond it. This is not beneficial but damaging.[46]

Such basic guidance by old-timers and their exchanges with beginners convey a spirit of a new era. The space previously occupied by few was now accessed by many. Obtaining knowledge through solitary reading was quite unlike getting together with other people to receive a message. Choosing reading materials on one's own from the ocean of printed works was equally novel, as was the need to distinguish, independently again, between truthful and fickle publications. Seasoned readers sensed that the tools the newcomers were bringing with them were inadequate for efficient reading. Basic counsel seemed in order, and was readily offered.

As ever, direct testimonies on actual reading are few. But many indirect references to the practice allow us to reconstruct a fairly meaningful picture of it. People read at home or away from it, privately and quietly or collectively and vocally. They read at home when conditions permitted, when the available space was comfortable enough and reading materials – books or journals, bought or borrowed – were at hand. This was conveniently done in the homes of the well-to-do, which had ample space, suitable lighting, and comfortable furniture, sometimes even a special reading section or a library. In the smaller and more crowded homes of others, people read as they could: by a table or on a kitchen

[45] E.g., *al-Muqtaṭaf*, 1 September 1894, 793–97; 1 August 1907, 671; 1 July 1913, 86; 1 October 1913, 349–53; 1 December 1932, 524. See also *al-Jarīda*, 25 September 1909, 2; 26 September 1909, 2; *al-Mawrid al-Ṣāfī*, Vol. 1, 2 (1910), 36–42.

[46] *Al-Muqtaṭaf*, 1 October 1913, 352.

chair, reclining or lying down (as noted in one reader's query above), sometimes sitting on the floor, and at other times by the doorway outside the house. Electric lighting was still in the future at that stage, and after sunset, homes were lit with oil lamps or, in more fortunate cases, gas light, both fatiguing to the eyes and neither fully adequate for convenient reading. People also read away from their homes, mostly newer practitioners whose homes had neither reading materials nor appropriate quarters. They read in shops, in cafés, or in the street, quietly to themselves or aloud and in groups. This was a new phenomenon, a striking mark of the cultural change which will be considered separately in the next chapter.

Retrospective memoirs by those who had made their first steps in reading during this period commonly emphasize the lure of the new pursuit and the joy it stirred in them. This was often the case with young people or schoolchildren, the vanguard of mass reading in the region. Let us look at a few examples. Yūsuf al-Ḥakīm, a child in Lādhiqiyya in the 1880s, was exposed to the new pursuit as a school student. In his memoirs, he recalled how he became attracted to it and came to "prefer reading of useful books during school breaks" to playing with his friends or any other activity. He used to read "in my small room, which was lit by a gas lamp that cast light on the desk."[47] Jurjī Zaydān, a teenager in Beirut around the same time, related how he used to read in his lamp-lit room, sitting on his bed. He was often so enamored with what he read that he went on and on for hours, sometimes through the night. He developed a passion for the world that was opened to him, so much so that he would not quit reading even when helping his father in his restaurant, standing in the kitchen among the rice and bean pots, and, "while watching them, I would open my English book and read from it." Zaydān recalled how, at the age of fifteen or sixteen, he was eager to possess a copy of *Majma^c al-baḥrayn* but could not afford its cost of four to five francs. One day, he managed to obtain a used copy of it for about half that price, something that filled him with immense joy. His father, however, was less thrilled and scolded his son for having wastefully "exchanged money for paper" – a trivial incident that highlights the generational gap then with regard to the value of books and reading.[48] In the Egyptian countryside in the early 1900s, Ṭaha Ḥusayn and his brothers would spend their summer vacation with books of all kinds, "serious and amusing, original and translated," reading during the day and much of the night and "drawing pleasure and joy from them far more than from schoolbooks." They

[47] Al-Ḥakīm, 108.
[48] Zaydān, *Mudhakkirāt*, 33–36. There are several works entitled *Majma^c al-baḥrayn*. Most likely, the young Zaydān was interested in Nāṣīf al-Yāzijī's collection of *maqāmāt* by that name, first published in 1856 and repeatedly thereafter.

would go on reading "whether the family approved of it or not" (another subtle hint to the generational gulf).[49] Around the same time, his younger fellow countryman Sayyid Quṭb used to cut on his meager money allocation and save for buying books. He collected them, until he managed to amass a "bulky library of ... twenty-five books!" which was massive enough to "fill an entire tin chest." Still a schoolchild, he became the local bookseller's best customer, and the latter's annual visits to his village became "the happiest days of the year" for him. The young Quṭb's obsession with reading and his book collection increased his local reputation, and village people predicted a glorious future for him.[50]

Women who began reading during this period likewise acknowledged their having been "passionately in love with reading, taking refuge in it."[51] Usually they had less freedom than men to choose their texts or even to engage in reading. But those whose testimonies came down to us reveal that they found ways to bypass restrictions and reach out to the reading materials they desired. History books, novels, poetry, the leading literary journals of the day, women's journals, and Qāsim Amīn's books on women emancipation are all mentioned in their accounts. ᶜAnbara Salām al-Kh ālidī, who grew up in a Muslim family in Beirut around 1900, at first had to make do with books she found at home and read them there. It was an intellectual home – ᶜAnbara's father was a member of the Ottoman parliament and her mother had her own book collection – so there was much in the house that was worth reading. Gradually the teenaged ᶜAnbara built her own collection and was permitted to buy books of her choice during a family trip to Cairo, which, she tells us, she read avidly.[52] Sometime earlier, in Egypt of the 1880s, Hudā Shaᶜrāwī had a similar experience with books. Her home education in Minyā focused on the Qur'ān, the basic text for training in reading, as well as on writing and some languages. Once she had acquired reading skills she became a curious girl:

> I began to buy books from peddlers who came to the door even though I was strictly forbidden to do so. I could not judge the quality of the book. If it was easy to read it was good. Otherwise I tossed it in the cupboard. But the books failed to satisfy me and I grew eager to read those of my father who had loved literature and had been surrounded by poets and learned men. At opportune moments I tried various keys to unlock his bookcase which stood in our lesson room, while our two companions kept watch in the corridor. One day when I finally succeeded ...

[49] Ḥusayn, part 2, 175–76.
[50] Quṭb, 110–14.
[51] Baron, *Women's Awakening*, 86, quoting ᶜAnbara Salām al-Khālidī. See also 84–88, where the stories of other reading women are discussed.
[52] Quoted in Baron, *Women's Awakening*, 85–86.

curiosity made me reach for the books. I grabbed two at random – the second volume of *al-Iqd al-Farid* (The Unique Necklace) and the *Diwan* of Abu al-Nasr (collected poems). I still have them to this day.[53]

Discovering the joys of reading by themselves, people bought, accessed, and read whatever was available, affordable, and befitting their tastes. We know a little more about the written works people purchased and possessed than of their actual reading of them. But we may assume that acquisition and possession were inspired by the buyers' sense that these works, which they could now decipher, promised to open to them exciting vistas. Writings on "heavy" subjects, such as the scholarly classics in theology, philosophy, language, and suchlike serious fields, went mostly to scholars and students, for their explorations. More modern books, both original and translated – in literature, poetry, epics, travel, or discussions of relevant social and cultural dilemmas – circulated more widely and were repeatedly mentioned in readers' accounts, from the tenth-century poetry of *al-ᶜIqd al-Farīd*, accessed by Hudā Shaᶜrāwī, to the popular ᶜAntara stories that reached Sayyid Quṭb's village, and from Qāsim Amīn to Sherlock Holmes.

An important channel of entry into the world of reading for a great many people was chapbooks, both spiritual and mundane. These seemingly trivial publications are seldom mentioned in the available accounts, but we may safely assume, though not yet prove, that they were widely circulated and read, plausibly even on a bigger scale than works of the previous kinds. That may have been so because of their cheapness and due to their usually lighter style, which was intended for mass publics. The relative ease with which such booklets were produced and purchased, and the focus of many of them on issues that mattered to the public, made them popular materials which helped instill reading habits in large sectors, probably more so than other books. To the same extent, if not more, journals and newspapers with their periodic appearance and crucial relevance played a special role in habituating Arab publics to reading at a tempo unimaginable before printing. Finally, the many other printed items that became closely interwoven into practices of daily life should be mentioned among the vehicles that initiated new readers, from holiday greeting cards to wall-affixed handbills. Designed for specific, usually utilitarian and mostly short-lived, purposes, they entailed a very different kind of reading, more hurried and practice-oriented. Such fleeting inspecting of a text might appear to have had little to do with the reflective delving into works of intellectual contents or even the lighter journals and newspapers. But it is relevant to our story

[53] Shaᶜrāwī, 39–41.

inasmuch as it represented one more form of training in reading, and conceivably a rather useful one at that.

Where people who wished to benefit from the multiplying written items of either type were yet unable to access them on their own, they fell back on the age-old convenient solution of collective reading. It will be examined in the next chapter.

7 Reading in Public

One noticeable change in popular reading habits which the entry of printing triggered was extending the practice on a big scale into the public domain, outside the privacy of one's home or the quiet of the library. Reading in public places, both silently and aloud, was not new in the Middle Eastern experience. But its extensive dimensions were, as were some social routines that came with it. By the eve of World War I, people reading in public locations were becoming a common sight in many parts of the region. It was seen mostly in urban areas but gradually also in rural ones. The practice had two main forms: individual and silent, of literate people (predominantly men) reading quietly to themselves; and collective-vocal, involving both literate and illiterate people going through a text in groups. Both forms resulted from the expanding availability of printed items and the rising public inquisitiveness about their contents. But each of the two forms had its own course and logic. They will be examined here separately for their cultural significance.

Self-Reading in Public: Café Reading

The growing ubiquity of printed texts drew people to reach out for them wherever they could be found out of the home, especially where they could be accessed free of charge. Library and public reading-room shelves were filling with new books that allured scholars, students, and other curious people; and newspapers, obtainable in public places, attracted everybody with their pertinent and practical contents.

A Khedivial Library operational report prepared in 1888, that is, nearly two decades after the library's inauguration, indicated that during the entire previous year the library had served a total of 331 users. This means six to seven readers per week on average, a rather modest pace. This rate increased in later years, reaching a total of 2,582 in 1903 and 3,331 in 1904, by another account. The last figure suggests a weekly average of roughly sixty-five users, a significant growth over the few of a decade and a half earlier.[1] Some of these visitors must have been scholars, who came to consult works in the collection as members of their ranks had done in the past. Others could be readers of a new type, students or recent graduates of the schooling systems who would be interested in more modern materials. By some testimonies that came down to us, many were visibly young people, the main category of new practitioners. Usually representing the first generation in their families to be schooled, they came from homes possessing little that they could read in them, so they had to look elsewhere to satiate their curiosity. Such, we may imagine, was the "youngster (*shāb*), no more than twenty years of age, a user or a student," who was spotted in the Cairo Khedivial Library in 1896 "with a book in his hand, absorbed in reading" and surrounded by other young men who were similarly engaged.[2] We have no similar data for other public libraries in the region. If the figures for the Khedivial Library are indicative of the general trend in library use – it is likely, but we cannot be sure of that – we may assume that public libraries represented a marginal channel of reaching to books, but were beginning during this period to serve customers who had not been among their users before, including newcomers to the world of reading.

Data concerning the activity in public reading rooms and book-lending shops are not extant. Their overall number seems to have been small at this stage, as we have seen. It stands to reason that private entrepreneurs, keen on identifying signs of public demand from which they could profit, would have opened more of them had they felt that the public interest in these institutions created a promising business potential. We may perhaps carefully assume that reading rooms and book-lending places, as well as public libraries, though offering a diverse set of avenues for accessing books, served only a small circle of Arab readers. Their limited contribution is especially noticeable when compared with the more substantial occurrence of public reading in other spaces, where the main practice was the reading not of books but of periodicals.

Unlike book reading in libraries, which had been a familiar phenomenon long before printing, the reading of periodicals in public places was a novelty. In the early years, the educated who subscribed to journals and newspapers received and read them in their homes, as a matter of course. But before long, these products, especially newspapers and light journals, came out of the home and began to be read in public sites that had not been the scene of such activity. Reading out became a popular habit

1 Rushdī, p. 5 of the Arabic text; *al-Hilāl*, 1 May 1905, 488 (quoting an unspecified account by Lord Cromer). A total of 926 books were borrowed in the latter year to be read out of the library.

2 *Al-Muqtaṭaf*, 1 October 1896, 769–70.

which entailed certain advantages over the reading of such publications in one's private quarters. Away from home, newspapers could be shared or exchanged with other readers, "rented" from the distributors, or listened to when read out loud. Out there, too, their pertinent and sometimes troubling contents could be discussed with others, something that turned their reading into a fuller experience. Public reading of journals, especially newspapers, became a routine choice all over the region. New in contents and pulse, they were also new in being commonly read in the café, in the barbershop (another routine socialization location)[3] and other shops, in the marketplace, and on the street. "People [are] eagerly reading newspapers in the street, the railway station, the houses, and shops,"[4] a German visitor to several Syrian towns in 1914 noted, and the scene was repeatedly reported in accounts from other parts of the region. The most widespread form of the practice was reading in cafés, the colorful quintessence of the new routine. It would be worth our while to examine it at some length.

That coffee and reading go together like a horse and carriage is a modern-time commonplace that has been given much attention in research and literature. As favorite public gathering spots in many cultures, starting in the early modern period, cafés offered a classic setting for circulating and debating news and gossip, scheming political action, and, of course, spending leisure time. Seats and coffee (or tea) were the two items essential for their operation; other features, such as smoking implements, table games, music, and performers of various kinds, were common but not indispensable. Similarly, written materials were not an essential ingredient of the setting, but they were often present in coffeehouses – in their European version – ever since the advent of newspapers. In seventeenth- and eighteenth-century Western Europe, cafés and publishing ventures developed in symbiosis, often adjacent to each other and relying on the same pool of eager audience. Given that juxtaposition, coffee shops may well have played a historic social role more significant than their modest image would suggest. As Adrian Johns has observed, the conjunction of print and coffee fostered "major changes in [Europe's] political and intellectual culture."[5] With the expansion of the European news press in the late seventeenth century, and especially the daily press in the eighteenth century, cafés came to serve as standard places for newspaper reading, thus becoming the habitual sites for spreading important public intelligence. Coffee and tea were effective stimulants for

[3] Sajdi, *The Barber*, 147. Sajdi calls the coffeehouse the "sibling institution to the barbershop"; Sajdi, *The Barber*, 74.
[4] Thomsen, 211.
[5] Johns, "Coffeehouses," 339 and passim. See also Johns, *Nature*, 111–13, 553–56.

reading and discussion, and coffee-shop owners made it a point to arrange a regular supply of papers as a means to lure clients. "No man," a writer in England remarked in 1829, "or no man who can read (and how few are there of those who go to coffee-shops who cannot read), thinks of calling for his cup of coffee without at the same time asking for a newspaper."[6]

In the Arabic-speaking provinces and other Ottoman parts, the café (*maqh^{an}* or more popularly *maqhā*) played a similar role as a public meeting place from the early sixteenth century onward. In urban areas, especially, it was a favorite space for social mingling, predominantly if not exclusively for men. News and views were exchanged here, future political action was plotted, and patrons were having pleasurable time smoking, playing table games, listening to storytellers, and watching assorted performers.[7] Here too, it has been shown, literary and poetic creativity was boosted and written texts were circulated already before printing.[8] Following the birth of the Arabic press, centuries after the appearance of Middle Eastern cafés, coffeehouses became standard sites for reading newspapers, individually and in groups. Here, as in Europe, their owners adopted the habit of furnishing their businesses with journals so as to meet the clients' new expectations. For the small price of a cup of coffee or tea, customers would have access to several papers in one visit or, as one observer of Egypt put it, "read the barman's paper."[9] In later years, café owners would continue to offer comparable attractions to visitors by equipping their shops with gramophones, radio, TV sets, cassette-players, and, recently, Internet.

With printed materials as common paraphernalia and newspaper reading as a typical form of pastime, coffee shops epitomized the gradual metamorphosis of the public domain. Having long served as prime institutions of public activity, along with mosques, the town or village square, the marketplace, and some other locales, they now took on a new form, adapting themselves to the changing demands. "We have opened a restaurant-and-coffeehouse," a newspaper advert in Damascus typically noted; "we have brought to it the most famous newspapers, most useful

[6] Quoted in Altick, 329. Altick, 342, reports that "London alone, by 1840, had between 1,600 and 1,800 coffeehouses. One of them attracted from 1,500 to 1,800 customers a day with a selection of forty-three copies of the dailies (half-a-dozen copies of a single paper were received) as well as several provincial and foreign papers, twenty-four magazines, four quarterlies, and eleven weeklies." See also Elliott, 139–45.

[7] The literature on Middle Eastern cafés is considerable and expanding. See, e.g., Hattox, especially chapters 7 and 8; Lane, 334–35; Marcus, 227, 231–35; Grehan, 135–46; Desmet-Grégoire and Georgeon; Kırlı; Marino; and Mikhail.

[8] Hanna, *In Praise*, 65–68, and see also Fahmy, 14 and passim.

[9] Crabitès, 1050. For a similar popular habit in Istanbul around the same time, see Emin, 132–39.

journals, and most up-to-date commercial telegrams (*tilighrāfāt*)."[10] Catering to what by then had become habitual customers' expectation, the proprietor's move mirrored the modified standards of his new business. As the public demand for newspapers grew, so did café owners' interest in making their shop a convenient reading place.

Egypt led the way, beginning around the turn of the century.[11] "No city has a more active café life than Cairo," a British visitor noted in 1911. "Even in the morning the little iron tables on the pavement are thronged. Whenever you pass a café there are numbers of tarbushes to be seen both outside and inside. A few people may be playing dice or dominoes. But the mass are reading newspapers and talking politics."[12] In a personal testimony on his childhood around the turn of the century, Egyptian writer Aḥmad Amīn related how, as a young boy, he was not exposed to newspapers because "they did not enter our [conservative] home, nor did I use to sit in a café where I could read them." But this changed when public life in the country became more excited, around 1904. "From that time on, I began to open myself to newspapers and read them. Having moved [from Cairo] to Alexandria, I would frequent the café of 'uncle Aḥmad al-Sharbatlī,' where I would read *al- Liwā'*, *al-Mu'ayyad* and *al-Muqaṭṭam*."[13] Amīn's experience embodied the novelty of this habit. For him, to begin visiting a café and read newspapers there meant leaving behind his parents' traditional routine, whereby newspapers "did not enter the home" – rigorously selective in its reading materials as it must have been – and adopting a new practice. Here is another recollection from around the same time by a compatriot, Egyptian historian ᶜAbd al-Raḥmān al-Rāfiᶜī:

> In 1904, I began to visit an old town café on Ra's al-Tīn Street, near Muḥsin Bāshā citadel [in Alexandria]. We used to go there every Friday. Its owner Ḥājj Aḥmad would serve us lemonade prepared so skillfully that it became his café's trademark. Then he would acquaint us (*yuṭliᶜunā ᶜalā*) with some of the daily newspapers in circulation at the time, including *al-Liwā'*, the paper of the leader, Muṣṭafā Kāmil. However, at that time I could not understand its ideas, or the ideas of the other papers . . . I was fifteen years old then . . .
>
> In October 1904, I entered law school [in Cairo] and it was there that I began to read newspapers in a comprehending manner. The students used to get together and . . . spend their free time and evenings in a fine café on ᶜAbdīn Street, corner of Ṣanāfīrī Street . . . named *qahwat al-ḥuqūq*, whose owner was Khawāja Andriyyā. We were impressed with the café's name and chose it as a meeting place, where we would read papers of all trends and viewpoints, most

[10] *Lisān al-ᶜArab*, Damascus, 18 November 1918, 2.
[11] Egypt's primacy will be further discussed in the next section.
[12] Fyfe, 113.
[13] Amīn, 88–90.

importantly *al-Liwā'*, *al-Mu'ayyad* and *al-Ahrām*. I thus moved from Ḥājj Aḥmad's café in Alexandria to that of Khawāja Andriyyā in Cairo. Both cafés played a great role in shaping my patriotic and political outlook.[14]

Rāfiʿī's description reveals an important facet of the practice. He came from a well-off family of scholars (his father was Mufti of Alexandria), a family that most likely owned a spacious home. Yet it was in a café, not at home, that he was first exposed to newspapers, and in another one that his "patriotic and political outlook" was later shaped by reading them. This was a typical situation: The café had by then come to be considered as the fittest place for reading and discussing newspapers, regardless of one's reading skills (or their absence) or the ability to purchase a copy. As conveyers of news and opinion that concerned all, newspapers were best read in a public place, not in the seclusion of one's home; more suitably in groups, not on one's own. Only in the café, in the company of other interested consumers, could they be absorbed to the full through reading and discussion. It was in coffee shops that collective reading aloud commonly rendered illiterate customers the great service of informing them and letting them partake in the debate. But they also attracted others who did have alternative options, like Rāfiʿī, yet chose to read their papers there. Here, the printed content was discussed by learned patrons conversing with their table partners and other readers around them. In that, newspapers were in a category unto themselves among printed publications. Only seldom do we hear about reading of more serious journals – cultural, historical, literary – in cafés, and only rarely about reading of books there (with the exception of public storytelling situations; in these, printed book copies often replaced story manuscripts or the *ḥakawātī*'s memory). Serious works that required contemplation were normally read in the quiet of one's home or in a library, as they had been in the preprinting era. Public places hosted mainly readers of newspapers and light journals.

The urban coffeehouses of the kind described by Amīn and Rāfiʿī seem to have been visited mostly by middle class, mostly educated people. They were popular and their number was rising, but they were not the only type of Arab café. Another kind, highly widespread, included institutions of an inferior quality, small places on street corners and market sites which attracted all manners of people, among them the poor and the uneducated. They often were – as a resident of Nablus around 1900 reported – "in dark and miserable corners, their straw chairs low, their tables low and filthy," and they were frequented mainly by

[14] Al-Rāfiʿī, *Mudhakkirātī*, 8–10. Ḥājj Aḥmad's café in Alexandria appears to have been that of "uncle" Aḥmad al-Sharbatlī, which Aḥmad Amīn used to frequent in the same year.

"youth, laborers, and the indigent."[15] Coffee shops of this kind were usually regarded by members of the more educated classes as debased places associated mostly with vain talk, wasteful pastime, and vulgarity.[16] Buṭrus al-Bustānī, advertising Khalīl Sarkīs's new library and reading room in 1876, added to it a note of his own describing the place as the cultural inverse of cafés. Go visit it, he urged his readers, for "it is better than getting together in cafés for a useless killing of time."[17] Two decades later, Jurjī Zaydān was more blatant when responding in his journal to a reader's query: "Staying in cafés for many hours day after day degrades the zeal of men and prevents them from focusing on their work. It is especially harmful for the young, who are on the verge of starting their working career."[18]

Such coffee shops, which to the refined Bustānī and Zaydān (and apparently to Aḥmad Amīn's conservative parents as well) implied excessive indulgence rather than more serious pursuits, were not places of typical public reading. Yet, the practice did seem to have taken place there too on a modest scale, at least in its collective form that would be discussed below. Such was also the case with cafés of a third type, more elitist and elegant than the ones serving the middle class, which had existed in the region both before and during the nineteenth century, a small number of exclusive places designed for the region's social elite. The extant evidence suggests that café reading of newspapers, and to some extent of journals, was practiced most commonly in institutions of the middle kind, those between the abject and the refined, mostly by members of the middle classes and the newly educated. They, like Aḥmad Amīn, let the cafés they regularly visited, and the papers they read there mold their worldview.

Commencing on a big scale in Egypt, café reading spread to other places where newspapers appeared after the fall of the Ḥamīdian censorship dam and became highly popular most everywhere after World War I. By then they had come to resemble the early nineteenth-century routine in London. The Arab *maqhā* as a reading location had a parallel in the

[15] Darwaza, 107, 114–15.

[16] Mikhail, 142–43 and passim; Sajdi, *The Barber*, 74–76.

[17] *Al-Jinān*, 29 February 1876, outside-back cover. Bustānī added this comment to an announcement by Khalīl Sarkīs.

[18] *Al-Hilāl*, 15 October 1897, 137–38. Zaydān also asserted:

> the opportunity given to young people to find work is short and precious, no longer than fifteen years, namely, between the ages of 20 and 35. This is the best, most valuable and most productive part of one's life. Why waste it sitting in cafés, drinking beer and playing backgammon and checkers? ... Moreover, these places are full of games to which one might become addicted, and then one's entire life might be wasted. This is a great disaster indeed.

For a similar depiction of cafés as places of "waste, idleness and stupidity," see *al-Karmil*, 4 October 1922, quoted in Naṣṣār, 15–16.

Turkish-speaking parts of the empire, beginning in the late nineteenth century (and still running in the early twenty-first, under the same name): the *kıraathane*, literally "reading house," a café-cum-reading room where coffee or tea and newspaper reading likewise complemented each other.[19] Newspaper reading in cafés was the archetypical mode of the new Arab reading experience, both when performed in silence and, still more so, when taking place as a vocal event, as we shall now see.

Collective Reading Aloud

Attaining universal literacy in the Arabic-speaking countries was a process that continued for many decades beyond the period examined here; in some places, for a century or more. Progress in education, we shall recall, was one of three factors mentioned above as responsible for the spread of reading, alongside public appetite for news and the ready availability of information in print (see previous chapter). Each of these evolved at its own pace. The public craving for news and the production of printed information rose fast; the advancement of education required more time and affected limited sections of the community in its early stage. This variance in stride spelled a gulf between people's public thirst for knowledge and their ability to quench it independently. Such a gulf was inevitable wherever both publishing and organized education began to grow at the same time. The solutions for this provisional difficulty in the Middle East resembled those devised in other places and were likewise based on an intuitive principle: collective consumption.

Group consumption of printed publications took on several forms. Among them were some of the mechanisms already considered above, which were based on collective acquisition and individual use, that is, buying a stock of books or journals jointly and reading them solitarily, for a fee. Libraries of scientific or literary association operated on this principle, their book collections being assembled through expense sharing and then put at their members' disposal to read and borrow. A similar mode of collective consumption was through forming up ad hoc groups to purchase a joint subscription for a periodical or for a book published by subscription, and sharing both the expenses and the use. This method had been common elsewhere and was reported in early nineteenth-century England and Canada, among other places.[20] In the Arab

[19] See François Georgeon's article in Desmet-Grégoire and Georgeon, 39–78.

[20] Altick, 323, describes "newspaper societies" in England of the early nineteenth century that were made up of families that grouped together to purchase newspaper subscriptions collectively. No fewer than 5,000 such "clubs" were reported there in the 1820s, according to one source, which together served some 50,000 families. See also Wiseman, 36:

provinces we hear of it occasionally, in Baghdad, Damascus, Sidon, and elsewhere.[21] Thus in al-Maḥalla al-Kubrā (Egypt), a group of twenty Egyptians teamed up in 1873 to purchase a twenty-franc subscription to the weekly *al-Kawkab al-Sharqī*, each paying one franc:

> They would wait the train every Friday as one would await the holiday moon. When the train arrived and mail was distributed, the literate one among them would stand [in front of] the post office, with the rest of the subscribers forming a long line behind him. One of them, at the farthest point, would then ask, shouting at the top of his voice: "Has the *Kawkab* arrived?"[22]

A different form of "collective" use, with multiple readers accessing the same text without purchasing it, was the "borrowing" of newspapers from their distributors for a fraction of the paper's price. In this practice, already mentioned above, a single copy changed many hands and eyes. Known in Europe before being adopted in the Middle East,[23] the routine obviously undermined the owner's profit but benefited both the lending distributor and his borrowing clients. It appeared in the region very early on: Already in 1876, a Beirut newspaper complained of the "*istiᶜāra* (borrowing/lending) of newspapers for reading them; the disgrace in such [acts] is all too obvious." Similarly, Iraqi papers sometime later carried front-page notices denouncing the habit: "Damn he who rents a paper from the distributor!" thereby suggesting that the practice was widespread.[24] In this, and in the other methods noted here, sharing was in purchasing, not in reading: Joint acquisition facilitated individual reading.

More popular, and far more significant as a social phenomenon, was the act of actual reading in groups. A time-honored ritual, it was carried into the age of printing as a useful way to enhance the spread of essential knowledge. To be sure, this was not a marginal conduit of access to texts. In all likelihood, during the early period we are examining here, printed

"Each issue would be delivered to the person closest to the main delivery route, who would read it first and then pass it to the next member of the 'club'."

21 *Al-Kitāb al-dhahabī*, 132; *al-ᶜIrfān*, 5 February 1909, 137; *Lisān al-ᶜArab* (Damascus), 21 October 1918, 4.

22 Ṭarrāzī, *Ta'rīkh al-ṣiḥāfa*, Vol. 3, 49–50.

23 Altick quotes many examples of such "hiring-out" of newspapers in England of the late eighteenth and early nineteenth century, which he depicts as "widely practiced": "A London newsman might make seventy of eighty lendings of the morning's *Time* in a day, at a penny an hour, after which he would post the used copies to subscribers in the country who paid him 3*d*. for a copy mailed the day of publication or 2*d*. for one mailed the day following." Altick, 323.

24 *Thamarāt al-Funūn*, 3 March 1876, 1; Iraqi journals from the early twentieth century, quoted in Abū al-Saᶜd, 150–51.

information reached many more people in the region through such mediated channels than through direct reading.

Vocal reading of written texts in groups had been a habit in many societies both prior to and following the introduction of printing. Here is Natalie Zemon Davis on one facet of this routine, taken from her oft-quoted pioneering study of print and popular reading in sixteenth-century France:

> The important social institution for this [practice] was the *veillée*, an evening gathering within the village community held especially during the winter months from All Saints' Day to Ash Wednesday. Here tools were mended by candlelight, thread was spun, the unmarried flirted, people sang, and some man or woman told stories – of Mélusine, that wondrous woman-serpent with her violent husband and sons; of the girl who escaped from incest to the king's palace in a she-donkey's hide; of Renard and other adventuresome animals. Then, if one of the men were literate and owned books, he might read aloud . . .
>
> *Reading* aloud? We might better say "translating," since the reader was inevitably turning the French of his printed text into a dialect his listeners could understand. And we might well add "editing."

In urban areas, likewise, books were "shared in reading groups which, as in the countryside, brought the literate and illiterate together."[25]

One written copy would enlighten a family, a street-corner crowd, and sometimes a whole village or urban community. The necessary elements of the event included a piece of written or printed text, at least one learned person with a reading ability, and an eager audience accustomed to receiving contents in a mediated aural way. Reports on this routine are recorded all over Europe and North America, at least from the sixteenth century (they were certainly much older than that) until well into the nineteenth, and we also hear of the practice in China, Central Asia, Latin America, and elsewhere. The scriptures and other religious texts, folk legends and literary works, government announcements, news bulletins, and, later, newspapers were all read collectively. It was done in the intimacy of home and in the public domain – in workplaces, markets and shops, taverns, cafés, and literary salons – involving all social classes and all trades.[26] Although schooling increased the number of people able to read, and the entry of printing infinitely increased the choice of affordable texts, the public habit of group reading aloud was slow to disappear. Rather, it persisted for a long time despite the expansion of quiet private reading, as a complement to it. For one thing, the long-winded spread of

[25] Davis, 201–2, 213.

[26] Chartier, "Practical Impact," 135–38; Chartier, "Leisure," 103–18; Henri-Jean Martin, 331–32; Altick, 35, 39, 250, 325, 330; Lyons, 340–44; Hall, 100, 104, 166–67; McLaren, esp. 167–73; Khalid, 197; Manguel, 109–23.

popular literacy, especially before universal education, left large sectors of the society everywhere out of the private-reading scene and in need of reading mediators. For another, the prices of books and even newspapers remained beyond reach for many. And there was another important reason why the old custom was not soon abandoned, even by those who could read and buy their own copies. More than just transmitting contents and messages, group reading had some other worthy advantages. It allowed listeners to ascertain that the text and its practical significance were fully understood, something that was not always obvious in individual reading; and it facilitated the exchange of thoughts and sharing of sentiments about the read material with other members of the crowd. Those assembled to listen could be utterly illiterate, semi-literate, and even fully literate people, who would receive the text with its many shades more comfortably through the ears than through the eyes. All stood to gain from the added value of group reading, which often turned the reading into a social (on occasion political) happening. Only gradually, and seldom before the nineteenth century, did collective reading fully give way to norms of solitary reading, which became prevalent in most societies except in some specific kinds of ceremonial events.

Arabic-speaking societies were used to receiving messages of many kinds vocally and in groups, including those that originated in written texts. In mosques, the Imam and *khaṭīb* regularly read out the contents of holy writings, or government notices, to attentive audiences. Shaykhs in *kuttāb*s and *madrasa*s read to their students or to followers who came to get an *ijāza* (license to serve as qualified transmitters of the text), using a written copy or reciting from their memory. The town or village announcer (*munādī*), usually a man with a thunderous voice, would read out official or other announcements to crowds that would gather around him when he called for their attention. And the storyteller (*ḥakawātī, rāwī*), an old and respected social calling, would entertain his audience by reading and performing legends and tales, with or without a written copy at hand. A few literate mediators thus played a key role in the different practices. In all of these events, the literacy level of attendees was irrelevant: The added value of sharing the text communally was as important in drawing many people into the gathering as was the illiteracy of many others. Texts were often composed in a style and rhythm that would make them fit for vocal reading: Whether epic stories or chronicles, they incorporated exclamation expressions, rhymed prose (*sajʿ*), or sections in a popular spoken-idiom register, revealing their being meant for oral performance.[27]

[27] Sajdi, *The Barber*, 158–62. For a similar practice in Europe, see Chartier, "Labourers," 50, 55.

When printing inundated the area with its products, society, though largely uneducated and poor, was ready to receive them with a tool of proven efficacy. While most community members were illiterate, the community as a unit had a "collective literacy" apparatus at hand, resting on the skills of few and sustained by centuries of operative experience. The community intuitively fell back on the accustomed oral-aural routine of transmitting messages of every kind, counting on its literate mediators to convey and elucidate the new contents – at least the most urgent parts – to those who lacked the required training. Relying on learned mediators proved an expedient solution when the hunger for knowledge surpassed the ability to reach it independently.

Before looking at some instances of the practice itself, one other factor that had a significant effect on it should be noted. The written language during the formative era of Arabic printing was marked by a structural problem that weighed down on its reception. It was a two-tier problem. One part of it was diglossia, the historic gap between the written or literary language (*fuṣḥā*), with its colorful and multilayer inventory, and the spoken vernacular (*ᶜāmīyya*), with its numerous regional and ethnic dialects. This gap was at times wide enough to render a written text all but incomprehensible to speakers of an Arabic dialect who had not been taught to read. The second tier of the problem comprised an additional difficulty that was superimposed on the first following the nineteenth-century Arab encounter with a world of foreign ideas and concepts. The contacts with new cultures and peoples exposed Arabic-speaking societies to new notions their language had not been equipped to express. Discussing the working of the British Parliament, reporting an elections campaign in the United States or describing the French Revolution required a semantic repertoire which at first did not exist in Arabic. (Needless to say, the problem was two-sided: Speakers of Western languages faced similar challenges when trying to describe and discuss Middle Eastern cultural, religious, social, or political ideas.) Already during the first half of the nineteenth century, the encounter initiated a process of linguistic adjustment, with many new expressions being added to the Arabic lexicon after an intricate process of verbal experimentations. These terminological trials – especially the bewildering application of terms with local associations to alien notions – rendered the written language of that time loose and sometimes ambiguous. Eventually Arabic adapted itself to the new needs, devising solutions that were often elegant and always serviceable. But during the decades after the entry of printing into the Middle East, this dual handicap of Arabic problem, especially the ongoing changes in its expressive capacity, made the reading of modern texts in that language a bigger challenge than before, or after. As in the above-quoted example from Natalie Zemon Davis, which noted that reading to a public entailed as well "translation" and "editing," in the Middle East too there was ever a need for interpretation by rephrasing the read text to listeners unaccustomed to the modernized vocabulary. This need redoubled the popular necessity for a collective transmission, guided by one who was better qualified than the others, and markedly increased its utility.

The practice started in the home, where the educated, typically of the younger generation, read aloud to the others, as in Davis's sixteenth-century France. It was then applied outside, in public places. The society resorted to these tools for circulating those texts that were of immediate relevance, above all the news of the day. The method of enlightening large audiences through vocal reading was fitter for discussing such matters than it was for heavy works of scholarship or complex socio-cultural dilemmas; a group reading setting would be too distracting for works requiring a serious reflection. The collective mode was suitable for the light stuff: newspapers, opinion and satirical journals, handbills, and proclamations. It was also fit for stories and legends designed to entertain. When texts that had been thus delivered before printing – stories from the "Thousand and One Nights" for example, or ᶜAntara eposes – appeared in print, the old practice of public reading continued unchanged.

Let us look at a few examples. In 1880–1881, written proclamations denouncing Sultan ᶜAbdülhamid's tyranny were clandestinely circulated in towns of Lebanon and Syria. Fāris Nimr, reportedly one of the "youth conspirators" who were involved in that activity in Beirut, later related how he and his friends,

> having drafted the text of an appeal . . . would spend long nightly vigils making out innumerable copies of it in disguised handwriting. Then at an agreed hour at dead of night, the younger members would go out with pots of glue in their pockets, and stick as many placards as they found time for on the walls of the city. In the morning, a crowd will collect around each poster while someone would read it out aloud, until the police would come.[28]

George Antonius, who quoted Nimr, saw no need to elaborate on the manner the handbills were transmitted to the public, except flatly noting that they were mediated vocally by the odd literate man around. An explanation was not needed: This was still the default mode of spreading

[28] Antonius, 80, quoting Fāris Nimr who is said to have taken part in this activity. Nimr, later a leading journalist and owner of both *al-Muqtaṭaf* and *al-Muqaṭṭam*, was Antonius's father-in-law. Abd al-Latif Tibawi raises doubts regarding his participation in this activity; Tibawi, *Arabic and Islamic Themes*, 309.

written information even when Antonius wrote his book, in the 1930s, let alone back in the 1880s. Such proclamations in public places were not a complete novelty in the region, nor were they a very common means of communication until around the end of the century.[29] When they were used, by the government or by its subjects (or opponents), those who posted them expected their contents to be publicly disseminated through the mediation of the few who could read, who were thus fulfilling a role akin to the *munādī*'s. This was so with other kinds of texts designed for mass consumption. When Arabic newspapers began to appear in the region, the only way they could become means of mass communication was through such communal vocal reading. Group consumption of newspaper typified the early decades of the Arab *nahḍa* in many places and remained a habit that would last well into the second half of the twentieth century.

Much of the evidence on the practice in the early period comes from Egypt. It was there that group reading began and continued for a few decades before spreading to other provinces. There were several reasons for that. Until 1908, newspapers were scarce in the provinces beyond Egypt and Lebanon. Copies of Egyptian and Lebanese journals that reached other places came in small numbers and usually went straight to subscribers' homes and were read there. Lebanon itself, where papers did appear and circulate, was – along with the rest of the Fertile Crescent – under the grip of a suspicious government that was hounding the private press and spying on its readers in the marketplace and cafés. This apparently discouraged the handing of newspapers and discussing their contents in the open.[30] By contrast, in Egypt, with its freer atmosphere under less rigid rulers and especially under British rule (1882 onward), newspapers and journals were read unrestricted, individually and in groups. In addition, an apparent disparity between Egyptian and Lebanese sociocultural norms might have also accounted for this variance (this assumption is, admittedly, easier to suggest than to prove): For Lebanese, perhaps more than for Egyptians, learnedness was an

[29] In the nineteenth century, the use of Arabic written proclamations was rather infrequent. Among the better-known instances are Buṭrus al-Bustānī's *Nafīr Sūriyā*; the Egyptian Khedive Tawfīq anti-ᶜUrābī proclamations (*manshūrāt*) during the latter's revolt; and, more intensively, handbills distributed by groups acting in opposition to Sultan ᶜAbdülhamid, on the eve of the Young Turk Revolution and subsequently. See al-Rāfiᶜī, *al-Thawra*, 366, 368, 370, 373, 385; Tauber, *The Emergence*, 238–41, and Chapter 3.

[30] Sehnaoui, 163–78. A somewhat aristocratic café in Beirut is said to have featured French journals already in 1832. But otherwise, in the detailed depiction of café routine in that city until the end of the century – drinking coffee and lemonade, smoking, storytelling, theater, music, performances of various kinds, and more – reading is not mentioned. Similarly, Qāsimī, Vol. 2, 367–68 – a detailed description of café life in Damascus around 1900, with no mention of reading or papers.

important determinant of social status, something that would make the uneducated less prone to expose publicly their dependence on reading mediators. (In the words of my mentor, the late Professor Charles Issawi – who had an unusually keen eye for human conditions and a close familiarity with both societies – a Lebanese would be "too vain to show he cannot read by himself.")[31] Be that as it may, the extant evidence suggests that Egypt was the first and most fertile ground for group reading in public, a habit that would later spread to other places in the region.

Egyptian and foreign observers in the late nineteenth century testified that the sight of "servants, donkey rearers, and others who cannot read gathering around one who reads while they listen" was highly common.[32] People were especially eager to hear the news of the day, just as they were attracted to satirical journals. "If you walked by a workshop, a low-class café or a carriage/transportation stop, you inevitably see someone surrounded by a crowd, and reading aloud from one or more of these newspapers. The listeners often laugh out-loud and uncontrollably pound the floor with their feet."[33] Foreign visitors to the region were struck by this habit, which by then had been long forgotten in their home countries and thus represented a curiosity worth reporting. It seemed to imply that "Arabs are inordinately proud of their voices." It often happens, an American observer noted, that "some Demosthenes is found reading to a group of myopic satellites who should buy their own copy of the paper."[34]

One of these accounts, by a Cairo resident around the turn of the century, described the common pattern of people gathering around "a man or a boy" who would read to them the local newspaper, or European ones in translation. One day, the observer related, he saw "a boy in a greengrocer's shop, with an Arabic newspaper in his hands. In front of the shop a large gathering of rabble crowded around the boy while he was reading the text to them."[35] The scene highlighted an important aspect of this routine: youth reading to the elders. This was common most everywhere. As we have seen, the spread of literacy through schooling, which rendered the overall readership constantly younger, also resulted in a decline in the age of mediators, while the sector that was dependent on their mediation was getting older (and in the long run dwindling).

[31] Issawi confirmed the impression that collective reading in public was much more common in Egypt than in Lebanon. He suggested that Egyptians "would be more easy-going about such matters." Talk with Charles Issawi, Princeton University, summer 1992.

[32] *Al-Hilāl*, 1 October 1897, 131: "The streets of Cairo and other towns of our country are full of this."

[33] Fahmy, 35, quoting Shārūbīm, Vol. 5, book 1, part 2, 660.

[34] Crabitès, 1050. Similarly Rae, 214.

[35] Shārūbīm, Vol. 4, 258–59.

In the initial phase of this long-term process, schoolchildren and school graduates played a key role in helping their society enter the world of reading via the collective channel.

In the family, younger members became the link to the written world outside. Niqūlā Khūrī, a child in Birzeit (Palestine) in the 1890s, recalled: "I acquired fluency in reading thanks to my father, who used to wake me up every day at dawn, take me by the hand to the church, and make me read for him the prayers, instructions, letters, and everything that needed to be taken care of." Muḥammad ᶜIzzat Darwaza, who grew up in Nablus around the same time, related how, "when spending an evening [in our place], my grandfather, his sisters, and his older cousins would ask me to read stories and books for them." And Elizabeth Cooper, a foreign visitor to Egypt in the early 1910s, described a young girl who was sent to school in the early twentieth century and noted that she was "the only member of the family who can read the evening paper." Thus, she related, "the father and mother and grandmother gather around her and listen with eagerness and astonishment to her marvelous tales, shaking their heads and perhaps murmuring, 'Is it possible that this is my daughter?'" Cooper commented that, as "a few of the women of the older day can read – the daughter and the grand-daughters can read to them the news of the world."[36] More testimonies of this kind reveal the prevalence of the custom, both at home and in public places. The reliance on this effective expedient for responding to the needs would continue for a long time. Many years later, in Syria of the late 1930s, when national news was a hot commodity, "newspaper hawkers (*al-bāᶜa al-mutajawwilūn*) would stop schoolchildren on their way to school and ask them to read out the paper for them."[37]

Adapted to the new needs, the old mechanism of sharing knowledge in groups permitted Arabic-speaking societies to distribute printed information and discuss it at the community's remotest corners. It was a useful bypass around the hurdles of pervasive illiteracy, penury, and the difficulties posed by rapid changes in the Arabic lexicon. The collective mode was at its utmost utility when applied in spreading the kind of knowledge that was of immediate relevance: news. As such, its use would be enhanced in times of dramatic events, such as wars.[38] It is important to note that this mediated format also had its limitations, most obviously the listeners' dependence on the reader's comprehension and selection.

[36] For these examples, see Niqūlā al-Khūrī, 64; Darwaza, 160; Cooper, 167, 241.

[37] Arsūzī, 296. For similar instances see: Abū Ḥannā, 70; Jabrā, 174–77; ᶜAbbās, 60; Dabbāgh, 117; ᶜAbd al-Raḥīm, 45–46; Zuᶜbī, 7.

[38] See e.g., the description of people gathering in a Hijaz marketplace during the 1911 Ottoman-Italian war and listening to the reading of news-agency reports on the battles – *al-Bilād al-Saᶜūdiyya* (Mecca), 30 January 1947, 3.

If skilled and knowledgeable, a mediator would offer a good solution to the gap between the flow of writings and the public inability to consume them. A perfect solution would be the complete eliminating of that gap, through schooling.

If collective reading in the Middle East was an advantageous response to the flood of publications, to historians of printing and reading, it poses a serious difficulty: It complicates their ability to assess the public consumption of the texts for its extent and quality and to reconstruct the social profile of the readership. Group-reading sessions, often spontaneous, hardly ever left a record of any kind. The magnifying potential of group reading and its extensive use would render futile any attempt to calculate the scope of circulation, let alone its impact. When a single copy of a newspaper or handbill – or, less often, a serious journal or book – is reached by an unspecified crowd through vocal mediation, sometimes on multiple occasions, the historian can more easily describe the phenomenon than assess its scope and effect. At best, we may responsibly postulate that the actual public exposure to a given text was many folds bigger than the number of its distributed copies (assuming we have a notion of that last figure) when some of them were read in groups. How many folds? Usually, there is no telling.

Conclusion

Many of the changes examined in this book are embodied, if we will, in one charming account: that of Sayyid Quṭb, telling about his youth as a book-loving boy in the Egyptian countryside of the early twentieth century (see Chapters 4 and 6). A roving bookseller making his living by vending and lending printed works in the villages, children as a prominent category of book-consumers, a teenager building his own book collection which buys him a local repute, ᶜAntara epics in print, and Sherlock Holmes in Arabic – all of these would have been inconceivable just several decades earlier. They reflected the change in the attitude of Arab society to written texts following the entry of printing into the region and the inception of a far-reaching cultural transformation. During the formative period explored here, tens of thousands of Arabic books and booklets were printed in the Middle East in millions of copies, a periodical and daily press was born and prospered, multiple channels were formed to route the mounting wave of publications to near and far places, and large publics of habituated readers emerged. These processes and practices, and the men and women engaged in them, together represented the foundations of the *nahḍa* edifice, known to us mostly through the written works of its luminaries.

The introduction of mass printing into the Middle East, like the entry of firearms, railways, or postal services, proved to be irreversible. World War I, a major watershed in the region's political history, did not mark an important turning point in that process of change or, more broadly, in the area's cultural development. Rather, it was an interval after which the momentum resumed with double vigor, an interval conspicuous enough to serve as a convenient cutting point of our story but little more than that. Contending with initial difficulties and overcoming many obstacles, the process continued to expand after the war. Developments which hitherto had taken place mostly in Egypt and Lebanon spread thereafter to other parts, in similar ways and with comparable results. Egypt and Lebanon would remain regional springs of literary resources for the entire area for many decades to come. But presses, newspapers, and bookshops would also burgeon in Syria, Palestine, Iraq, Transjordan, and parts of the Arabian Peninsula, as would schooling systems and reading publics. The seeds sown during the *nahḍa* began to sprout most everywhere already before World War I, and would later yield a colorful garden.

These developments were an integral part of the broad changes of the last Ottoman century, affecting and being affected by them. The advent of printing, diffusion systems, and readership rested on progress in transportation and postal services, the upgrading of urban infrastructures, and educational reforms, and were influenced by economic changes and administrative adjustments, the expansion of foreign presence, and historic shifts such as the substantial Lebanese emigration to Egypt. At the same time, these developments had their profound effect on the wider changes of the time. They modified the operation of social, political, and cultural systems; altered modes of interpersonal relations; and converted people's everyday life in endless ways. Such had been the consequences of the entry of printing in Europe earlier on, but in the Middle East, the changes were more striking, as they took less time to unfold. The rapid pace with which the region embraced tools and practices that had taken long to develop in Europe had an impact on its societies evocative of shock treatment. Its wide-ranging results are a matter for another study, or studies. Here we may only briefly point to some of them, by way of concluding the book.

A major result of mass printing was the transformation of the public role of written texts, from a realm of small groups into a public sphere reachable by all. Spiritual and mundane knowledge, much of it enclosed in state files and old books, had previously been reachable primarily by political, bureaucratic, and pious leaders. Routes to some of that wisdom had existed, and sometimes been accessed by others; but on the whole, a distinction between those who employed the instruments of knowledge, and hence power, and the rest of society had typified the public system. It had been generally accepted and seldom contested. Printing opened the door to a change in this structure, by allowing not only easy popular admission to knowledge but also its large-scale reproduction and dissemination by anyone. The musical instruments used by the band on the stage became available to all members of the audience, who could employ them as they pleased. Anyone with small resources could obtain one of those tools and air his melody to others in the hall; if enterprising, one could even become a builder of such instruments and let them be heard by many, near and far. In other words, anyone could now print a proclamation or a pamphlet, skinny or substantial, in multiple copies and spread them around with a potentially robust effect.

With the growing ease of issuing books, newspapers, and handbills, and with more and more people able to read them, the old structure of political and spiritual authority in Arab societies began to crack. Whether or not sultans and *ᶜulamā'* had once worried about the danger printing posed to their standing, such a worry would have been justified: Newspapers came to compete with the official *munādī* and the pulpit and in some ways even replaced them. Political and religious leaders whose authority was being challenged tried to check that trend: the state with strong-arm measures and religious guides by embracing the modern tools and applying them in counteroffensive. Both the state and the religious leadership had to resort to new methods in order to retain their long-acknowledged standing in the new game; both scored merely partial success, something that had become quite evident by 1914. Printing facilitated the circulation of ideas that led to organized political action of new kinds in the region. There can be no doubting its major role in generating the processes which gave birth to the Egyptian nationalist movement around the turn of the century, for example, or to the Young Turk Revolution of 1908.

The impact of printing on social relations was equally profound. With access to written knowledge becoming more vital than ever before, acquisition of the key to it became a major criterion for social status, alongside traditional criteria such as descent, wealth, or old age. The new rules modified relations within the family as well: As younger members were taught to obtain intelligence that was beyond reach to their illiterate elders, the traditional locus of authority in the family was beginning to shake. Similarly, when women began to read, lured by available books and journals at home and the bold call for emancipation by members of their gender, this began to challenge their old unprivileged place in the family and society. Finally, the introduction of many printed items of various uses, from legal notices to commercial receipts, modified people's daily routine in many small ways and gradually made them dependent on it for practical and mental navigation in the shifting surroundings. Typical of urban more than of rural areas at first, these developments would gradually affect the entire society.

All of these changes were long-term processes. Most of them would become visible only at a later time, and in some areas – for instance, the reform in the standing of women – the process is still under way. But printing, publishing, and the new systems for training consumers started off these changes during the phase explored here, and their repercussions could be observed already at that early stage. Many other factors that were at play beside the entry of printing played an equal or bigger role in generating these changes. The impact of those other factors on individual and group functioning was in itself often facilitated by printing in one way or another, in the Middle East as elsewhere.

Finally, we may return to the question posed in a previous chapter: Would it be suitable to designate these substantial changes as "revolutionary"? Since "revolutionary," especially in this adjectival form, is essentially a relative term, the question is one of the historian's semantic preferences. My sense is that the changes whose formative phase has been examined in this book were sufficiently profound, and their implications sufficiently far-reaching, to merit being labeled revolutionary. During the early stage studied here, the engine of change began rolling slowly, gathering speed and reaching a vigorous momentum in its irreversible course on the eve of World War I. It might not have seemed as a revolutionary journey then in certain parts of the region, but with the benefit of hindsight, we now know that it was portending one, in a big way.

If we choose to apply such a tag, we must also keep in mind that the Arab printing and reading revolution, like all revolutions, did not obliterate the past but rather retained much of it. The embracing of many innovations was accompanied by a good measure of continuity in the contents and genres of written works, their form and style, the methods of their retention and diffusion, and the modes of their reading. Some of these, not all, would change over time. Bearing that in mind, and given the unfolding implications, the mass adoption of printing and reading from the late nineteenth century onward may well be counted as a truly major revolution in modern Arab cultural history – as would be the later-generation entry of media such as Internet, smartphones, and Facebook.

Bibliography

Newspapers and Journals Quoted in the Book

(place and year of launching)
al-Ahrām (Alexandria/Cairo, 1876)
al-ᶜAlam (Cairo, 1910)
al-Bayān (Cairo, 1897)
al-Bilād al-Saᶜūdiyya (Mecca, 1932)
Filasṭīn (Jaffa, 1911)
Ḥadīqat al-Akhbār (Beirut, 1858)
al-Hilāl (Cairo, 1892)
al-Iskandariyya (Alexandria, 1878)
al-Janna (Beirut, 1879)
al-Jarīda (Cairo, 1909)
al-Jawā'ib (Istanbul, 1861)
al-Jinān (Beirut, 1870)
Journal des Debats (Paris, 1860)
Lisān al-ᶜArab (Alexandria, 1894)
Lisān al-ᶜArab (Damascus, 1918)
Lisān al-Ḥāl (Beirut, 1877)
al-Manār (Beirut, 1898)
al-Manār (Cairo, 1898)
al-Mashriq (Beirut, 1898)
al-Mawrid al-Ṣāfī (Beirut, 1909)
Miṣr al-Fatāt (Cairo, 1908)
al-Mu'ayyad (Cairo, 1889)
al-Muqaṭṭam (Cairo, 1889)
al-Muqtaṭaf (Beirut/Cairo, 1876)
al-Nafā'is al-ᶜAṣriyya (Haifa/Jerusalem, 1908)
al-Naḥla (Beirut, 1870)
al-Najāḥ (Beirut, 1870)
New York Tribune (New York, 1841)
Nūr al-Islām (Cairo, 1930)

al-Qibla (Mecca, 1916)
al-Rā'id al-Miṣrī (Cairo, 1896)
al-Rā'id al-Tūnisī (Tunis, 1860)
Rawḍat al-Akhbār (Cairo, 1874)
al-Ṭabīb (Beirut, 1878)
Thamarāt al-Funūn (Beirut, 1875)
al-^{c}Urwa al-Wuthqā (Paris, 1884)
al-Waṭan (Cairo, 1877)
al-Ẓāhir (Cairo, 1903)
al-Zahra (Beirut, 1870)
al-Zamān (Cairo, 1882)

Works in Arabic

^{c}Abbās, Iḥsān. *Ghurbat al-rā^{c}ī: sīra dhātiyya*. Amman: dār al-shurūq, 1996.
^{c}Abd al-Masīḥ, Ibrāhīm. *Dalīl wādī al-nīl li-^{c}āmay 1891, 1892*. Cairo, 1892.
^{c}Abd al-Raḥīm, Maṭar. *Idfinūnī hunāk. Sīrat filasṭīnī yaḥlum bi'l-waṭan*. Damascus: ^{c}Abd al-Raḥīm, 1995.
^{c}Abduh, Ibrāhīm. *A^{c}lām al-ṣiḥāfa al-^{c}arabiyya*. Cairo: maktabat al-ādāb, 1944.
Ta'rīkh al-waqā'i^{c} al-miṣriyya. 3rd printing. Cairo: mu'assasat sijill al-^{c}arab, 1983.
Taṭawwur al-ṣiḥāfa al-miṣriyya, 1798–1981. 4th edn. Cairo: mu'assasat sijill al-^{c}arab, 1982.
Abū al-Sa^{c}d, ^{c}Adnān ^{c}Abd al-Mun^{c}im. *Taṭawwur al-khabar wa-asālīb taḥrīrihi fī al-ṣiḥāfa al-^{c}irāqiyya mundhu nash'atihā ḥattā sanat 1917*. Baghdad: wizārat al-thaqāfa wa'l-i^{c}lām, 1983.
Abū Ḥannā, Ḥannā. *Ẓill al-ghayma*. Nazareth: dār al-nahḍa li'l-ṭibā^{c}a wa'l-nashr, 1997.
Amīn, Aḥmad. *Ḥayātī*. Cairo: maktabat al-nahḍa al-miṣriyya, 1966.
al-Arsūzī, Zakī. *Al-Mu'allafāt al-Kāmila*. Vol. 4. Damascus: maṭābi^{c} al-idāra al-siyāsiyya li'l-jaysh wa'l-quwwāt al-muṣallaḥa, 1972.
Āṣāf, Yūsuf and Qayṣar Naṣr. *Dalīl miṣr li-^{c}āmay 1889–1890*. Cairo: al-maṭba^{c}a al-^{c}umūmiyya, 1889.
al-Batanūnī, Muḥammad Labīb. *Al-Riḥla al-ḥijāziyya li-walī al-ni^{c}am al-ḥājj ^{c}abbās ḥilmī bāshā al-thānī khadīw miṣr*. Cairo: maṭba^{c}at al-jamāliyya, 1911.
Buḥayrī, Muḥammad Kāmil. *Siyāḥat ithnayn wa-thalāthīn yawm^{an} fī ḥumṣ wa-ba^{c}albak wa-dimashq wa-bayrūt*. Tripoli: maṭba^{c}at al-balāgha, 1320/1902.
[al-Bustānī, Buṭrus]. *I^{c}lān al-kawthar*. Beirut: maṭba^{c}at al-ma^{c}ārif, 1874.
al-Bustānī, Buṭrus, and others. *Dā'irat al-ma^{c}ārif*. 11 vols. Beirut: maṭba^{c}at al-ma^{c}ārif, 1876–1900.
al-Dabbāgh, Ibrāhīm. *Ḥadīth al-ṣawma^{c}a: rasā'il fī al-adab wa'l-fukāha wa'l-naqd wa'l-falsafa*. Jaffa: maktabat al-ṭāhir ikhwān, n.d.
Dabbās, Anṭuwān Qayṣar and Nakhla Rashshū. *Ta'rīkh al-ṭibā^{c}a al-^{c}arabiyya fī al-mashriq. Al-baṭrik athanāsyūs al-thālith dabbās (1685–1724), mu'assis awwal maṭba^{c}a ^{c}arabiyya lughat^{an} wa-ḥirf^{an} fī al-mashriq*. Beirut: dār al-nahār, 2008.

Dalīl wādī al-nīl 1891–1892. Cairo, [1892].

Dār al-Kutub al-Miṣriyya. *Fihris al-kutub al-ᶜarabiyya al-maḥfūẓa bi'l-kutubkhāna al-khidīwiyya al-miṣriyya*. 7 vols. Cairo: Dār al-kutub, 1306–1310/1888–1892.

Darwaza, Muḥammad ᶜIzzat. *Mudhakkirāt 1305–1404/1887–1984*. Vol. 1. Beirut: dār al-gharb al-islāmī, 1993.

Ghālib, ᶜAbd al-Raḥīm. *Mi'at ᶜām min ta'rīkh al-ṣiḥāfa: lisān al-ḥāl*. Beirut: Jarrūs Press, 1988.

al-Ghasānī, Muḥammad bin ᶜAbd al-Wahhāb, al-Wazīr. *Riḥlat al-wazīr fī iftikāk al-asīr*. Ed. Alfredo Bustani. Tangier: mu'assasat al-jinirāl frānkū, 1940.

al-Ḥakīm, Yūsuf. *Dhikrayāt al-ḥakīm: sūriya wa'l-ᶜahd al-ᶜuthmānī*. Beirut: al-maṭbaᶜa al-kāthūlikiyya, 1966.

al-Ḥammād, Ḥamad bin ᶜAbdāllāh. *Maṭbaᶜat al-jawā'ib: nash'atuhā, ta'rīkhuhā, maṭbūᶜātuhā*. Riyad: dār al-fayṣal al-thaqāfiyya, 2002.

Ḥamza, ᶜAbd al-Laṭīf. *Adab al-maqāla al-ṣaḥafiyya fī miṣr*. 3 vols. Cairo: al-hay'a al-miṣriyya al-ᶜāmma li'l-kitāb, 1995.

Ḥusayn, Ṭaha. *Al-Ayyām*. Cairo: dār al-maᶜārif, 1960.

Jabrā, Jabrā Ibrāhīm. *Al-Bi'r al-ūlā*. London: riyāḍ al-rayyis li'l-kutub wa'l-nashr, 1987.

al-Jāmiᶜa al-amīrikiyya fī bayrūt. Muqābala maᶜa al-sayyida ᶜanbara salām al-khālidī, 13 March 1970 – http://ddc.aub.edu.lb/projects/cames/interviews/anbara_salam/ [viewed 16 September 2015].

al-Jamᶜiyya al-sūriyya li'l-ᶜulūm wa'l-funūn, 1848–1852. Beirut: dār al-ḥamrā', 1990.

Jayyid, Ramzī Mikhā'īl. *Taṭawwur al-khabar fī al-ṣiḥāfa al-miṣriyya*. Cairo: al-hay'a al-miṣriyya al-ᶜāmma li'l-kitāb, 1985.

Kaḥḥāla, Jūzīf Ilyās. *ᶜAbdāllāh zākhir, mubtakir al-maṭbaᶜa al-ᶜarabiyya*. Aleppo: markaz al-inmā' al-ḥaḍārī, 2002.

al-Khūrī, Mārūn ᶜĪsā. *Malāmiḥ min al-ḥarakāt al-thaqafiyya fī ṭarābulus khilāl al-qarn al-tāsiᶜ ᶜashar*. Tripoli: Jarrūs Press, 1983.

al-Khūrī, Niqūlā. "Mudhakkirāt kāhin al-quds al-khūrī niqūlā al-khūrī, bīrzayt 1885- bayrūt 1954," *Dirāsāt ᶜArabiyya*, 30, 5–6 (March–April 1994), 62–76.

Khūrī, Yūsuf Quzmā. *Rajul sābiq li-ᶜaṣrihi: al-muᶜallim buṭrus al-bustānī*. Beirut: bīsān, 1995.

Al-Ṣiḥāfa al-ᶜarabiyya fī filasṭīn 1876–1948. Beirut: mu'assasat al-dirāsāt al-filasṭīniyya, 1986.

al-Kitāb al-dhahabī li-yūbīl al-muqtaṭaf al-khamsīnī 1876–1926. Cairo: maṭbaᶜat al-muqtaṭaf, 1926.

Kurd ᶜAlī, Muḥammad. *Mudhakkirāt*. Vol. 1. Damascus: maṭbaᶜat al-taraqqī, 1948.

al-Maktaba al-Khālidiyya. *Barnamaj al-maktaba al-khālidiyya al-ᶜumūmiyya*. Jerusalem: maṭbaᶜat jūrjī ḥabīb ḥanāniyā, 1900.

al-Maktaba al-Miṣriyya. *Qā'imat al-kutub al-mawjūda fī al-maktaba al-miṣriyya bi-miṣr, khāṣat ᶜazīz zand wa-shurakā'ihi*. Cairo: al-maktaba al-miṣriyya, 1878.

Muḥyi al-Dīn, Ḥāzim Zakariyā. *Al-Shaykh ṭāhir al-jazā'irī 1268–1338/1852–1920*. Damascus: dār al-qalam, 2001.

Mūsā, Salāma. *Al-Ṣiḥāfa ḥirfa wa-risāla*. Cairo: maṭbaᶜat miṣr, 1958.

Tarbiyyat Salāma Mūsā. Cairo: mu'assasat al-khānjī, 1962.

Naṣṣār, Najīb. *Rasā'il ṣāḥib al-karmil: al-masīra al-maydāniyya fī arjā' filasṭīn wa-sharq al-urdunn*. Ed. Walīd Khulayf. Nazareth: matbaᶜat al-ḥakīm, 1992.

Nuṣayr, ᶜĀyida Ibrāhīm. *Ḥarakat nashr al-kutub fī miṣr fī al-qarn al-tāsiᶜ ᶜashar*. Cairo: al-hay'a al-miṣriyya al-ᶜāmma li'l-kitāb, 1994.

al-Qāsimī, Muḥammad Saᶜīd. *Qāmūs al-ṣināᶜāt al-shāmiyya*. 2 vols. Paris: Mouton, 1960.

Quṭb, Sayyid. *Ṭifl min al-qarya; ḥayāt sayyid quṭb bi-qalamihi*. Beirut: dār al-ḥikma, 196–?

al-Rāfiᶜī, ᶜAbd al-Raḥman. *Mudhakkirātī 1889–1951*. Cairo: dār al-hilāl, 1952.

Al-Thawra al-ᶜurābiyya wa'l-iḥtilāl al-injlīzī. Cairo: dār al-maᶜārif, 1983.

Riḍwān, Abū al-Futūḥ. *Ta'rīkh maṭbaᶜat būlāq wa-lamḥa fī ta'rīkh al-ṭibāᶜa fī buldān al-sharq al-awsaṭ*. Cairo: al-maṭbaᶜa al-amīriyya, 1953.

Rushdī, ᶜAbd al-Raḥman. *Tarjamat taqrīr marfūᶜ ilā al-aᶜtāb al-khadīwiyya al-ᶜaliyya min niẓārat al-maᶜārif al-ᶜumūmiyya ᶜan ḥālat al-kutubkhāna al-khadīwiyya fī sanat 1887 mīlādiyya*. Būlāq: al-maṭbaᶜa al-ahliyya, 1888.

Ṣābāt, Khalīl. *Ta'rīkh al-ṭibāᶜa fī al-sharq al-ᶜarabī*. Cairo: dār al-maᶜārif, 1958.

Ṣāliḥ, Sulaymān. *Al-Shaykh ᶜalī yūsuf wa-jarīdat al-mu'ayyad*. Cairo: al-hay'a al-miṣriyya al-ᶜāmma li'l-kitāb, 1995.

al-Sāmarā'ī, Qāsim. "Al-Ṭibāᶜa al-ᶜarabiyya fī ūrūbbā," in *Nadwat ta'rīkh al-ṭibāᶜa al-ᶜarabiyya ḥattā intihā' al-qarn al-tāsiᶜ ᶜashar*. Abū Ẓābī: al-mujtamaᶜ al-thaqāfī, 1996, 45–109.

Sāmī, Amīn. *Al-Taᶜlīm fī miṣr fī sanatay 1914, 1915*. Cairo: maṭbaᶜat al-maᶜārif, 1917.

Sarkīs, Khalīl. *Al-ᶜĀdāt fī al-ziyārāt wa'l-walā'im wa'l-aᶜrās wa'l-maᶜātim wa-ādāb al-maḥāfil wa-ghayrihā mimma huwwa Jār^in wa-muṭallaᶜ ᶜalayhi ᶜinda al-shuᶜūb al-mutamaddina*. Beirut: al-maṭbaᶜa al-adabiyya, 1909.

Mukhtaṣar ustādh al-ṭabbakhīn. Beirut: al-maṭbaᶜa al-adabiyya, 1905.

Riḥlat mudīr al-lisān khalīl sarkīs ilā al-īstāna wa-ūrūbbā wa-āmīrikā. Beirut: al-maṭbaᶜa al-adabiyya, 1893.

Ta'rīkh ūrshalīm ayy al-quds al-sharīf. Beirut: maṭbaᶜat al-maᶜārif, 1874.

Sarkīs, Yūsuf Ilyān. *Muᶜjam al-maṭbūᶜāt al-ᶜarabiyya wa'l-muᶜarraba*. 2 vols. Cairo: maktabat yūsuf ilyān sarkīs, 1928.

al-Ṣāwī, Aḥmad Ḥusayn. *Fajr al-ṣiḥāfa fī miṣr*. Cairo: al-hay'a al-miṣriyya al-ᶜāmma li'l-kitāb, 1975.

Sayyid, Ayman Fu'ād. *Dār al-kutub al-miṣriyya, ta'rīkhuhā wa-taṭawwuruhā*. Beirut: awrāq sharqiyya, 1996.

Shalfūn, Yūsuf. *Al-Shirāka al-Shahriyya*. A monthly series of 8 booklets. Beirut: al-maṭbaᶜa al-ᶜumūmiyya, January–August 1866.

Shārūbīm, Mīkhā'īl. *Al-Kāfī fī ta'rīkh miṣr al-qadīm wa'l-ḥadīth*. Vol. 4. Būlāq: al-maṭbaᶜa al-kubrā al-amīriyya, 1900.

Shaykhū, Lūīs. *Ta'rīkh fann al-ṭibāᶜa fī al-mashriq*. Beirut: dār al-mashriq, 1995.

Sulaymān, Muḥammad. "Al-Maṭābiᶜ al-filasṭīniyya wa-athruhā al-thaqāfī fī al-ᶜahd al-turkī," *Ru'ya* (Gaza), 2, 13 (October 2001), 72–98.

al-Ṣulḥ, ᶜImād. *Aḥmad fāris al-shidyāq, āthāruhu wa-ᶜaṣruhu*. Beirut: sharikat al-maṭbūᶜāt li'l-tawzīᶜ wa'l-nashr, 1987.

al-Ṣulḥ, Sāmī. *Mudhakkirāt sāmī bak al-ṣulḥ, 1890–1960.* 4 vols. Beirut: maktabat al-fikr al-ᶜarabī wa-maṭbaᶜatuhā, 1960.

Tamīmī, Muḥammad Rafīq and Muḥammad Bahjat. *Wilāyat bayrūt.* 2 vols. Beirut: maṭbaᶜat al-iqbāl, 1335 [1917].

dī Ṭarrāzī, Fīlīb. *Khazā'in al-kutub al-ᶜarabiyya fī al-khāfiqayn.* 3 vols. Beirut: wizārat al-tarbiyya al-waṭaniyya wa'l-funūn al-jamīla, dār al-kutub, 1948.

Ta'rīkh al-ṣiḥāfa al-ᶜarabiyya. 4 vols. Beirut: al-maṭbaᶜa al-adabiyya, 1913, 1914, 1933.

al-ᶜUrwa al-wuthqā wa'l-thawra al-taḥrīriyya al-kubrā, li'l-sayyid jamāl al-dīn al-afghānī wa'l-shaykh muḥammad ᶜabduh. Cairo: dār al-ᶜarab, 1958.

Yāghī, ᶜAbd al-Raḥman. *Ḥayāt al-adab al-filasṭīnī al-ḥadīth, min awwal al-nahḍa ḥattā al-nakba.* Beirut: al-maktab al-tijārī li'l-ṭibāᶜa wa'l-nashr wa'l-tawzīᶜ, 1968.

al-Yāzijī, Kamāl. *Ruwwād al-nahḍa al-ᶜarabiyya fī lubnān al-ḥadīth, 1800–1900.* Beirut: maktabat ra's bayrūt, 1962.

Yehoshuᶜa, Yaᶜqūb. *Ta'rīkh al-ṣiḥāfa al-ᶜarabiyya fī filasṭīn fī al-ᶜahd al-ᶜuthmānī (1908–1918).* Jerusalem: maṭbaᶜat al-maᶜārif, 1974.

Yūbīl lisān al-ḥāl al-dhahabī 1877–1927. Beirut: al-maṭbaᶜa al-adabiyya, 1927.

Zaᶜrūr, Ḥasan. *Bayrūt, al-ta'rīkh al-ijtimāᶜī 1864–1914 min khilāl al-wathā'iq wa'l-ṣiḥāfa al-lubnāniyya.* Beirut: al-markaz al-islāmī li'l-iᶜlām wa'l-inmā', 199–?.

Zaydān, Jurjī. *Mudhakkirāt.* Ed. Ṣalāḥ al-Dīn al-Munajjid. Beirut: dār al-kitāb al-jadīd, 1968.

Ta'rīkh ādāb al-lugha al-ᶜarabiyya. Vol. 4. Beirut: maktabat al-ḥayāt, 1967.

Ziyāda, Mayy. *Warda al-yāzijī.* Beirut: mu'assasat nawfal, 1980.

Zuᶜbī, Sayf al-Dīn. *Shāhid ᶜiyyān: mudhakkirāt.* Shafāᶜamr: dār al-mashriq li'l-tarjama wa'l-ṭibāᶜa wa'l-nashr, 1987.

Works in Other Languages

Abu-Lughod, Ibrahim. *Arab Rediscovery of Europe.* Princeton: Princeton University Press, 1963.

Abu Manneh, Butrus. "The Christians between Ottomanism and Syrian Nationalism: The Ideas of Buṭrus al-Bustānī," *International Journal of Middle East Studies*, 11 (1980), 287–304.

"Sultan Abdülhamid II and Shaikh Abulhuda al-Sayyadi," *Middle Eastern Studies*, 15 (1979), 131–53.

Allen, James Smith. *In the Public Eye. A History of Reading in Modern France 1800–1940.* Princeton: Princeton University Press, 1991.

Alston, R. C., F. J. G. Robinson, and C. Wadham. *A Check-List of Eighteenth-Century Books Containing Lists of Subscribers.* Newcastle: Avero, 1983.

Altick, Richard D. *The English Common Reader. A Social History of the Mass Reading Public 1800–1900.* Columbus, OH: Ohio State University Press, 1998.

Antonius, George. *The Arab Awakening.* New York: Capricorn, 1965.

Atiyeh, George N., ed. *The Book in the Islamic World. The Written Word and Communication in the Middle East.* Albany: SUNY Press, 1995.

"The Book in the Modern Arab World: The Case of Lebanon and Egypt," in George N. Atiyeh, ed., *The Book in the Islamic World. The Written Word and Communication in the Middle East*. Albany: SUNY Press, 1995, 233–53.

Auji, Hala. *Between Script and Print: Exploring Publications of the American Syria Mission and the Nascent Press in the Arab World, 1834–1860*. Unpublished Ph.D. thesis, Binghamton University, 2013.

Ayalon, Ami. "Arab Booksellers and Bookshops in the Age of Printing, 1850–1914," *British Journal of Middle Eastern Studies*, 37, 1 (April 2010), 73–93.

"The Arab Discovery of America in the Nineteenth Century," *Middle Eastern Studies*, 20, 4 (October 1984), 5–17.

"Hassun and Shidyaq: Pencraft and Survival in Mid-Nineteenth Century Istanbul," in Jayne L. Warner, ed., *Cultural Horizons. Festschrift in Honor of Talat S. Halman*. Syracuse: Syracuse University Press, 2001, 59–68.

"Modern Texts and Their Readers in Late Ottoman Palestine," *Middle Eastern Studies*, 38, 4 (October 2002), 17–40.

The Press in the Arab Middle East; A History. New York: Oxford University Press, 1995.

"Private Publishing in the Nahḍa," *International Journal of Middle East Studies*, 40 (2008), 561–77.

Reading Palestine. Printing and Literacy 1900–1948. Austin: University of Texas Press, 2004.

"The Syrian Educated Elite and the Literary *Nahda*," in Itzchak Weismann and Fruma Zachs, eds., *Ottoman Reform and Muslim Regeneration; Studies in Honour of Butrus Abu Manneh*. London: I. B. Tauris, 2005, 127–48.

Ayalon, Yaron. "Richelieu in Arabic: The Catholic Printed Message to the Orient in the Seventeenth Century," *Islam and Christian-Muslim Relations*, 19, 2 (April 2008), 151–65.

Aymes, Marc. "Introducing 'Ill-Literate Knowledge'," *European Journal of Turkish Studies*, 6 (2007), 1–7.

Al-Bagdadi, Nadia. "From Heaven to Dust: Metamorphosis of the Book in Pre-Modern Arab Culture," *The Medieval History Journal*, 8, 1 (January–June 2005), 83–107.

Balagna, Josée. *L'imprimerie arabe en Occident: XVIe, XVIIe et XVIIIe siècles*. Paris: Maisonneuve & Larose, 1984.

Barak, On. *On Time. Technology and Temporality in Modern Egypt*. Berkeley: University of California Press, 2013.

Barbéris, Pierre and Claude Duchet, eds. *Manuel d'histoire littéraire de la France. Vol. 4: 1789–1848*. Paris: Editions Sociales, 1972.

Barolini, Helen. *Aldus and the Dream Book*. New York: Ithaca Press, 1992.

Baron, Beth. "Readers and the Women's Press in Egypt," *Poetics Today*, 15, 2 (Summer 1994), 217–40.

The Women's Awakening in Egypt: Culture, Society and the Press. New Haven: Yale University Press, 1994.

Baruchson, Shifra. *Sefarim ve-kor'im; tarbut ha-keri'a shel yehudey iṭaliya be-shilhey ha-renesans*. Ramat Gan: Bar Ilan University, 1993.

Bawardi, Basiliyus. "First Steps in Writing Arabic Narrative Fiction: The Case of *Ḥadīqat al-Akhbār*," *Die Welt des Islams*, 48 (2008), 170–95.

Ben-Bassat, Yuval and Fruma Zachs, "Correspondence Manuals in Nineteenth-Century Greater Syria: Between the *Arzuhalcı* and the Advent of Popular Letter Writing," *Turkish Historical Review*, 4 (2013), 1–25.

Berger, Lutz. "Zur Problematik der späten Einführung des Buchdrucks in der islamischen Welt," in Ulrich Marzolph, ed., *Das gedruckte Buch im Vorderen Orient*. Dortmund: Verlag für Orientkunde, 2002, 15–28.

Berkey, Jonathan P. *Popular Preaching and Religious Authority in the Medieval Islamic Near East*. Seattle: University of Washington Press, 2001.

The Transmission of Knowledge in Medieval Cairo: A Social History of Islamic Education. Princeton: Princeton University Press, 1992.

Bilici, Faruk. "Les bibliothèques vakıf-s à Istanbul aux XVIe siècle, prémices de grandes bibliothèques publiques," *Revue des mondes musulmans et de la Méditerranée*, 87–88 (September 1999), 39–59.

Blake, N. F. *William Caxton and English Literary Culture*. London: Hambledon, 1991.

Bloom, Jonathan. *Paper before Print: The History and Impact of Paper in the Islamic World*. New Haven: Yale University Press, 2001.

Booth, Marilyn. *Classes of Ladies of Cloistered Spaces; Writing Feminist History through Biography in Fin-de-Siècle Egypt*. Edinburgh: Edinburgh University Press, 2015.

May Her Likes Be Multiplied: Biography and Gender Politics in Egypt. Berkeley: University of California Press, 2001.

Bowring, John. *Report on the Commercial Statistics of Syria*. New York: Arno Press, 1973 (reprint of the 1840 edition).

Brewer, John. *The Pleasures of the Imagination: English Culture in the Eighteenth Century*. Glasgow: HarperCollins, 1997.

"British Circulating Libraries: 1725–1966," http://britishcirculatinglibraries.weebly.com [viewed 16 September 2015].

Brooks, Jeffrey. *When Russia Learned to Read: Literacy and Popular Literature 1861–1917*. Princeton: Princeton University Press, 1985.

Burak, Guy. "Reliable Books: Islamic Law, Canonization and Manuscripts in the Ottoman Empire (16th–18th Centuries)." Forthcoming.

Burton, Richard Francis, trans. *A Plain and Literal Translation of the Arabian Nights Entertainments*. Vol. 1. n.p.: The Burton Club, 1885.

Cavallo, Guiglielmo and Roger Chartier, eds. *A History of Reading in the West*. Amherst: University of Massachusetts Press, 1999.

Chartier, Roger. *The Author's Hand and the Printer's Mind*. Cambridge: Pility Press, 2014.

Histoire de la lecture: un bilans de recherches, actes du colloque des 29 et 30 janvier 1993, Paris. Paris: Institut mémoires de l'édition contemporaines, 1995.

"Labourers and Voyagers: From the Text to the Reader," in David Finkelstein and Alistair McCleery, eds., *The Book History Reader*. London: Routledge, 2006, 47–58.

"Leisure and Sociability: Reading Aloud in Early Modern Europe," in Susan Zimmerman and Ronald F. E. Weissman, eds., *Urban Life in the Renaissance*. Newark: University of Delaware Press, 1989, 103–20.

"The Practical Impact of Writing," in David Finkelstein and Alistair McCleery, eds., *The Book History Reader*. London: Routledge, 2006, 118–42.

Claire, Colin. *Christopher Plantin*. London: Cassell, 1960.

Cole, Juan R. I. "Printing and Urban Islam in the Mediterranean World, 1890–1920," in Leila Tarazi Fawaz and C. A. Bayly, eds., *Modernity and Culture from the Mediterranean to the Indian Ocean*. New York: Columbia University Press, 2002, 344–64.

Collins, Norman J. and Anton Steichele. *The Ottoman Posts and Telegraph Offices in Palestine and Sinai*. London: Sahara Publications, 2000.

Commins, David Dean. *Islamic Reform. Politics and Social Change in Late Ottoman Syria*. New York: Oxford University Press, 1990.

Conrad, Lawrence I. "The Khalidi Library," in Sylvia Auld and Robert Hillenbrand, eds., *Ottoman Jerusalem*. Vol. 1. London: Altajir World of Islam Trust, 2000, 191–209.

Cooper, Elizabeth. *The Women of Egypt*. New York: F. A. Stokes, 1914.

Crabitès, Piérre. "Journalism along the Nile: The Press in a Country Where Editors Often Put Politics Before Business," *Asia*, 27 (December 1927), 992–1052.

Curwen, Henry. *A History of Booksellers, the Old and the New*. First published 1873. London: Thoemmes Press and Tokyo: Kinokuniya, 1996.

Darnton, Robert. *The Business of Enlightenment. A Publishing History of the Encyclopédie 1775–1800*. Cambridge, MA: Harvard University Press, 1979.

"First Steps toward a History of Reading," in *The Kiss of Lamourette: Reflections in Cultural History*. New York: Norton, 1990, 136–53.

"The Forgotten Middlemen of Literature," in *The Kiss of Lamourette: Reflections in Cultural History*. New York: Norton, 1990, 154–87.

"What Is the History of Books?" in *The Kiss of Lamourette: Reflections in Cultural History*. New York: Norton, 1990, 107–35.

"'What Is the History of Books?' Revisited," *Modern Intellectual History*, 4, 3 (2007), 495–508.

Davis, Natalie Zemon. "Printing and the People," in *Society and Culture in Early Modern France*. Stanford: Stanford University Press, 1975, 189–226.

Davison, Roderic H. "The Advent of the Electric Telegraph in the Ottoman Empire," in *Essays in Ottoman and Turkish History, 1774–1923*. Austin: University of Texas Press, 1990, 133–65.

Delanoue, Gilbert. *Moralistes et politiques musulmans dans l'Egypte du XIXe siècle (1798–1882)*. Cairo: Institut français d'archéologie orientale du Caire, 1982.

Demeerseman, A[ndré]. *L'Imprimerie en Orient et au Maghreb*. Tunis: Institut des Belles Lettres Arabes (IBLA), 1954 (reprint of an article published in *IBLA Revue* 17 [1954], 1–48, 113–40).

Desmet-Grégoire, Hélène and François Georgeon, eds. *Cafés d'Orient revisitée*. Paris: CNRS éditions, 1997.

Dondi, Cristina. "The European Printing Revolution," in Michael F. Suarez and H. R. Woudhuysen, eds., *The Book, a Global History*. Oxford: Oxford University Press, 2013, 80–92.

Eche, Yousef. *Les bibliothèques arabes publiques et semi-publiques en Mésopotamie, en Syrie et en Égypte au Moyen Age*. Damascus: Institut Français de Damas, 1967.

Egyptian Government, Ministry of Finance, Statistical Department. *The Census of Egypt, Taken in 1907*. Cairo, 190–?

The Census of Egypt, Taken in 1917. 2 vols. Cairo, 1920–1921.

Eich, Thomas. "Abū l-Hudā, the Rifāʿīya and Shiism in Ḥamīdian Iraq," *Der Islam*, 80 (2003), 142–52.

"The Forgotten Salafī Abū l-Hudā aṣ-Ṣayyādī," *Die Welt des Islams*, 43 (2003), 61–87.

Eisenstein, Elizabeth L. "The Early Printer as a 'Renaissance man'," *Printing History*, 3, 1 (1981), 6–17.

The Printing Press as an Agent of Change. Cambridge: Cambridge University Press, 1979.

The Printing Revolution in Early Modern Europe. 2nd edn. Cambridge: Cambridge University Press, 2005.

Elliott, Blanche B. *A History of English Advertising*. London: Business Publications, 1962.

Emin, Ahmed. *The Development of Modern Turkey as Measured by Its Press*. New York: Columbia University, 1914.

Establet, Colette and Jean-Paul Pascual. "Les livres des gens à Damas vers 1700," *Revue des mondes musulmans et de la Méditerranée*, 87–88 (1999), 143–69.

Evered, Emine Ö. *Empire and Education under the Ottomans*. New York: I. B. Tauris, 2012.

Fahmy, Ziad. *Ordinary Egyptians*. Stanford: Stanford University Press, 2011.

Farah, Mounir A. "Syria Reborn: American Missionaries, Education, and the Literary Revival of the Nineteenth Century," in Adel Beshara, ed., *Butrus al-Bustani, Spirit of the Age*. Melbourne: Iphoenix, 2014, 26–48.

Febvre, Lucien and Henri-Jean Martin. *The Coming of the Book*. London: Verso, 2000.

Feodorov, Ioana. "The Romanian Contribution to Arabic Printing," in Institut des Études Sud-Est Européennes, ed., *Impact de l'imprimerie et rayonnement intellectual des Pays Roumaines*. Bucarest: Editura Biblioteca Bucureştitor, 2009, 41–59.

Finkel, Caroline. *Osman's Dream: The Story of the Ottoman Empire 1300–1923*. New York: Basic Books, 2006.

Finkelstein, David and Alistair McCleery. *An Introduction to Book History*. New York: Routledge, 2013.

Fortna, Benjamin C. *Imperial Classroom. Islam, the State, and Education in the Late Ottoman Empire*. Oxford: Oxford University Press, 2000.

Learning to Read in the Late Ottoman Empire and the Early Turkish Republic. New York: Palgrave-Macmillan, 2012.

Frankel, Miryam. "Reshimot min ha-geniza ke-makor le-historya ḥevratit ve-tarbutit shel ha-yehudim ba-agan ha-yam ha-tikhon," in Mordechai

Akiva Friedman, ed., *Ḥeker ha-geniza le-akhar mea shana*. Tel Aviv: Tel Aviv University, 1999, 333–49.
Fyfe, Hamilton H. *The New Spirit in Egypt*. London: William Blackwood, 1911.
Galland, A[ntoine]. "Discourse pour server de preface à la Bibliothèque orientale," in Barthelèmy d'Herbelot, ed., *Bibliothèque orientale*. Paris: Compagnie des Libraires, 1697, xix.
Gdoura, Wahid. *Le début de l'imprimerie arabe à Istanbul et en Syrie: evolution de l'environment culturel (1706–1787)*. Tunis: Institut Supérieur de Documentation, 1985.
Georgeon, François. "Lire et écrire à la fin de l'Empire ottoman: quelques remakes introductives," *Revue des mondes musulmans et de la Méditerranée*, 75–76 (1995), 169–79.
Gerçek, Selim Nüzhet. *Türk Matbaacılığı*. Istanbul: Matbaᶜat Ebu Ziyya, 1928.
"Gesellschaft der Künste und Wissenschaften in Beirut," *Zeitschrift der Deutschen Morgenländischen Gesellschaft*, 2 (1848), 378–88.
Ghobrial, John-Paul. *Diglossia and the "Methodology" of Arabic Print*. Paper presented at the second international symposium on "The History of Printing and Publishing in the Languages and Countries of the Middle East," Paris, 2–4 November 2005.
Gidal, Nachum Tim. *Jerusalem in 3000 Years*. Edison, NJ: Knickerbocker Press, 1996.
Giladi, Avner. "Three *Fatāwā* on 'Lending Libraries' in North Africa and Spain," *Arabica*, 44, 1 (1997), 140–43.
Ginzburg, Carlo. *The Cheese and the Worms. The Cosmos of a Sixteenth Century Miller*. Baltimore: Johns Hopkins, University Press, 1980.
Glass, Dagmar. *Malta, Beirut, Leipzig and Beirut Again: Eli Smith, the American Syria Mission and the Spread of Arabic Typography*. Beirut: Orient-Institut der Deutschen Morgenländischen Gesellschaft, 1998.
Göçek, Fatma Müge. *East Encounters West. France and the Ottoman Empire in the Eighteenth Century*. New York: Oxford University Press, 1987.
Gordon, Gil. "Ha-ṭov mi-kullam ba-'umanut ha-sheḥora': beit ha-dfus shel ha-mision ha-germani shel Schneller bi-yerushalayim be-shilhey ha-tequfa ha-othmanit," *Cathedra*, 138 (2011), 83–110.
Gouvernement Egyptien, *Recensement général de l'Egypte, 1 Juin 1897 – 1er Moharrem 1315*. 3 vols. Cairo, 1898.
Grafton, Anthony T. "The Importance of Being Printed," *Journal of Interdisciplinary History*, 11, 2 (autumn 1980), 265–86.
Green, Nile. "Journeymen, Middlemen: Travel, Transculture, and Technology in the Origins of Muslim Printing," *International Journal of Middle East Studies*, 41 (2009), 203–24.
Grehan, James. *Everyday Life & Consumer Culture in 18th-Century Damascus*. Seattle: University of Washington Press, 2007.
Griffiths, Paul J. *Religious Reading: The Place of Reading in the Practice of Religion*. New York: Oxford University Press, 1999.
Gulick, John. *Tripoli, a Modern Arab City*. Cambridge, MA: Harvard University Press, 1967.

Halevi, Shoshana. *Sifrey yerushalayim ha-rishonim*. Jerusalem: Ben-Zvi Institute and the Hebrew University, 1975.

Hall, David. *Cultures of Print. Essays in the History of the Book*. Amherst: University of Massachusetts Press, 1996.

Hanania, Mary. "Jurji Habib Hanania; History of the Earliest Press in Palestine, 1908–1914," *Jerusalem Quarterly*, 32 (autumn 2007), 51–69.

Hanebutt-Benz, Eva, Dagmar Glass and Geoffrey Roper, eds. *Middle Eastern Languages and the Printing Revolution; a Cross Cultural Encounter*. Mainz: Gutenberg Museum, 2002.

Hanna, Nelly. *In Praise of Books. A Cultural History of Cairo's Middle Class, Sixteenth to the Eighteenth Century*. Syracuse: Syracuse University Press, 2003.

"Literacy and the 'Great Divide' in the Islamic World, 1300–1800," *Journal of Global History*, 2 (2007), 175–93.

Hanssen, Jens. *Fin de Ciècle Beirut. The Making of an Ottoman Provincial Capital*. Oxford: Oxford University Press, 2005.

Harding, Çiğdem Balım. "Turkish Literature," in *The New Cambridge History of Islam*, Vol. 4. Cambridge: Cambridge University Press, 2011, 424–33.

Harris, Michael. "Collecting Ephemera," in Michael F. Suarez and H. R. Woudhuysen, eds., *The Book, a Global History*. Oxford: Oxford University Press, 2013, 205–19.

Hattox, Ralph S. *Coffee and Coffeehouses. The Origins of a Social Beverage in the Medieval Near East*. Seattle: University of Washington Press, 1985.

Heffening, W. and J. D. Pearson. "Maktaba," in *Encyclopaedia of Islam*, 2nd edn.

Henkin, David M. *City Reading. Written Words and Public Space in Antebellum New York*. New York: Columbia University Press, 1998.

Heyberger, Bernard. "Livres et pratiques de la lecture chez les chrétiens (Syrie, Liban) XVIIe-XVIIIe siècles," *Revue des mondes musulmans et de la Méditerranée*, 87–88 (September 1999), 209–23.

Heyworth-Dunne, J[ames]. *An Introduction to the History of Education in Modern Egypt*. London: Luzac, 1938.

"Printing and Translation under Muḥammad ʿAlī: The Foundation of Modern Arabic," *Journal of the Royal Asiatic Society*, Part 3 (July 1940), 325–49.

Hirschler, Konrad. *The Written Word in the Medieval Arabic Lands. A Social and Cultural History of Reading Practices*. Edinburgh: University of Edinburgh Press, 2012.

Holt, Elizabeth M. "Narrative and the Reading Public in 1870s Beirut," *Journal of Arabic Literature*, 40 (2009), 37–70.

Hourani, Albert. "Bustānī's Encyclopaedia," *Journal of Islamic Studies*, 1 (1990), 111–19.

Hsu, Cheng-Hsiang. "A Survey of Arabic-Character Publications Printed in Egypt during the Period of 1238–1267 (1822–1851)," *Journal of Semitic Studies*, Suppl. 15 (2004), 1–16.

Huber, Valeska. *Channelling Mobilities; Migration and Globalisation in the Suez Canal Region and Beyond, 1869–1914*. New York: Cambridge University Press, 2013.

Huff, Toby E. *Intellectual Curiosity and the Scientific Revolution. A Global Perspective*. Cambridge: Cambridge University Press, 2001.

Ibn Dohaish, Abdul Latif Abdullah. "Growth and Development of Islamic Libraries," *Der Islam*, 66 (1989), 289–302.

Issawi, Charles. "Asymmetrical Development and Transport in Egypt, 1800–1914," in William R. Polk and Richard L. Chambers, eds., *Beginnings of Modernizations in the Middle East*. Chicago: University of Chicago Press, 1968, 383–400.

An Economic History of the Middle East and North Africa. New York: Columbia University Press, 1982.

The Economic History of the Middle East 1800–1914; a Book of Readings. Chicago: Chicago University Press, 1966.

The Fertile Crescent 1800–1914. A Documentary Economic History. New York: Oxford University Press, 1988.

Jandora, John W. "Unity through Patriotism: The Butrus al-Bustani Approach," in Adel Beshara, ed., *Butrus al-Bustani, Spirit of the Age*. Melbourne: Iphoenix, 2014, 166–87.

Johns, Adrian. "Coffeehouses and Print Shops," in L. Daston and K. Park, eds., *Cambridge History of Science*. Vol. 3. Cambridge: Cambridge University Press, 2006, 320–40.

The Nature of the Book. Print and Knowledge in the Making. Chicago: University of Chicago Press, 1998.

Jouhaud, Christian. "Readability and Persuasion: Political Handbills," in Roger Chartier, ed., *The Culture of Print; Power and the Uses of Print in Early Modern Europe*. Princeton: Princeton University Press, 1987, 235–60.

Kaestle, Carl F. "The History of Readers," in *Literacy in the United States*. New Haven and London: Yale University Press, 1991, 33–72.

"Studying the History of Literacy," in *Literacy in the United States*. New Haven and London: Yale University Press, 1991, 3–32.

Kark, Ruth. *American Consuls in the Holy Land 1832–1914*. Jerusalem: Magnes Press, 1994.

Yafo, Tsemihata shel ʿir, 1799–1917. Jerusalem: Ariel, 2003.

Khalid, Adeeb. "Printing, Publishing, and Reform in Tsarist Central Asia," *International Journal of Middle East Studies*, 26, 2 (1994), 187–200.

Khalidi, Rashid. *Palestinian Identity; the Construction of Modern National Consciousness*. New York: Columbia University Press, 1997.

Khayyat, Latif. "The Style and Contents of Arabic Folk Material in Chapbooks Found in the New York Public Library," *Fabula*, 28, 1 (January 1987), 59–71.

King, Carole. "The Rise and Decline of Village Reading Rooms," *Rural History*, 20, 2 (2009), 163–86.

Kırlı, Cengiz. "Coffeehouses: Public Opinion in the Nineteenth Century Ottoman Empire," in Armando Salvatore and Dale F. Eickelman, eds., *Public Islam and the Common Good*. Leiden: Brill, 2004, 75–97.

Klancher, Jon P. *The Making of English Reading Audiences, 1790–1832*. Madison: University of Wisconsin Press, 1987.

Kohlberg, Etan. *A Medieval Muslim Scholar at Work: Ibn Ṭāwūs and His Library*. Leiden: Brill, 1992.

Krymskii, Agathangel Efimovich. *Istoriia Novoi Arabskoi Literaturyi*. Moscow: Nauka, 1971.

Kunt, Metin I. "Reading Elite, Elite Reading," *Journal of Semitic Studies*, Suppl. 25 (2008), 89–100.

Kut, Turgut and Fatma Türe. *Yazmadan Basmaya: Müteferrika, Mühendishane, Üsküdar*. Istanbul: Yapı Kredi, 1996.

Landau, Jacob M. "An Arab Anti-Turk Handbill, 1881," *Turcica*, 9, 1 (1977), 215–27.

Landes, David S. "Why Europe and the West? Why Not China?" *Journal of Economic Perspectives*, 20, 2 (Spring 2006), 3–22.

Lane, Edward William. *Manners and Customs of the Modern Egyptians*. Cairo: East-West Publications, 1978 (first published 1836).

Leder, Stefan. "Charismatic Scripturalism, the Hanbali Maqdisis of Damascus," *Der Islam*, 74 (1997), 279–304.

Lewis, Bernard. *The Middle East, 2000 Years of History*. London: Wiedenfeld and Nicolson, 1995.

The Muslim Discovery of Europe. New York: Norton, 1982.

Lowry, Martin. *The World of Aldus Manutius; Business and Scholarship in Renaissance Venice*. Oxford: Blackwell, 1979.

Lyons, Martin. "New Readers in the Nineteenth Century: Women, Children, Workers," in Guiglielmo Cavallo and Roger Chartier, eds., *A History of Reading in the West*. Amherst: University of Massachusetts Press, 1999, 313–44.

Makdisi, Usama. *Artillery of Heaven. American Missionaries and the Failed Conversion of the Middle East*. Ithaca: Cornell University Press, 2008.

The Culture of Sectarianism. Community, History and Violence in Nineteenth-Century Ottoman Lebanon. Berkeley: University of California Press, 2000.

Manguel, Alberto. *A History of Reading*. New York: Penguin, 1996.

Marashi, Afshin. "Print Culture and Its Publics: A Social History of Bookstores in Tehran, 1900–1950," *International Journal of Middle East Studies*, 47 (2015), 89–108.

Marcus, Abraham. *The Middle East on the Eve of Modernity. Aleppo in the Eighteenth Century*. New York: Columbia University Press, 1989.

Marino, Brigitte. "Cafés et cafeteries de Damas aux xviiie et xixe siècles," *Revue des Mondes Musulmans et de la Méditerranée*, 75–76 (1995), 272–92.

Martin, Henri-Jean. *The History and Power of Writing*. Trans. Lydia G. Cochrane. Chicago: University of Chicago Press, 1994.

Marzolph, Ulrich. "Still the Same Old Jokes: The Continuity of Jocular Tradition in Early Twentieth-Century Egyptian Chapbooks," in Cathy Lynn Preston and Michael J. Preston, eds., *The Other Print Tradition; Essays on Chapbooks, Broadsides and Related Ephemera*. New York: Garland, 1995, 161–79.

McHenry, Elizabeth. "'An Association of Kindred Spirits': Black Readers and Their Reading Rooms," in Shafquat Towheed, Rosalind Crone and Katie Halsey, eds., *The History of Reading*. New York: Routledge, 2011, 310–22.

McLaren, Anne E. "Constructing New Reading Publics in Late Ming China," in Cynthia J. Brokaw and Kai-wing Chow, eds., *Printing and Book Culture in Late Imperial China*. Berkeley: University of California Press, 2005, 152–83.

Messick, Brinkley. "On the Question of Lithography," *Culture and History*, 16 (1997), 158–76.

Mikhail, Alan. "The Heart's Desire: Gender, Urban Space and the Ottoman Coffee House," in Dana Sajdi, ed., *Ottoman Tulips, Ottoman Coffee*. New York: I.B. Tauris, 2007, 133–70.

Nasrallah, Joseph. *L'imprimerie au Liban*. Harissa: Imprimerie St. Paul, 1948.

Neumann, Christoph K. "Books and Newspaper Printing in Turkish, 18th–20th Century," in Eva Hanebutt-Benz, Dagmar Glass and Geoffrey Roper, eds., *Middle Eastern Languages and the Printing Revolution; a Cross Cultural Encounter*. Mainz: Gutenberg Museum, 2002, 227–48.

Ochsenwald, William. *Religion, Society and the State in Arabia. The Hijaz under Ottoman Control, 1840–1908*. Columbus: Ohio State University Press, 1984.

O'Fahey, R. S. "'His Masters Voice': The Sufis, the Mahdists and Printing," *Culture and History*, 16 (1997), 136–44.

Okan, Ayşegül. *The Ottoman Postal and Telegraphic Services in the Last Quarter of the Nineteenth Century*. Unpublished M.A. thesis, Istanbul, Boğaziçi University, 2003.

Oman, G. et al., "Maṭbaᶜa," in *Encyclopaedia of Islam*, 2nd edn.

Patel, Abdulrazzak. *The Arab Nahḍah. The Making of the Intellectual and Humanist Movement*. Edinburgh: Edinburgh University Press, 2013.

Pedersen, Johannes. *The Arabic Book*. Trans. Geoffrey French. Princeton: Princeton University Press, 1984.

Perron, A. "Lettres sur les écoles et l'imprimerie du Pacha d'Egypte," *Journal Asiatique*, 4th series, 2 (1843), 5–60.

Petrozzi, M. T. "The Franciscan Printing Press," *Christian News from Israel*, 20, 26 (1971), 64–69.

Philipp, Thomas. *The Syrians in Egypt 1725–1975*. Stuttgart: Steiner, 1985.

Pinto, Olga. "The Libraries of the Arabs during the Time of the Abbasids," *Islamic Culture*, 3 (1929), 210–43.

Porter, Josias Leslie. *A Handbook for Travellers* [sic] *in Syria and Palestine*. Part 1. London: John Murray, 1868.

Preston, Cathy Lynn and Michael J. Preston, eds. *The Other Print Tradition; Essays on Chapbooks, Broadsides and Related Ephemera*. New York: Garland, 1995.

Proudfoot, I. "Lithography at the Crossroads of the East," *Journal of the Printing Historical Society*, 27 (1998), 113–31.

"Mass Producing Houri's Moles, or Aesthetics and Choice of Technology in Early Muslim Book Printing," in P. G. Ridell and J. Street, eds., *Islam: Essays on Scripture, Thought, and Society*. Leiden: Brill, 1997, 161–84.

Rae, W. Fraser. "The Egyptian Newspaper Press," *The Nineteenth Century*, 32 (July–December 1892), 213–23.

Reid, Donald. *The Odyssey of Faraḥ Anṭūn. A Syrian Christian's Quest for Secularism*. Minneapolis: Bibliotheca Islamica, 1975.

Richter, Noë. *La lecture & ses institutions. Vol. 1: La lecture populaire 1700–1918.* Paris: Université de Maine, 1987.

Roberts, R. J. "The Greek Press at Constantinople in 1627 and Its Antecedents," *The Library*, 5th series, 22 (1967), 13–43.

Robinson, Francis. "Technology and Religious Change: Islam and the Impact of Print," *Modern Asian Studies*, 27, 1 (1993), 229–51.

Roper, Geoffrey. "Arabic Books Printed in Malta 1826–42: Some Physical Characteristics," *Journal of Semitic Studies*, Suppl. 15 (2004), 111–29.

Arabic Printing in Malta 1825–1845: Its History and Its Place in the Development of Print Culture in the Arab Middle East. Unpublished Ph.D. thesis, University of Durham, 1988.

"Arabic Printing: Printing Culture in the Arabic and Islamic Context," in Houari Touati, ed., *Encyclopedia of Mediterranean Humanism*, spring 2014 – www.encyclopedie humanisme.com?/Arabic-printing [viewed 16 September 2015].

"The Beginnings of Arabic Printing by the ABCFM, 1822–1841," *Harvard Library Bulletin*, 9, 1 (Spring 1998), 50–68.

"Early Arabic Printing in Europe," in Eva Hanebutt-Benz, Dagmar Glass and Geoffrey Roper, eds., *Middle Eastern Languages and the Printing Revolution; a Cross Cultural Encounter.* Mainz: Gutenberg Museum, 2002, 129–50.

"Fāris al-Shidyāq and the Transition from Scribal to Print Culture in the Middle East," in George N. Atiyeh, ed., *The Book in the Islamic World. The Written Word and Communication in the Middle East.* Albany: SUNY Press, 1995, 209–31.

"The History of the Book in the Muslim World," in Michael F. Suarez and H. R. Woudhuysen, eds., *The Book, a Global History.* Oxford: Oxford University Press, 2013, 524–52.

Rosenthal, Franz. "'Of Making Many Books There Is No End'; the Classic Muslim View," in George N. Atiyeh, ed., *The Book in the Islamic World. The Written Word and Communication in the Middle East.* New York: SUNY Press, 1995, 33–55.

The Technique and Approach of Muslim Scholarship. Analecta Orientalia No. 24. Rome: Pontificium Institutum Biblicum, 1947.

Russell, Mona L. *Creating the New Egyptian Woman. Consumerism, Education, and National Identity, 1863–1922.* New York: Palgrave-Macmillan, 2004.

Ryad, Umar. "A Printed Muslim 'Lighthouse' in Cairo: *al-Manār's* Early Years, Religious Aspirations and Reception," *Arabica*, 56 (2009), 27–60.

Sabev, Orlin. "The First Ottoman Turkish Printing Enterprise: Success or Failure?" in Dana Sajdi, ed., *Ottoman Tulips, Ottoman Coffee.* New York: I.B. Tauris, 2007, 63–89.

"Formation of Ottoman Print Culture (1726–1746): Some General Remarks," in *Regional Program 2003–2004, 2004–2005.* Bucharest: New Europe College, 2007, 293–333.

In Search of Lost Time Waiting for Godot: How "Late" Was the Introduction of Ottoman Printing? Paper presented at the third international symposium on the History of Printing and Publishing in the Languages and Countries of the Middle East, Leipzig, 25–27 September 2008.

"A Virgin Deserving Paradise or a Whore Deserving Poison: Manuscript Tradition and Printed Books in Ottoman Turkish Society," in Jaroslav Miller, ed., *Friars, Nobles and Burghers – Sermons, Images and Prints*. Budapest: Central European University Press, 2010, 389–409.

"Waiting for Godot: The Formation of Ottoman Print Culture," in Geoffrey Roper, ed., *Historical Aspects of Printing and Publishing in Languages of the Middle East*. Leiden: Brill, 2014, 101–20.

Saenger, Paul Henry. "Books of Hours and the Reading Habits of the Later Middle Ages," in Roger Chartier, ed., *The Culture of Print: Power and the Use of Print in Early Modern Europe*. Cambridge: Polity Press, 1989, 141–73.

Space between Words: The Origins of Silent Reading. Stanford: Stanford University Press, 1997.

Sajdi, Dana. *The Barber of Damascus. Nouveau Literacy in the Eighteenth Century Ottoman Levant*. Palo Alto: Stanford University Press, 2013.

"Print and Its Discontents," *The Translator*, 15 (2009), 105–38.

"A Room of His Own: The 'History' of the Barber of Damascus 9fl. 17620," *The MIT Electronic Journal of Middle East Studies*, 4 (2003), 19–35.

Sālnāme-i vilāyet sūriye. [Damascus], 1317/1899.

Schaefer, Karl R. *Enigmatic Charms: Medieval Arabic Block Printed Amulets in American and European Libraries and Museums*. Leiden: Brill, 2006.

Schultze, Reinhard. "The Birth of a Tradition and Modernity in 18th and 19th Century Islamic Culture – The Case of Printing," *Culture and History*, 16 (1997), 29–72.

Schwartz, Kathryn Anne. *Meaningful Mediums: A Material and Intellectual History of Manuscript and Print Production in Nineteenth Century Ottoman Cairo*. Unpublished Ph.D. thesis, Harvard University, 2015.

Sedra, Paul. *From Mission to Modernity; Evangelical, Reformers and Education in Nineteenth Century Egypt*. London and New York: I. B. Tauris, 2011.

Sehnaoui, Nada. *L'Occidentalisation de la vie quotidienne à Beyrouth 1860–1914*. Beirut: Éditions dar an-nahar, 2002.

Servantie, Alain. "Development of Steamship Travelling in the Mediterranean (1833–1860)," in Dejanirah Couto, Feza Gunergun and Maria Pia Pedani, eds., *Seapower, Technology and Trade; Studies in Turkish Maritime History*. Istanbul: Piri Reis University Publications, 2014, 504–14.

Shaᶜrāwī, Hudā. *Harem Years: The Memoirs of an Egyptian Feminist 1879–1924*. Trans. Margot Badran. New York: Feminist Press at the City University of New York, 1987.

Shaylor, Joseph. *The Fascination of Books*. New York: G. P. Putnam's Sons, 1912.

Shechter, Relli. "From Journalism to Promotion of Goods: Why and How Did Press Publishers Establish Advertising Agencies in Egypt, 1890–1913?" *Journal of Semitic Studies*, Suppl. 15 (2004), 179–91.

Sheehi, Stephen. "Butrus al-Bustani's *Nafir Suriyah* and the National Subject as Effect," in Adel Beshara, ed., *Butrus al-Bustani, Spirit of the Age*. Melbourne: Iphoenix, 2014, 275–309.

Sibai, Mohamed Maki. *Mosque Libraries: An Historical Study*. London and New York: Mansell, 1987.

Skovgaard-Petersen, Jakob. "Fatwas in Print," *Culture and History*, 16 (1997), 73–88.

Stallybrass, Peter. "'Little Jobs'; Broadsides and the Printing Revolution," in Sabrina Alcorn Baron, Eric N. Lindquist and Eleanor F. Shevlin, eds., *Agent of Change; Print Culture Studies after Elizabeth L. Eisenstein*. Amherst: University of Massachusetts Press, 2007, 315–41.

Steele, Robert. *A Bibliography of Royal Proclamations of the Tudor and Stuart Sovereigns and of Others Published under Authority 1485–1714*. Vol. 1: England and Wales. New York: Burt Franklin, 1967.

Strauss, Johan. "Who Read What in the Ottoman Empire (19th–20th Centuries)?" *Arabic and Middle Eastern Literatures*, 6, 1 (2003), 39–76.

Street, Brian V. *Literacy in Theory and Practice*. Cambridge: Cambridge University Press, 1984.

Suit, Natalia Kasprzak. *Qur'anic Matters: Media and Modernity*. Unpublished Ph.D. thesis, University of North Carolina at Chapel Hill, 2014.

Szyliowicz, J. S. "Functional Perspectives on Technology: The Case of the Printing Press in the Ottoman Empire," *Archivum Ottomanicum*, 9 (1986), 249–59.

Tauber, Eliezer. *The Emergence of the Arab Movements*. London: Frank Cass, 1993.

"Four Syrian Manifestos after the Young Turk Revolution," *Turcica*, 19 (1987), 195–213.

Tebbel, John. *A History of Book Publishing in the United States. Vol. 1: The Creation of an Industry 1630–1865*. New York and London: R. R. Bowker, 1972.

Thevet, André. *Le vrais pourtraits et vies des homes illustrés*. Delmar, NY: Scholars Facsimiles & Reprints, 1973 (a facsimile reproduction of the Paris 1584 book).

Thomsen, P[eter]. "Verzeichnis der arabischen Zeitungen und Zeitschriften Palästinas," *Zeitschrift des Deutschen Palästina-Vereins*, 37 (1914), 211–15.

Tibawi, A[bdul] L[atif]. *American Interests in Syria 1800–1901*. Oxford: Clarendon Press, 1966.

"The American Missionaries and Buṭrus al-Bustānī," in *Saint Antony's Papers 16: Middle Eastern Affairs*. Vol. 3. London: Chatto and Windus, 1963, 137–82.

Arabic and Islamic Themes: Historical, Educational and Literary Studies. London: Luzac, 1976.

Touati, Houari. "Pour une histoire de la lecture au Moyen Âge musulman: à propos des livres d'histoire," *Studia Islamica*, 104–05 (2007), 11–44.

Tzorref, Mira. *Salonim sifrutiyim be-mitzrayim mi-shenot ha-ᶜesre ᶜad shenot ha-arbaᶜim – perek be-historiya hevratit-tarbutit*. Unpublished M.A. thesis, Tel Aviv University, 1999.

Van den Boogert, Mauritz. "The Sultan's Answer to the Medici Press? Ibrahim Müteferrika's Printing House in Istanbul," in Alastair Hamilton, Mauritz van den Boogert and Bart Westerweel, eds., *The Republic of Letters in the Levant*. Leiden: Brill, 2005, 265–92.

Visser, Rogier W. *Identities in Early Arab Journalism: The Case of Louis Ṣābūnjī*. Unpublished Ph.D. thesis, University of Amsterdam, 2013.

Warren, Charles. *Underground Jerusalem*. London: Richard Bentley, 1876.
Whitmore, Harry E. "Readers, Writers, and Literary Taste in the Early 1830s: The *Cabinet de lecture* as Focal Point," *Journal of Literary History*, 13, 2 (Spring 1978), 119–30.
Wilson, M. Brett. *Translating the Qur'an in the Age of Nationalism; Print Culture and Modern Islam in Turkey*. Oxford: Oxford University Press, and London: Institute of Ismaili Studies, 2014.
Wiseman, John A. "Silent Companions: The Dissemination of Books and Periodicals in Nineteenth Century Ontario," *Publishing History*, 12 (1982), 17–50.
Wishnitzer, Avner. *The Transformation of Ottoman Temporal Culture during the Long Nineteenth Century*. Unpublished Ph.D. thesis, Tel Aviv University, 2009.
Wittmann, Richard. "Was There a Printing Revolution at the End of the Eighteenth Century?" in Guiglielmo Cavallo and Roger Chartier, eds., *A History of Reading in the West*. Amherst: University of Massachusetts Press, 1999, 282–313.
Worldcat, provided by OCLC Online Computer Library Center – www.worldcat.org.
Yousef, Hoda. *Composing Egypt; Reading, Writing, and the Emergence of a Modern Nation, 1870–1930*. Redwood City, CA: Stanford University Press, 2016.
Zachs, Fruma. *The Making of a Syrian Identity. Intellectuals and Merchants in Nineteenth Century Beirut*. Leiden: Brill, 2005.
"Subversive Voices of Daughters of the *Nahḍa*: Alice al-Bustani and *Riwayat Sa'iba* (1891)," *Hawwa*, 9 (2011), 332–57.
Zachs, Fruma and Sharon Halevi. "From *Difāᶜ al-Nisā'* to *Mas'alat al-Nisā'* in Greater Syria: Readers and Writers Debate Women and Their Rights, 1858–1900," *International Journal of Middle East Studies*, 41 (2009), 615–33.
Gendering Culture in Greater Syria; Intellectuals and Ideology in the Late Ottoman Priod. London: I.B. Tauris, 2015.
Zeidan, Joseph T. *Arab Women Novelists: The Formative Years and Beyond*. Albany: SUNY Press, 1995.
Zentrum Moderner Orient (Berlin). *A Chronology of Nineteenth-Century Periodicals in Arabic (1800–1900)* – www.zmo.de/jaraid/index.html.

Index

ᶜAbduh, Muḥammad, 88, 89
ᶜAbdülhamid II, sultan, 30, 31, 42, 49, 53, 66, 67, 189
Acre, 126, 130
adab, 70, 74, 121, 142
adīb, udabāʾ, 118, 138, 139
advertising, 30, 39, 48, 135–40
al-Afghānī, Jamāl al-Dīn, 89
al-Aḥdab, Ibrāhīm, 59
Ahmet III, sultan, 1, 19, 22
al-Ahrām, 50, 83, 84, 88, 130, 182
Aldus Manutius, 47, 48, 69, 71
Aleppo, 1, 25, 29, 50, 101, 102, 105, 112, 123, 127, 128, 130, 132, 166
Alexandretta, 134
Alexandria, 22, 56, 62, 82, 99, 102, 112, 121, 126, 127, 130, 132, 134, 140, 166, 181, 182
Alf layla wa-layla, 43, 44, 70, 72, 73, 74
Algiers, 134
Amerbach, Johann, 47
American Board of Commissioners for Foreign Missions (ABCFM), 27
American Press (Beirut), 27, 40
Amīn, Aḥmad, 181, 182, 183
Amīn, Qāsim, 174, 175
Anglicans, 26, 27, 52
al-Anjā, ᶜAbd al-Qādir, 103, 104
Antioch, 1
Anṭūn, Rūza, 169
Arabic language, 6, 9, 10, 13, 14, 28, 33, 38, 70, 137, 138, 188
Armenian, 2, 19, 52, 53, 70, 102
Asia, 13, 14, 186
ᶜAslūj, 100
Asyūṭ, 127
Āthār al-adhār (encyclopedia), 79
Austria, 99, 100, 128
ᶜAyn Waraqa, 28
al-ᶜAẓm, Rafīq, 58
al-Azhar, 90
al-Azharī, Khālid, 72
Baalbek, 113
Badius (Bade), Jodocus, 47
Baghdad, 29, 50, 101, 112, 127, 128, 130, 185
Bākūs, 170
Baron, Beth, 166
al-Bashīr, 89, 169
Bashīr II, amir, 28
Bashīr III, amir, 142
Baṣra, 101, 126, 127, 128
al-Baṭalyawsī, Ibn al-Sayyid, 60
al-Bayḍāwī, 72
Bāyezid II, sultan, 6, 8
Bayt al-Dīn, 28, 142, 144
Beauvoir, Roger de, 138
Beirut, 25, 27–29, 37, 38, 40–42, 43, 49, 50, 58, 59, 60, 63, 65, 66, 67, 72, 73, 79, 82, 83, 84, 86, 89, 91, 99, 100, 102, 103, 104, 105, 106, 108, 109, 110, 111, 112, 117, 118–19, 120, 122, 123, 126, 127, 128, 130, 131, 132, 139, 140, 142–46, 165, 166, 173, 174, 185, 189
  sūq al-ᶜaṭṭārīn, 104
  sūq al-ḥamīdiyya, 108
  Zuqāq al-Blāṭ, 41
Berkey, Jonathan, 158
Bethlehem, 126
bidᶜa, 6, 15, 88
binders, binding, 42, 43, 46, 48, 51, 69, 95, 102, 112
Birzeit, 192
bookshops, 28, 29, 30, 32, 40, 41, 48, 59, 85, 91, 101–14, 121, 122, 125, 127, 132, 133, 140, 154, *See also* under individual shop names (*maktaba*)
Booth, Marilyn, 166
Bowring, John, 102
al-Buḥayrī, Muḥammad Kāmil, 108, 117
al-Bukhārī, 73, 77
Būlāq press, 22, 23, 24, 44, 62, 72, 75
Burak, Guy, 8

Lightning Source UK Ltd.
Milton Keynes UK
UKHW022217160419
341152UK00020B/443/P